CHAUCER STUDIES XX

CHAUCERIAN REALISM

Chaucerian Realism is concerned with the understanding of
Chaucer and of his age of the intentionality, or object-
directedness, of thought and language. It considers how intentionality was considered and understood in the middle ages, the
sources of this understanding, how intentionality is considered
today, and how Chaucer's 'modern' understanding of the
intentionality of language makes his fiction psychologically
realistic – a view of Chaucer's writing previously thought to be
untenable.

Where modern criticism has tended to see Chaucer as a
nominalist, that is, anti-realist, this book demonstrates that he is a
realist in many senses of the term, a foundational realist, an
epistemological realist, a semiotic and linguistic realist, an ethical
realist, as well as a writer of realistic fiction. Through the
introduction of the term 'intentionalist realism', the author offers
a means of considering these realisms.

The book refers to many of Chaucer's texts while making its
conclusive demonstration with an examination of the thorough
and deliberate play with three-level semantics in the *Friar's Tale*,
the very subject of which is intentionality.

CHAUCER STUDIES
ISSN 0261-9822

CHAUCERIAN REALISM

ROBERT MYLES

D. S. BREWER

First published 1994
D. S. Brewer, Cambridge

ISBN 0 85991 409 7

D. S. Brewer is an imprint of Boydell & Brewer Ltd
PO Box 9, Woodbridge, Suffolk IP12 3DF, UK
and of Boydell & Brewer Inc.
PO Box 41026, Rochester, NY 14604-4126, USA

British Library Cataloguing-in-Publication Data
Myles, Robert
    Chaucerian Realism. – (Chaucer Studies,
    ISSN 0261-9822; Vol. 20)
    I. Title II. Series
    821.1
    ISBN 0-85991-409-7

Library of Congress Cataloging-in-Publication Data
Myles, Robert, 1947–
    Chaucerian realism / Robert Myles.
        p. cm. – (Chaucer studies, ISSN 0261-9822 ; 20)
    Includes bibliographical references and index.
    ISBN 0-85991-409-7 (hardback : alk. paper)
    1. Chaucer, Geoffrey, d. 1400 – Philosophy. 2. Chaucer, Geoffrey,
d. 1400 – Criticism and interpretation. 3. Intentionality (Philosophy) in
literature. 4. Semantics (Philosophy) in literature. 5. Philosophy,
Medieval, in literature. 6. Realism in literature. I. Title. II. Series.
PR1875.P5M95 1994
821'.1–dc20   94-5852

The paper used in this publication meets the minimum requirements
of American National Standard for Information Sciences –
Permanence of Paper for Printed Library Materials, ANSI Z39.48-1984

Printed in Great Britain by
St Edmundsbury Press Ltd, Bury St Edmunds, Suffolk

CONTENTS

TO
Susan Keys
AND
David Williams

ACKNOWLEDGEMENTS

This book would not have been begun nor completed without the support of two people: my wife, Susan Keys, to whom I owe, as she tells me only half-jokingly, 'more than you can ever repay'; and my teacher, Professor David Williams, McGill University, who provoked and supervised the doctoral dissertation from which this book is developed.

There are many other people I thank for their encouragement and/or assistance: Professor (retired) Ben Weems and Professor Gary Wihl of the Department of English, McGill; Professor Emeritus Raymond Klibansky of McGill and Oxford Universities; Professor Guy H. Allard of L'Institut Médiévale, Université de Montréal; Professor Douglas Wurtele of Carleton University, Ottawa; Dr Richard Cooper; Dr Victor Haines, Dawson College, Montreal; Dr Nini Pal, Marianapolis College, Montreal; Professor Patrick J. Gallacher of the University of New Mexico; and my colleagues and friends at the English and French Language Centre, McGill. For technical assistance I thank Caitlin Myles and Emily Myles.

Finally, but not in order of importance, I thank my always faithful parents, Erminia Paolini (Polly) Myles and Clifford J. Myles.

Aspects of my description of existential metaphysics have appeared formerly in my article, ' "This litel worde IS": The Existential Metaphysics of the *Cloud* author,' *Florilegium* 8 (1986): 140–168.

EDITION

Chaucer, Geoffrey. *The Riverside Chaucer*. 3rd ed. Ed. Larry D. Benson. Boston: Houghton, 1987.

ABBREVIATIONS

Works of Geoffrey Chaucer:

RC	*The Riverside Chaucer*
Bo	*Boece*
ClT	*Clerk's Tale*
FrT	*Friar's Tale*
GP	*General Prologue*
ManT	*Manciple's Tale*
MerT	*Merchant's Tale*
NPT	*Nun's Priest's Tale*
PardT	*Pardoner's Tale*
ParsT	*Parson's Tale*
Ret	Chaucer's Retraction
RR	*The Romaunt of the Rose*
Sted	'Lak of Stedfastnesse'
SumT	*Summoner's Tale*
Tr	*Troilus and Criseyde*
WBT	*Wife of Bath's Tale*

Other:

BPC	*Cloud* author, *The Book of Privy Counselling*
DDC	St Augustine of Hippo, *De doctrina christiana*
DT	St Augustine of Hippo, *De Trinitate*
EETS	Early English Text Society
PL	*Patrologia Latina*
SCG	Thomas Aquinas, *Summa Contra Gentiles*
ST	Thomas Aquinas, *Summa Theologica*

CHAPTER ONE

Chaucerian Realism

CONTRARY TO MUCH current opinion, Chaucer is a realist in many senses: Chaucer's works reveal a foundational realist, an epistemological realist, an ethical realist, a semiotic and linguistic realist, an intentionalist realist and an author capable of creating psychologically real characters. Together these realisms compose 'Chaucerian realism.'

The general concept of realism need not be confusing. Anyone who believes, as Chaucer did, that we dwell in a dimension of beings created by a unique transcendent Being is already a realist, a type of *foundational realist* (Drummond 239–242). Because creation is an intentional act, a person believing in such a cosmogony, as Chaucer did, is also an *intentionalist realist*. Chaucer is even more of an intentionalist realist because he believes that all created beings (or, at the very least, human beings) naturally intend back towards their creator. If one further assumes that the proper order of this universe may be subject to acts (speech acts, or other human actions) which are either 'proper' (in line with a 'natural' order) or 'improper' (the natural order is 'turned up-so-doun' [Sted 5], as Chaucer puts it), one is, like Chaucer, an *ethical realist*. If one assumes, as Chaucer did, that the foundation of beings, Being, 'Reality' itself, can be known to some degree, one is an *epistemological realist*. Furthermore, if one assumes, as Chaucer did, that signs, including all created reality and language in particular, are, to some degree, a reliable means of knowing this extramental reality, one is a *semiotic* and *linguistic realist*. Also if one believes, as Chaucer did, that signs may reveal, to some degree, the real mental or spiritual condition of individual human beings one is also a *psychological realist*. And, finally, if one deliberately uses play with signs to develop characters in a complex way, as Chaucer does, one may be said to be developing psychologically real characters.

'REALISMS' AND NOMINALISM: SOURCES OF CONFUSION

A common error of many critics – and not just critics of medieval literature – is to equate linguistic realism with a *form* of linguistic realism, 'Cratylic realism'

1

(defined below), and both of these with a *form* of epistemological realism, 'scholastic realism.' Because Chaucer can definitely be shown *not* to be a Cratylic realist, many critics assume, wrongly, that he must be a type of nominalist, anti-realist, or relativist, terms that are often used loosely and interchangeably. Furthermore, some also misidentify scholastic nominalism as being necessarily anti-realist in the foundational and epistemological senses. Rather than understanding realism in its general sense, some critics have simplistically associated Chaucer with one side or the other of the narrow scholastic nominalist-realist debate on the nature of the universals and used this as a litmus test to decide whether he is a 'realist' or 'nominalist.' The potential for error in such a method is evident in the fact that there is perfect disagreement in the criticism which has used this approach. There one finds Chaucer-as-nominalist, Chaucer-as-realist, and Chaucer as a confused Mr In-Between.

Cratylic realism holds that there is a natural, real relationship between a word and a thing – that somehow the essence of a chair is reflected or contained in the sound of the word 'chair.' Cratylic realism has nothing to do with 'scholastic realism,' which makes 'a claim to the effect that certain ways of classifying things are right, in the sense that they classify together things which really, i.e., independently of our activity of classification, are alike, and others are wrong' (Haak 282). According to two versions of this theory, universals or concepts, for example, those described by the words 'chair' or 'justice,' exist either in the things so classified or independently of the things so classified. This is opposed to nominalism, which in both its scholastic and modern forms

> claims . . . that there is no 'right' or 'correct' scheme of classification, and that the things that we happen to classify together have as it were, only the name in common. All schemes of categorization or classification, according to this view, are optional, and the choice between them is a matter rather of convenience than of objective rightness and wrongness.
>
> (Haak 281)

It does not follow that a scholastic realist must hold a Cratylic position on language. Indeed, some may find it surprising that someone like Ockham, who is usually considered the arch-nominalist on the question of universals, is not only a foundational realist, but may also be considered to be an epistemological and linguistic realist.

As I use the term, 'scholastic realism' includes two theses of the independence of universals applicable also to pre-scholastics, most importantly, Augustine. An 'independence thesis' of universals holds simply that universals are not 'convenient' and 'optional' classifications created by human reason but that universals which describe individual things ('a tree') or acts ('a just act') exist somehow in reality independent of our classification of them – 'tree' and 'justice' are not mere concepts, man-made classes, but somehow *really* exist: hence, of course, the term 'realism.' Nominalism, on the other hand, believes that universals are convenient and optional classifications.

Nominalism and realism in the Middle Ages may be reduced to four major positions on the nature of the existence of universals: (1) Realism: the universals classified by the terms 'man,' 'horse,' 'justice,' 'white,' are real and 'before the thing,' *ante rem*; in the Platonic conception, 'humanness' is a prior and independent form, or, in the Augustinian conception, 'humanness' exists in the mind of God, so that the 'idea' or essence 'humanness' precedes its creation in the individual 'thing,' a human being. Extreme or Platonic realism, the belief that universals have some kind of independent, prior, and superior form of existence, and that individual entities are but inferior copies of those universals, was not considered seriously in the Middle Ages; however, the Augustinian version, in various forms, was and is still held by many. John Duns Scotus, for example, a scholastic realist, offered sophisticated arguments to prove that words primarily signify essences or concepts; these are the first real things, and they exist independently of man and human consciousness (see Maurer 1:799). (2) Moderate realism (Aristotle and Aquinas): universals are somehow 'in the thing,' *in rem*, so that the essence 'humanness' exists somehow in each individual human being. Aquinas unlike Scotus: 'does not attribute a positive reality to essences themselves. The only real beings, in his view, are individuals. These share a form or essence, as all men participate in human nature, but this nature has no real being or community distinct from individuals' (Maurer 1:800). (3) Extreme nominalism: universals are merely logical beings 'after the thing,' *post rem*, concepts which are signs of things, but which, unlike particular things, do not exist apart from our thinking of them, so that 'humanness' is a mental creation that we abstract from particulars. An extreme nominalist position (held by no one of importance in the Middle Ages) would say that these universal concepts have no bearing on external reality – this may also be called a conceptual idealist position. Ilham Dilman describes such nominalism generally:

> According to the most extreme form [of nominalism], which is perhaps the only position that deserves to be called nominalism, a name is all that different things we call by the same name [man, horse, justice, white] have in common. In other words, the application of every name, and indeed of every word, is arbitrary. It is not based on any reality outside purely human conventions.   (48–49)

This is not the nominalism of Ockham who, strictly speaking, does not deserve to be called a nominalist at all. (4) Moderate nominalism or conceptual realism (Ockham), which does not accept the conceptual idealism of extreme nominalism. A moderate nominalist position holds that while such universal concepts as 'man,' 'horse,' 'white,' and 'justice,' do not properly have an existence of their own, these concepts succeed in describing extramental reality. Philotheus Boehner argues that this 'conceptual realist' (310) position is that of Ockham, for whom there 'is a foundation [for universals] in the [extramental] things themselves' (310).

While there are similarities, it is simply wrong and misleading to closely equate scholastic nominalism with modern extreme nominalism (Gosselin). Critics who do, such as Robert M. Jordan who misassociates Chaucer with extreme nominalism simply because he is not a Cratylist, often make the further misstep of associating him with anti-realism and relativism, making of Chaucer a proto-constructivist or proto-deconstructionist (which may amount to the same thing).[1] On the other hand, the one critic, David Williams, who connects Chaucer with realism, defines the term incompletely and allows only a exegetical interpretation of character. Williams' Wife of Bath and Pardoner, for example, are interpreted only as types (negative) in the Robertsonian mode (*The Canterbury Tales* 64–88). Unfortunately, critics who argue, quite rightly I believe, that such characters are complex and memorable individuals as well as universal types, may tend to throw out Williams' baby (realism) with the bath water (the simplification of character to type).

Many critics, including Jordan and Williams, have ignored or misinterpreted the fact that, as Eugene Vance puts it, 'people of the Middle Ages were basically anti-Cratylistic . . . holding that the bond between signifier and signified . . . was merely conventional' (Vance, *Signals* 258). Such a position necessarily implies that signs are arbitrary, but this was not a problem for scholastic philosophers; they all agreed that language is conventional.[2]

In addition to the errors of simplistically misequating modern nominalism with scholastic nominalism, extreme nominalism with scholastic nominalism, linguistic conventionalism with nominalism, and identifying Cratylism as the sole form of linguistic realism, there is a further common misconception, namely, falsely identifying the doctrine of the primacy of the will – the belief that the action of the will precedes the action of the intellect – as exclusively or principally a nominalist position. In Chaucer criticism this error is found initially in David C. Steinmetz and Russell E. Peck. Because Chaucer can be shown to understand language to be conventional and/or to understand and stress the importance of the function of the will in all conscious acts, many critics have been led to believe that he was ipso facto a 'nominalist' (read, 'relativist'), even while others hold (Gardner), or demonstrate (Williams), that Chaucer satirizes extreme nominalist positions. Moreover, as we shall see, the misunderstanding of 'nominalism' leads some critics to misidentify it with post-Saussurian language theory, and, in turn, to create an overly exclusive association of these with postmodern literature.

The starting point of 'intentionalist realism' is the 'thesis of intentionality'; in its medieval version: 'the object-directedness of all being'; and in its more limited modern version: 'the object-directedness of all conscious acts.'[3] In the Middle Ages, it was commonly held that there was a fundamental connection

---

[1] 'Nominalism' is a term mis-equated in some peoples minds with 'constructivism,' 'Creative Idealism' (Haak 282), or relativism, 'radical' or 'extreme' (Haak 276–78). This mis-equation occurs because a nominalist may often also be a relativist, etc.; this is not the case with 'scholastic nominalists.' 'Constructivism' (which, according to Devitt, would apply to such literary critics as Stanley Fish [234, 256 n. 2, 256 n. 10]) holds that: 'The only independent reality is beyond the reach of our knowledge and language. A known world is partly constructed by the imposition of concepts. These concepts differ from (linguistic, social, scientific, etc.) group to group, and hence the worlds of groups differ. Each such world exists only relative to an imposition of concepts' (Devitt 302). I believe that many deconstructionists, including Derrida, hold this same basic assumption and attempt to demonstrate it by unveiling the conceptually and linguistically-based 'theoretical fiction' (Derrida 150) underlying the oppositions upon which particular 'realities' are constructed. Adding to the confusion is the use of the term 'conventionalism' in modern philosophy which may be associated with 'constructivism' and 'nominalism.'

[2] Language is conventional: see pages 6–16.

[3] Thesis of intentionality: see pages 33–39, 47–54.

between will and language, derived, in turn, from a belief in the necessary connection between God's will and all creation, and the ultimate directedness of all created beings towards Being or God. On the level of language, people in the Middle Ages understood, as we understand today, that the speech act is an intentional act.[4]

The dynamic of created beings within a creationist, foundational metaphysics, such as that of Judeo-Christianity, is intentionalist (created beings are object-directed) and realist (that which created beings intend is real and is, in fact, Reality): this is *intentionalist realism*. Here 'being' is to be considered in its classic metaphysical sense of 'anything that in any way is,' and so may include not only what we consider normally to be individual beings, such as an individual person or thing, but words, thoughts, feelings, and anything else that in any way is. At a certain point intentionalist realism may define a general medieval attitude toward the movement of return of created beings towards the creative Being, God. Furthermore, created beings, simply because they are created, are also signs of the creative intentionality of Being.[5] As *imago Dei* a human being is the sign *par excellence* of Being. All signs, including human language, always reveal reality to some degree (the here and now of beings and their world) and, to some degree, transcendent 'Reality' (the interpretation of beings as signs of Being). The 'to some degree' qualification is very important for it was generally understood and believed in the Middle Ages that Being, or Reality, in totality, is not absolutely knowable – a very common view (Augustine, Aquinas), and a realist view ('Transcendentalism: truth may outrun us' [Haak 283]) that is often confused with nominalism.

For all practical purposes, the attitudes towards signs discussed above were widely held in the Middle Ages. While differing on how 'things' exist (universals and particulars) and how language intends these things, both scholastic nominalists and realists would agree that somehow language always intends things. This is also a given of modern theories of intentionality, arising out of phenomenology. Whether or not many of these modern thinkers of the phenomenological tradition would be content to be described as 'linguistic realists,' many are certainly in opposition to a conceptualism or an idealism that argues that the human mind creates what we believe to be real and then calls into question all of the 'reality' which the mind 'constructs.' Such extreme idealism or conceptualism was also simply not part of the baggage of respected medieval thinkers, including Ockham (Boehner 307–10).

Both scholastic realists and scholastic nominalists believe in divine ideas, but in different ways. The realist believes that universals subsist in God. In Augustine's realism, for example, *rationes aeternae* are universals, the equivalent of the Platonic Forms, and are the patterns of individual things (Nash 6). So too in Ockham's scholastic nominalist view, God 'has ideas as exemplars of real beings, as any craftsman has in knowing what he is to make' (Leff 440); however, Ockham's nominalist 'ideas' exist in the mind of God in a scholastic nominalist fashion, as particulars rather than as universals (Leff 440). Despite the considerable difference in the nature of divine ideas for scholastic realists and scholastic nominalists, their very belief in them reveals that they share the

---

[4] Speech act an intentional act: see particularly pages 27–32, 37–39.
[5] See pages 45–48, 55–62.

foundational realist view that there is 'something' which, as far as the perceiving, thinking, speaking, human subject is concerned, is 'preintentional.'[6] All this should clarify the paradox: scholastic nominalists are realists.

Another element that adds to the confusion is that Cratylic realism may be called a 'natural' attitude towards language, and that for some critics, John A. Alford, for example, Cratylic realism seems to be *the* natural attitude towards language rather than a mere form of it. The source of confusion lies, probably, in the fact that the term 'Cratylic realism' is derived from the name of Plato's Cratylus, who espouses a 'natural,' inherent, direct relationship between a word and a thing, regardless of the will or intention of the person who speaks that word. Here the concept of 'intentionalist realism' can come to the rescue.

Intentionalist realism understands all speech acts to be conscious, willful, intentional acts, that is, acts that have a directedness towards those 'things' which precede them. Unlike Cratylic linguistic realism, intentionalist realism does not see the directedness of language to lie within the nature of language itself, but in the *natural relationship* between the human will and language. Rather than a *direct* relationship between word and thing, intentionalist realism sees a *directed* relationship between word and thing – the key element is the will or intention of the director of language, each individual speaker who directs conventional signs according to his or her will.

The importance of this difference between a *direct* and a *directed* view of language is that for the believer of the latter position, who is an intentionalist realist, there is absolutely no contradiction between understanding language to be conventional and being a linguistic realist; the 'natural' relationship begins in the will. On the other hand, for the Cratylic realist, who believes that there is a direct relationship between word and thing, language cannot be conventional because the 'natural' relationship resides in both word and thing. Because many critics misequate medieval and in some cases modern linguistic realism with the Cratylic or 'natural' (as defined above) variety, they tend to misinterpret as 'confused' anyone in whom is found simultaneously an understanding of the conventionality of language and a linguistic realist belief that language may reveal reality. Such critics are wrong.

The source of the (modern) confusion over linguistic realism lies in Plato's *Cratylus*, where Cratylus and Hermogenes argue opposing views of language. The long reach of those views is indicated by the fact that today the names of these characters are still used to classify positions on language. Perhaps, in part, it is this reduced classification, one which does not consider other forms of linguistic realism, that has led some interpreters to have a simplistic view of linguistic realism.

The dialogue begins with Hermogenes summarizing for Socrates the position of his opponent, Cratylus:

> I should explain to you, Socrates, that our friend Cratylus has been arguing about names. He says that they are natural and not conventional – not a portion of the human voice which men agree to use – but that there is a

6 On the 'preintentional' see Searle, *Intentionality* 141–159.

truth or correctness in them, which is the same for Hellenes as for barbarians.   (383 a)

Hermogenes then presents the conventionalist view:

I have often talked over this matter, both with Cratylus and others, and cannot convince myself that there is any principle of correctness in names other than convention and agreement. Any name which you give, in my opinion, is the right one, and if you change that and give another, the new name is as correct as the old – we frequently change the name of our slaves, and the newly imposed name is as good as the old.   (394 c–d)

The talk of 'slaves' and 'imposing' names raises interesting questions about the use and abuse of power when one willfully manipulates language to attain selfish ends – ends unrelated to any concern for a connection between language and truth: the 'things' language *should* name or attempt to name.[7] The abuse of power through the abuse of language, particularly by the Sophists, was also a Platonic concern and seems to be a concern for Socrates in the *Cratylus*. These concerns are ethically based, part and parcel of an ethical realism.

After the opening positions of Cratylus and Hermogenes are put, Socrates leads a discussion that causes the debaters to see weaknesses in each other's point of view. While Plato's *Cratylus* is indeed the battleground between extreme conventionalist and extreme Cratylic realist views of language, it is not necessarily true, as John A. Alford asserts, that the position of Cratylus is the one that 'Plato seems to favor' (736). This is the view also of P.B. Taylor (317) who extends it to Platonists in general. But thinkers as diverse as Marcia Colish (9), Paul Ricoeur (*Rule* 70), and Roy Harris and Talbot T. Taylor (18) would all disagree, arguing the current widespread view: a lack of resolution in the *Cratylus*. While such a 'failure' may offend some modern sensibilities, Harris and T. Taylor suggest, reasonably, that no resolution is necessary because Plato's concern was not primarily with defining the nature of language as conventionalist or Cratylic, but, rather, with asserting the epistemological realist concern with the primacy of 'things' over words.

It seems that while the conventionalist argument can never be dismissed, many, like Socrates, are reluctant to admit it fully, for they are aware that to do so is to open the door to skepticism, private language worlds, and the idealist view that extramental 'reality' is an unreliable, subjective projection. Indeed, given Socrates' theistic concerns, a case in point justifying his hesitation to admit wholly the view of Hermogenes would be the extreme nominalist or conceptual idealist position arrived at by Robert Jordan, who, as we shall see, seems to doubt the very possibility of the referentiality of language. According to Harris and T. Taylor, what is at stake for Socrates, Plato, Aristotle, and Augustine (and one could add, Boethius, Chaucer and all foundational realists) is the 'truth' that

---

[7] David Williams has argued that a critique of such an abuse of man's power over language occurs in Chaucer's *Friar's Tale* ('Intentionality,' 85–92). I agree that a reading of the *Friar's Tale* as an attack on the abuse of language is a fruitful one; indeed, the reading of this tale in the present book supports such a view. However, one need not infer, as Williams does, that such an attack is simultaneously an attack on the common-sense view that language is conventional.

an objective, extramental reality is prior to any individual and is revealed, not created by language.

In the *Cratylus*, Plato or Plato's Socrates is able to show some limitations in both an exclusively Cratylic and an exclusively conventionalist view of language. However, he wishes to maintain a certain order of nature:

> Plato's point is that it does not matter whether language is conventional or mimetic [i.e., Cratylic], or to what extent it is a mixture of both. Since these are the only possibilities we can imagine, we are driven in the end to realize that language reaches both beyond our opinions and beyond itself. (Harris and Taylor 19)

This is where the realism of both the Cratylic variety and the intentional variety coincide – an ontological and temporal priority of things over words.

Aristotle's famous statement, transmitted to the Middle Ages by Boethius: 'A noun is a vocal sound which is significant by convention' (*On Propositions* 16a) would seem to make of Aristotle a follower of Hermogenes. From such an easy identification springs a further misconceived opposition that recurs among a number of critics: Plato-as-linguistic-realist versus Aristotle-as-linguistic-conventionalist. So Alford, for example, correctly points out that Aristotle is 'usually associated with the conventionalist point of view' (736), but proceeds to oppose this position to the 'natural' position he thinks that only Plato leans towards. Aristotle's conventionalism makes him an anti-Cratylist, but it does not necessarily make him an anti-naturalist or anti-realist. To understand this distinction let us consider Aristotle's definition of metaphor, remembering that for Aristotle 'metaphor' is a generic term under which one finds many species of tropes – synecdoche, metonymy, analogy – as well as the more restricted sense of 'metaphor' we understand today: 'a metaphor is a name *belonging* to one thing but applied to another' (*Poetics* 1457b, emphasis added). This definition shows him to share the realistic presupposition of Plato: the name *belongs* to the thing:

> Aristotle's concept of metaphor is clearly based on Socrates' concept of names [in the *Cratylus*]. A name is a word which 'belongs to' something or someone. The debate which Socrates referees in Plato's dialogue is a debate about how names 'belong to' the objects, persons, actions, qualities, etc. with which they are correlated [that is, by nature, or by convention] . . . Aristotle's definition of metaphor bypasses this controversy, and rests content with identifying metaphor as the transference of a name to something it does *not* 'belong to.' But this definition would hardly make sense without the Socratic assumption that names *do* (either by nature or convention) 'belong to' something or other in the first place. (Harris and T. Taylor 20)

There is a 'proper' way of naming and an 'improper' way of naming. While one need not invest these two modes of naming with an ethical value, the fact of the belief in their existence signals an ethical realism and a linguistic realism: a belief in a *natural* order between words and things. This is a wider view of 'natural' in relation to language than that admitted by Alford; it is one assumed by both Plato and Aristotle (and Chaucer), for whom there is a natural, *real*, ethical order, but one that does not exclude the possibility of language being conventional.

We should also consider the description of the beginning of things which the Middle Ages considered historical:

> And out of the ground the Lord God formed every beast of the field, and every fowl of the air; and brought them unto Adam to see what he would call them: and whatsoever Adam called every living creature, that was the name thereof. (Gen. 2:19)

Foundational metaphysics and realist views of language would seem to be supported by Genesis: here things definitely precede their names. Socrates, too, in the *Cratylus*, refers to an originary 'name-giver.' Harris and T. Taylor devote an interesting chapter to Genesis where, among other things, they compare the 'name-giver' of the *Cratylus* with Adam (Chapter Three). While we know that God leaves it to Adam to create the words to name God's creation, Genesis does not inform us whether the name used by Adam somehow mirrored the essence of the animal named, or if he just made sounds which for ever after became the conventional name for the thing in Hebrew. However, as it is argued by Harris and T. Taylor, the omission of the issue here, the inconclusive stand of the *Cratylus*, and Aristotle's bypassing of the issue are not necessarily indications of their authors' inadequate treatment of linguistic theory, but rather, indications of the relative unimportance of this particular issue to them. What is finally important for all three authors is not whether the name in some way necessarily and naturally imitates the thing named, but rather the foundational and linguistic realist understanding that 'things' precede the human conception of them, that language intends towards reality and reveals it, but that language does not create reality. To have such a view of language does not necessarily imply that one must eschew a belief in the conventionality of language. One can still have a conventionalist view of language and be capable of thinking that language can be used 'unnaturally,' that is, in a way other than in its conventional manner. Whether this 'unnatural' usage constitutes a good, bad, or morally neutral act depends largely on the good or bad intent of the language user.

One of the consistent and most obvious arguments in support of conventionalism has been the existence of many languages. The traditions which share the Old Testament have the Tower of Babel narrative to explain the multiplication of languages. This story also contains an intentionalist realist view of language: after Babel, while the words may change, the things they are directed towards and attempt to name and reveal remain the same. In medieval thought, while spoken languages may differ, a unique 'mental language' is the common foundation of all languages. And so, too, Chomskian linguistics, with its sense of the common 'deep structure' which unites all languages, is a modern realist view of language which never denies that at the surface phonological level languages are principally conventional.

The failure to recognize that language can at once be considered conventional and to have a natural order is also caused by misinterpretation of such dicta as *nomina sunt consequentia rerum.* Ernst Curtius states that this dictum was 'familiar to the entire Latin Middle Ages' (499). But rather than consider it as advocating a Cratylic view of language and denying a conventionalist view, one should see it simply as a foundational realist statement on the natural order: things before words.

John A. Alford argues that 'Augustine is able to combine two opposing views of language, the natural and the conventional, without any sense of contradiction' (737). But Alford himself confuses an Augustinian interest in etymology as a sign of contradiction, because he, Alford, falsely assumes as correct his own presuppositions, namely, that a 'naturalist' or realist position on language is necessarily Cratylic, and that a conventionalist position is necessarily opposed to any 'naturalism' or realism – these are false oppositions.[8] Etymology can be considered a study of the history of linguistic conventions, and/or of 'proper' and 'natural' usage, without holding that the natural connection between a word and a thing is necessarily inherent in a word. Furthermore, one may hold a partial 'Cratylic' view, as in the case of onomatopoeia, where there is obviously a natural mimetic relationship between a word and a thing, without surrendering a general view of language being conventional.

This same tendency to oppose, falsely, conventionalism and realism has led to R. Howard Bloch's statement, which generalizes for medieval thinkers a schizophrenic 'confusion' which some critics also find in Chaucer:

> The dominant attitude toward the question of beginnings [of language] was, in fact, one of anguished ambiguity provoked by a deep split between what medieval writers *knew* about verbal signs [i.e., their conventionalism] and what they *desired* to believe about them [i.e., their Cratylic realism]. (44)

---

[8] To show where the assumption of such false presuppositions could lead consider the following: Alford could have used the passage he cites from Augustine (Alford 737; Augustine, *City* 13.11) in order to 'deconstruct' Augustine; that is, to show an inherent contradiction between what Augustine's statement asserts, but his rhetoric contradicts. Augustine is arguing for what Alford calls a 'natural' relationship between the word 'moritur' ('dies') and that which it signifies, namely, 'death.' But the passage depends for its success on that which Alford *purports* that 'naturalism,' or, for Robert M. Jordan a 'rhetoric of realism,' opposes necessarily, that is, conventionalism.

Perhaps the ultimate exemplar of the conventionality of language, in fact one which Socrates grants to the opponent of Cratylus, Hermogenes (434d–435b), is the perfect homonym: two words pronounced and spelled identically but which have different meanings. It seems that in the very passage in which Augustine argues a 'naturalist' or 'realist' position, he uses a trope dependent on that which such a view purportedly opposes. In arguing, rather playfully, I would say, for a natural or real relationship between a particular word ('moritur,' 'dies') and a 'thing' (death), Augustine puns on two totally different meanings of the identical word *declinare*: 'to decline' as in 'to decline a verb,' and 'to avoid,' as in 'to avoid death.' While such a deconstruction might delight some in exposing a fallacy in Augustine's 'logocentrism,' it more readily shows a weakness of the deconstructive method: the 'deconstructor' may be belied by his or her own presuppositions. The fact is, Augustine did not assume, as critics such as Alford and other critics I consider in this chapter do assume, that 'naturalism' and 'conventionality' are necessarily opposed. Therefore, there is no contradiction or confusion in the passage from Augustine.

When we see the same 'confusion' in such widely different authors – Plato, Aristotle, Augustine, Chaucer – should we not be led to question the actual source of the confusion?

and that despite a

> general agreement that verbal signs are socially, not naturally, determined
> . . . [there is] a profound resistance to breaking entirely with the wish for
> continuity between language and matter along with a radical denial of the
> practical consequences of such a rupture.   (46)

Bloch points to Abelard and John of Salisbury, both of whom evince what he
calls a 'moderate conventionalism' which seems 'typical of medieval sign
theory' (49). For example, although Abelard says 'voces sunt emulae rerum'
(Bloch 48), he also admits that signification is conventional. Although there may
be some confusion inherent in this statement, it largely disappears if one
considers it as a reaffirmation of the 'natural' order: things before words.

While Bloch offers a citation from John of Salisbury that suggests a view
similar to but more qualified than that of Abelard, he exaggerates the importance
of a minor issue (48). He can present no evidence for a great medieval debate on
the issue of mimetic, Cratylic realism versus Aristotelian conventionalism
because there is none. Certainly, there is no one who holds that a belief in the
conventionality of language is an anti-realist position, as Bloch implies.
Nevertheless, Bloch feels free to diagnose some kind of group neurosis or
sublimation, some kind of 'radical denial' of reality. While the evidence leaves
no doubt that in the Middle Ages there was a great interest in both the mimetic
and etymological aspects of language, it is wrong to reduce the medieval
understanding of 'realism' to such interests, just as it would be wrong to equate
similar interests in etymology or onomatopoeia among linguists today with a
commitment to Cratylism.

The conclusion, then, should be that Plato's Socrates, the author of Genesis,
St Augustine, Boethius, Anselm, John of Salisbury, and, as we shall see, Dante
and Geoffrey Chaucer, are not primarily concerned with Cratylism versus
conventionalism; rather they are concerned with linguistic realism, the priority
of things over words.

Intentionalist, linguistic realism is a dimension of a larger foundational
realism. In its understanding of language intentionalist realism has no concern
with a conflict between realism and conventionalism because there is no need to
consider these to be 'mutually exclusive,' nor is there a 'pervasive dichotomy
between semiological theory and practice' as Bloch claims (44). If there is any
'anguish' in Chaucer it is not over the question of realism and conventionalism,
or scholastic realism and scholastic nominalism, it is over the 'improper'
application of words to 'things.'

MAJOR MISUNDERSTANDINGS: ROBERT M. JORDAN

Because it contains so many of the different misunderstandings about the
medieval view of the conventionality and intentionality of language, and
because is shows where these often lead in Chaucer criticism, a case worth
considering in detail is Robert M. Jordan's *Chaucer's Poetics and the Modern*

Reader. Many of these misunderstandings can be extrapolated from the following statement:

> Rhetoric provides the basis for a poetics of uncertainty – or to put it more positively, a pluralistic poetics – because of its primary and always manifest presupposition that language is conventional and inevitably ambiguous; it is a system devised and managed by man, rather than a univocal emanation from God and the created world. The crucial difference between rhetoric and realism in this regard is dramatically illustrated in the career of St Augustine.   (Jordan 10)

Jordan asserts, but fails to argue, that Augustine's religious turn from the Manichaean religion to Christianity is accompanied by a linguistic turn. Supposedly, Augustine's early view, that of 'rhetoric' and his pre-conversion period, is grounded in the 'manifest presupposition' that 'language is conventional.' Augustine's later view, that of 'realism' and his post-conversion phase, is supposedly grounded in a naturalistic/Cratylic view that '[language is] a univocal emanation from God and the created world.' Inexplicably, Jordan does not present any evidence from Augustine's writings to demonstrate this fundamental and dramatic change in language theory; nor does he present any evidence from any scholar who has written on Augustine's understanding of language. Marcia Colish's landmark study of Augustine's 'verbal epistemology' receives no reference in the book, nor do other respected studies of Augustine's sign theory.[9]

While, of course, there is no doubt that Augustine turned from skepticism and Manichaeanism to a form of Christian Neoplatonism and, simultaneously, from being a teacher of rhetoric to a Christian apologist, there is no evidence to suggest that he ever ceased to consider language to be primarily conventional (see Chydenius, *Theory* 5–8), a theory he inherited from Cicero, derived ultimately from Aristotle (Colish 13; 10–11). For Augustine, language in itself has no necessary connection with either thought or extramental reality – a position he argues after his conversion in both *De magistro* and *De doctrina christiana*, II. Undoubtedly, at the same time, he

---

[9] Those interested in medieval epistemology in general and/or Augustine's sign theory in particular should consider the following, all of them ignored by Jordan: First, Colish's seminal study of medieval epistemology. In a series of case studies she demonstrates that, whatever their differences, Augustine, Anselm, Aquinas, and Dante share 'Augustine's verbal epistemology.' Words are 'the fundamental kind of epistemic signs to which other kinds of signs can be reduced' (205–206). Such ideas in Augustine (e.g., *De doctrina christiana* 2.3.4) are well-known, but Colish is able to generalize the situation up to Dante. Eugene Vance, following Colish, speaks of the 'semiological consciousness' (*Signals* 294) and 'metalinguistic consciousness' (305) of the Middle Ages. Patrick J. Gallacher using documentation that is 'substantially different' from that of Colish, arrives 'independently' (162 n. 4) at an understanding similar to Colish's of what he calls the 'Verbum tradition' (2). Thus, Colish and Gallacher corroborate each other. See especially Gallacher's excellent first chapter, 'The Rhetoric of the Word.' On Augustine in particular see R.A. Markus and Darrel B. Jackson. For an historical perspective see Johan Chydenius, *Theory*.

holds a Christian version of the Platonic realist position that language may reveal to us truths which we already unknowingly possess (Nash 84–92). However, Jordan does not seem to understand that such foundational and epistemological realist positions do not necessarily require a Cratylic view of language. It is this faulty assumption on which Jordan bases his scenario of Augustine playing an up-side-down Adam of the philosophy of language, for whose sin (precipitated by his conversion) the understanding of language suffered for centuries.

Jordan's narration of the history of ideas leaves western civilization wallowing in the confusion wrought by Augustine until the genius of Chaucer, enabled for vague reasons connected with the 'realist-nominalist situation in the fourteenth century' (25), is able to overcome the retrograde, so-called Augustinian view of language and he becomes a pioneer practitioner of a 'rhetorical poetics.' Bringing the narrative up to date, Jordan argues that, generally, only today is the rest of western civilization catching up to Chaucer in the widespread understanding that language is conventional and hence ambiguous. Chaucer's 'poetics of rhetoric' becomes synonymous with a 'poetics of uncertainty' or a 'pluralistic poetics.' Chaucer is not only modern, he is state of the art: ' "Postmodern" writers – Barthes, Calvino, Beckett, and a host of others – have reconditioned us to a poetics of uncertainty, where the givens are not unity and coherence but multiplicity and contingency' (20). Since this postmodern 'poetics of uncertainty' is, according to Jordan, 'counter-realist' (25), by implication Chaucer too is a 'counter-realist.' So the purported postmodern return to the pre-Augustinian state of a clear understanding of how language really functions was announced six centuries ago by Chaucer, who had the genius to extract the 'poetics of rhetoric' from the linguistic debates swirling about him. It is indeed true that Augustine's position on the nature of spoken signs – their conventionality – is the view shared generally by the Middle Ages, but this position is exactly the opposite of that which Jordan claims for him.

The understanding that language is conventional is explicitly expressed not only by thinkers from Aristotle, Cicero, and Augustine to Aquinas, Burley, Duns Scotus and Ockham,[10] but also by Geoffrey Chaucer. Although not cited by Jordan, the following verse from *Troilus and Criseyde* is frequently invoked to demonstrate Chaucer's belief that language is conventional:

> Ye knowe ek that in forme of speche is chaunge
> Withinne a thousand yeer, and wordes tho
> That hadden pris, now wonder nyce and straunge
> Us thinketh hem, and yet thei spake hem so,
> And spedde as wel in love as men now do;
> Ek for to wynnen love in sondry ages,
> In sondry londes, sondry ben usages. (2: 22–28)

But in this very verse in which Chaucer asserts linguistic conventionalism, he also asserts a form of linguistic realism. If one were to be consistent with the type of analysis offered by Alford, Bloch, and Jordan, such mingling should be

---

[10] On Aquinas, Scotus, Ockham and conventionality of signs see pages 27–28, 28n22.

considered to be a sign of linguistic confusion. If this is the case this 'confusion' is widespread, for this verse contains the common classical-medieval view of language and its relation to extramental reality. Lines very similar to those of the passage above were written by Horace, Seneca, John of Salisbury, and Dante (RC 1031n22–28). But there is no confused position between 'conventionalism' and 'realism' for Chaucer, or for any of these authors whom, consciously or not, he echoes, if the linguistic realism is understood in a foundational and intentionalist context. The passage from *Troilus and Criseyde* asserts the view that that which language intends, names, reveals, and may even evoke actually precedes language: in this case, 'love.' The 'londes' and 'ages' in which love is spoken of may change, and even the 'wordes' may change, but the experience of love does not change, because, these authors believe, love is before language, before space, before time; love is something that transcends particular experiences of it. Such a position conforms to a theory of the independence of universals, a realist position. Chaucer, here, is like Dante, who believed 'the Augustinian principle that the object is prior to its verbal sign, and that the sign must be judged true or false in terms of its object' (Colish 167). Chaucer, like Dante and Augustine, is a realist who believes not only that extramental reality precedes language, but also that extra-subjective reality can be named, revealed by language, and known to some degree by the human subject – epistemological realism.

Bearing in mind this common understanding of foundational, epistemological, and intentionalist realism expressed by Chaucer, let us return again to Jordan who states that with Dante the 'realist tradition . . . reached an apogee' (Jordan 23). Jordan's confusion on Dante is consistent with his confusion on Augustine and Chaucer. If 'realism' means a belief that language 'is a univocal emanation from God and the created world' (Jordan 10), a form of Cratylism, then how can Dante, who explicitly states that he understands language to be conventional (Colish 176–77), and in the *Convivio* makes statements similar to Chaucer's 'in forme of speche is chaunge' (RC 1031n22–28), be, according to Jordan's definition, a realist? Of course Dante, like Chaucer, *is* a linguistic realist, but he is one in contradiction of Jordan's definition, according to which Dante should be a 'counter-realist' (Jordan 25). While setting up Chaucer as opposed to Augustine and Dante, Jordan ignores the fact that Augustine, Dante, and Chaucer have basically similar understandings of language: all three are at once linguistic conventionalists and linguistic realists.

Beyond the errors of equating belief in the conventionality of language with nominalism and identifying all theories of linguistic realism with Cratylism, we find a third error in Jordan's analysis (found in other critics as well), namely, finding a source of post-Saussurian language theory in scholastic nominalism:

> The analytical separation of language from its object [occurs in Saussure's work] . . . Like the nominalist movement in the fourteenth century, Saussure's work exerted a strong influence on the development of new avenues of intellectual investigation . . . (14–15)

Elsewhere Jordan speaks of 'the [misdirected] realist pursuit of referentiality' (24). The associations made by Jordan are: (a) Saussure (his purported non-referentiality) with nominalism; (b) both of these with postmodern literature; and (c) referentiality with realism. In place of the term 'nominalist' Jordan uses the term 'counter-realist' (25) and includes in this camp all who write in a postmodern style:

> The postmodernists' rejection of the old verities of recognizable characters, logical plots, and unambiguous meaning . . . has generated a critical climate of controversy and uncertainty in many ways analogous to the realist-nominalist situation in the fourteenth century. (25)

Clearly to be inferred from this analogy is that Chaucer is the fourteenth-century equivalent of a postmodern writer, and that such a writer is necessarily a champion of nominalism. Because of the fact that the exclusive association of nominalism with post-Saussurian language theory is a misidentification, Jordan's sweeping generalizations about classes of literature, medieval and modern, are seriously undermined.

Interestingly, this same misidentification has also been made by some of those in an opposing – and equally reductionist – ideological camp; one might call them 'anti-modernists,' who also see Saussure as a descendant of Ockham and a nominalist, but hold this in an entirely negative light. For example, Marion Montgomery, described as 'poet, novelist, critic, and philosopher . . . one of the foremost interpreters of the spiritual crisis of modernity' (book jacket), sweepingly links, negatively and totally incorrectly, Saussure with Ockham and nominalists on the grounds that Saussure's understanding of the arbitrary nature of the sign is 'an obvious derivative of Occam' (78).

There are many analogies that can be made between the modern and medieval understanding of the sign. However, the nominalist parallel with post-Saussurian linguistics made by both Montgomery and Jordan is based on a false analogy and a false association. The false association is the consideration of Saussure's axiom of the 'arbitrariness of the sign' as an exclusively nominalist position. 'The arbitrariness of the sign' is indeed a concept that is absolutely necessary for understanding not only Saussure's insights into the structure of language but the traditional understanding that language is conventional; however, neither of these theories have much to do with the nominalist understandings of the nature of universals, or, for that matter, with 'anti-realism,' as Jordan's work implies. The false analogy is made between the nominalist doctrine that concept words or universals do not refer directly to real things and the Saussurian belief that the science of linguistics should be primarily concerned with the internal structure of signs rather than the question of reference. One of Saussure's successors, Stephen Ullmann, states this position: 'Since the "thing" is non-linguistic, it has no place in a purely linguistic analysis' (*Meaning* 6). Such bracketing of reference is questionable and a source of confusion, but it does not necessarily call into doubt the possibility that accurate reference may occur in a speech act, as some, such as Jordan, seem to infer.

Jordan's interpretation of Chaucer seems to be conditioned by the fact that in Chaucer's writing there is both a concern with and an exploitation of the genuine uncertainty that may occur in interpreting linguistic reference. But this should not necessarily be connected, as it is by Jordan, with an 'anti-realist' position or a 'poetics of uncertainty, where the givens are not unity and coherence but multiplicity and contingency' (Jordan 20). As already argued, the uncertainty and multiplicity of reference that is potential in any use of signs is not an understanding that is exclusive to 'anti-realists.' Such a position does not exclude a realist belief that in their reference signs reveal extramental reality with some degree of accuracy.

MAJOR MISUNDERSTANDINGS: NINE MORE CRITICS

If we consider briefly nine other critics who have taken a position on or made reference to Chaucer and 'nominalism' and/or 'realism,' we will again see the misequation of Cratylism with realism, and linguistic conventionalism with nominalism. We also see another area of confusion in the discussion of nominalism and realism, namely, the misidentification of the primacy of the will as exclusively or principally a nominalist position.

Perhaps the major source of a 'nominalist Chaucer' has been Russell A. Peck. His article 'Chaucer and the Nominalist Questions' usually finds its way into footnotes whenever the words 'Chaucer' and 'nominalist' come together. This is not surprising, for after much argument, and considerable qualification, Peck dramatically concludes his article by declaring, in the same breath, that Chaucer and Ockham are ' "nominalist" thinkers' (760). Here Peck's scare quotations around 'nominalist' are very important, but they are usually ignored by those who use him as an authority. They are there because Peck calls Chaucer a 'nominalist' thinker even while granting that Chaucer does not enter directly into the scholastic debate on the subject:

If nominalism is to be understood as that ontological exercise which refutes realist premises that universals are things of creation, proving to the contrary that only individual things exist and are experienced, and that concepts beyond the individual are names only (concepts which exist exclusively in our heads), then nominalism is probably a matter which lies apart from Chaucer's particular interests. He shows little concern with that problem as such. (745)

While Peck denies Chaucer's 'particular interests' in the central question of the nominalist-realist debate, he nevertheless moves on quickly to identify 'nominalist questions,' and argues that Chaucer is preoccupied with the 'moral implications' of these (745).

The leading 'nominalist question' which Peck considers to be 'at the center of his [Chaucer's] epistemology' is 'the efficacy of the will' (746). However, this is another unfortunate misidentification which has misled critics. While 'the efficacy of the will' – the view of one camp in medieval faculty psychology that the will has primacy over the intellect, that in any human act the will acts before the intellect or the reason acts – may well be central to Chaucer's epistemology, it is not a position peculiar to either nominalism or realism. Indeed, if this view is named with its origin in mind, the primacy of the will should be called an 'Augustinian' position, and Augustine was a realist on the question of the universals. We see Peck doing with this issue what Jordan does with the belief in the conventionality of signs, that is, ascribing exclusively to nominalism a position common to fourteenth-century nominalists and scholastic realists alike. Interestingly, Peck quickly associates Chaucer's position on the function of the will with Ockham and Boethius. Boethius, like Augustine a realist on the question of universals, believed that the will had primacy over the intellect. Moreover, Duns Scotus, the highly regarded 'subtle doctor,' whose metaphysical position is often taken to epitomize the fourteenth-century scholastic realist position on universals, was the major proponent in his century of the primacy of the will, a position sometimes known as 'voluntarism' (Arendt 125-148). Katheryn L. Lynch has reiterated the universally accepted modern understanding of Scotus's importance to this movement and also links it with Chaucer:

> The most widely known and influential proponent of voluntarism in the late Middle Ages was John Duns Scotus, who had been a member of the faculty at both the universities of Paris and Oxford, and whose works continued to be an important part of the university curriculum in Chaucer's time. (86)

Peck does not even mention Scotus, but seems to fudge in his notes by generalizing the interest in 'efficacy of the will' to '14th-century theologians' (746n7). Peck's misidentification of the primacy of the will as a purely nominalist position is without historical support; unfortunately, it has been widely accepted. A typical example occurs in the work of Judith Ferster who, with reference to Peck, asserts that 'Fourteenth-century nominalism paid special attention to Boethius because of his interest in the human will' (Ferster 14). While this is true, it is also true of fourteenth-century scholastic realists, but by now the association has become established between human will, nominalism, Boethius, and Chaucer.

The negative effect of Peck's misequation is partially mitigated by the fact that he draws attention to the centrality of the will as an issue for Chaucer and his period, and in doing so suggests that one reason for the entire 'period's enormous interest in Boethius' (Peck 746n7), including that of Chaucer, may have been Boethius's advocacy of the primacy of the will. For some critics, such as John Gardner, Rodney Delasanta, and P.B. Taylor, the 'Boethian Chaucer' is staid, conservative, even atavistic, while the Chaucer who reveals himself in the 'nominalist narrator' of *The Canterbury Tales* is fresh and modern, a liberal-humanist. While Chaucer's interest in Boethius may indeed suggest a conservatism, it was a conservatism of his century. Pre-Thomist positions on the will, such as those of Boethius and Augustine, were given new life and considered from new perspectives by many fourteenth-century theologians. While Chaucer's interest in both Boethius and the function of the will is not an index of Chaucer's 'nominalism,' as Peck argues, or of his 'modernity,' as others would suggest, it is certainly an index of his contemporaneity.

We saw above that in order to explain a confusion that is their own Alford and Bloch discover confusion, and even schizophrenia, in the understanding of signs by medieval theorists. Bloch and Alford succeed in this by constructing an opposition that simply did not exist for the authors they consider, namely, linguistic realism versus the conventionality of language. This same model has been widely applied by other critics to Chaucer. Rodney Delasanta uses it in an attempt to explain how Peck's Chaucer can be at once a nominalist thinker and a Boethian realist. Delasanta is justifiably uneasy with Peck: 'his [Peck's] identification of voluntarist epistemology with "Chaucer's strongly Boethian orientation" is at odds with my own interpretation, which sees Ockham and Boethius on opposite sides of the philosophical fence' ('Chaucer' 162n4). Boethius *is* Augustinian in his understanding of universals, and on this particular issue he *is* on the other side of the philosophical fence from Ockham. But like so many others Delasanta misses the point that, while thinkers may be divided on the question of the nature of the universals, it does not necessarily follow that they are opposed on all other issues – the primacy of the will or intellect, for example. Indeed, the position of Aquinas on the issue of the primacy of the intellect is opposed to the position of Augustine, Boethius, Scotus, and Ockham. Seemingly unable to sort this all out, Delasanta, like other critics discussed above, resorts to the 'confusion' argument: 'it is not me who is confused, it is those whom I am reading.' Consequently Delasanta comes up with a split Chaucer, who displays 'a nominalist surface cozening a realist depth.' This is an unsupported suggestion that Delasanta considers a 'paradox [which] must be pursued elsewhere' (Delasanta, 'Chaucer' 160). However, when he does return to it in another article he simply repeats the arguments for a split Chaucer, and argues, incorrectly, like Peck, that the primacy of the will is an exclusively nominalist issue ('Nominalism' 126).[11]

One of the initial propagators of the schizophrenic Chaucer is John Gardner, who generalizes it for medieval poetry: 'Medieval poetry commonly expresses a tension between an orthodox theory of reality and an unorthodox intuition of reality' (xxvi). Delasanta takes this statement, quotes part of it out of context ('Chaucer' 154), and then goes on to 'vindicate John Gardner's . . . observation' on 'Chaucer's [sic] art' (160).

What Gardner does argue is that Chaucer, because of 'the arguments offered by the philosophical position called nominalism, [knew] that quite possibly all truth is relative' (ix). Gardner, then, does identify the slogan 'all truth is relative' with the now catch-all term 'nominalism.' There is a basic error here, for 'Nominalism and Scholastic Realism are really theses about predicates, rather than truth' (Haak 283). Gardner is describing an anti-realism which may be called 'Creative Idealism,' but it is certainly not identical with scholastic nominalism.[12] 'Truth is relative' is certainly not a view held by any scholastic

---

11 Another misinterpretation of a philosophical position occurs in another area in this article ('Nominalism' 124) when Delasanta incorrectly associates the Thomistic epistemological primacy of existence over essence with a moderate realist attempt to deal with the problem of the universals, rather than as an existentialist development of Neoplatonism by Aquinas. See my article,' "This litel worde is,".'

12 See Haak's definitions and examples of nominalism and scholastic realism (281–82) which lead to her conclusion: 'Nominalism seems sometimes to have been confused with Creative Idealism,

philosopher, and so it is certainly wrong to assert that such a view could be held by Chaucer because it was current in 'the philosophical position called nominalism.' More adaptable to medieval thinking, and so more readily applicable to Chaucer's undeniable play with ambiguity, is that type of *realism* which Haak calls 'Transcendentalism: truth may outrun us' (283; 280). Such a view was widespread in the Middle Ages and had its theoretical base in Christian Neoplatonism, not in nominalism. Elsewhere I describe this attitude towards reality as being 'anti-essentialist,' not because it denies that essences exist, but because it asserts that absolute knowledge of essences, absolute Truth, is not possible for human beings.[13] Indeed, given man's inferior status to absolute Being, as well as the belief in man's fallen nature which has debilitated his cognitive abilities, the view that man is unable to attain absolute knowledge of the truth through language or thought was one held by all medieval Christian thinkers, be they scholastic nominalists or scholastic realists on the question of the universals. Moreover, the objective accuracy of knowledge which is acquired through the senses had been questioned since classical times, and new studies and speculations in optics in the thirteenth and fourteenth centuries increased such questioning, giving scientific support to the theoretical view of the limits of human cognitive capacities (Tachau). However, none of these inquiries or their conclusions had much to do with the logical pursuits of scholastic nominalists and realists.

Connected with new or renewed epistemological speculations and Christian assumptions was a medieval interest in intentionality. Medieval thinkers, just like some modern thinkers, focused on the epistemological consequences of subjective intentionality. Medieval thinkers understood intentionality, or the object-directedness of thought, to be a function of the intellect governed by the individual human will, and so also understood that the same object could be perceived differently by different people: one observer might see a different aspect or *actualitas* of an object than another observer, a medieval version of what phenomenological psychology now refers to as 'mode of presentation.'[14] One could arrive at this understanding without becoming a relativist. From a Chaucerian and fourteenth-century perspective, indeed from an Augustinian perspective, two people could observe the same object and see different things, or read the same texts and arrive at different meanings, all of which are 'there' in the object. Furthermore, it is a commonplace and orthodox medieval point of view that man is temporarily imprisoned in this earthly sphere in which miscommunication, misapprehension, and misinterpretation occur constantly. Anyone who has followed the comically naive Chaucer-narrator on his flight to *The House of Fame* will find difficulty in disputing that Chaucer, while believing that the senses are the ports of knowledge, also believed that absolute truth in the realm of being inhabited by man is impossible to attain, particularly through the use of language. But, again, this is not an exclusively nominalist insight.

---

and hence to have been thought more of a threat than it really is to the independence of factual truth' (282).

[13] Anti-essentialism: see page 63, 63n11, and my article ' "This litel worde IS".'

[14] Mode of presentation: see particularly pages 75–86.

Perhaps it is some kind of awareness of the inadequacy of the 'nominalist' explanation that finally leaves Gardner uncertain as to Chaucer's realist or nominalist tendencies:

> Chaucer would make it [nominalism] the very heart of his comedy, dramatizing the nominalist position by means of his squinting, dim-witted narrator in the *House of Fame*, or such other later 'unreliable narrators' as the Physician, Prioress, and Manciple in the *Canterbury Tales*. This is not necessarily to say that Chaucer was himself a nominalist. His comedy may have been, at least in his own mind, a way of making fun of the nominalist view of man; and even if he was a nominalist, he was never in his life thrown into self-pity or despair on account of a conviction that nothing can be known for certain. (xviii)

Seeing Chaucer as 'making fun of the nominalist view of man' is, as Gardner himself admits, not a strong argument for seeing Chaucer as a nominalist.

Delasanta's characterization of Chaucer as 'a nominalist surface cozening a realist depth' ('Chaucer' 160) is succinctly summarized by P.B. Taylor as follows: '[according to Delasanta] Chaucer the poet is a Boethian realist while Chaucer the pilgrim-reporter of the tales is a confused nominalist' (318). Taylor refines this position and suggests that in Chaucer's works a 'realistic view of language' is confused with a 'nominalist view' (323). He does, however, make an observation similar to that of Gardner: 'In general, . . . Chaucer's emphasizing of nominalist views on language are [sic] found more often in comic and satiric contexts than in serious ones, and considerations of linguistic realism occur in serious contexts' (318). Taylor, like Gardner, sees Chaucer mocking nominalist views. Finally, however, Taylor, like most critics, finds it necessary to retreat to the fence between realism and nominalism, seeing in Chaucer's poetry 'doubts and confusions about the complex relations between intent, word, and deed' (319). This move might be due in part to the fact that, like Peck and Ferster, Taylor sees, reasonably, in Chaucer's works a manifestation of the belief in the efficacy or primacy of the will. But Taylor's identification of such a position as belonging exclusively 'to that branch of nominalism known as voluntarism' (318) is, for the same reasons as outlined in the discussion of Peck above, a misidentification. Unlike Ferster's case, Peck is not cited as a support for this misidentification, but David C. Steinmetz is (316n7); unfortunately, Steinmetz is an equally perilous source.

Is the *Clerk's Tale* focused on a nominalist issue? Steinmetz thinks it is because he sees it as centered on the question of the function of the human will. While Steinmetz does succeed in showing that the function of the will is a focus of the tale, we see here the same type of error of definition of 'nominalism' as we have seen practiced by Peck, Ferster, and Taylor, that is, the mistaken understanding that an interest in the topic of will is exclusively a nominalist interest. We saw that Peck incorrectly makes 'the efficacy of the will' a 'nominalist question,' while allowing in a footnote that the issue is of interest to '14th-century theologians' (746n7) in general, *not* '14th-century *nominalist* theologians,' though one could easily miss this. Steinmetz fudges in a similar manner. He incorrectly asserts that what he sees as the central issue of the

Clerk's Tale is also primarily a nominalist issue, while simultaneously allowing that it is not solely a nominalist issue: 'The story is an illustration of the axiom, common to all medieval scholastics but of particular importance for Occamists, "facientibus quod in se est Deus non denegat gratiam" ' (38). Steinmetz renders the Latin as 'God does not deny His grace to those who do what is in them' (58n5). In fact the formula does not refer to what is 'in' anybody, but to those who do good 'in itself' (*in se*), and it is a position common not 'to all medieval scholastics,' nor to nominalists ('Occamists'), but to Franciscans regardless of their position on universals.[15]

Steinmetz concludes that 'The Clerk has elaborated on an allegorical level the main elements of the nominalist doctrine of justification . . . Conformity of our will to the will of God, not in order to obtain temporal or eternal benefits from Him but out of love for Him alone . . . will be rewarded' (58n5). Yet this 'nominalist' division and doctrine on types of willing is also one discussed and advocated by the realist and Franciscan, Duns Scotus. God gives man a power whereby he may choose a good greater than himself, and ultimately the Good *in se*, God. *The Clerk's Tale* may well consider and take to absurd lengths a very serious question of two different intentionalities, that of the human will and that of the divine will. This question of will, human and divine, together with the related topics of grace and justification, was a topic of great interest in the fourteenth century, but interest in this question is not necessarily a signal of the nominalist-realist opposition.

A view which directly opposes the nominalist Chaucer, nominalist-leaning Chaucer, or schizophrenic Chaucer of the critics considered above is that of David Williams. Though Williams would, I think, agree with Peck that Chaucer was not immediately concerned with the philosophical issues of nominalism and realism, he does see in Chaucer's writings 'the beginnings of a realist theory of fiction' ('Intentionality' 92). If 'realist' means here that Chaucer believes that his fiction reveals a pre-existing reality, Williams has, I believe, an arguable case. However, while this meaning seems to be intended, Williams also clearly uses 'realist' in its Cratylic sense, committing the same error as Robert M. Jordan, to whose approach that of Williams is diametrically opposed. However, Williams' work is more directed at disproving that Chaucer is a 'nominalist' than at proving that he is a 'realist' in the scholastic sense of the term – and in this I believe he succeeds, particularly in his reading of the *Pardoner's Tale* (*Pilgrimage* 73–88). Satire tends to take positions to extremes, and so the 'nominalism' which Chaucer develops is closer to that type of conceptual idealism which, in Philotheus Boehner's description, 'severs the bond between thought and reality' (307). Such an extreme conceptual idealism was not the position of any major nominalist, as Boehner points out, but may be a consequence of nominalism taken to its limits – something Chaucer appears to do. As we have seen in the comments of John Gardner and P.B. Taylor above,

---

[15] I thank Patrick J. Gallacher for pointing this out to me and referring me to William J. Courtenay's discussion of this axiom. Courtenay writes that *facientibus quod in se est, Deus non denegat gratium* expresses a 'view, encountered often in Franciscan theology, that man can initiate the return to God, and that God will reward with grace and final acceptation those who do their best' (*Schools* 296–97).

Williams is not alone in the observation that Chaucer parodies extreme nominalism, but he is the first to demonstrate it.

A satire of extreme scholastic nominalism may exist in Chaucer's writings; however, to associate Chaucer with *scholastic* realism as a necessary consequence of this, as does Williams, undermines Williams' credibility. Because the sheer volume of the criticism which indicates that Chaucer is a nominalist, or nominalist-leaning, far outweighs the work of Williams and the glancing observations of Gardner and P.B. Taylor, it is not surprising that many have followed Peck, Steinmetz, et al., and we have a situation today where a nominalist Chaucer is sprouting from much critical literature. Often, as in the case of Judith Ferster, the roots of the nominalist Chaucer are firmly buried in footnotes referring to the works of the critics just discussed.

In other cases such desultory views have led to total confusion. The danger, both for academics and students, of relying on the general criticism on Chaucer to arrive at a view of his understanding of language can be seen in the following statement by Philip Pulsiano:

> Although Chaucer nowhere directly addresses the leading language theorists of his day, his poetry reflects an intense awareness of the moral and philosophical dimensions of language . . . And while one cannot say with any certainty whether Chaucer allied himself with the realists or the nominalists on the issue of verbal epistemology, clearly his ideas on language are compatible with those of a wide range of writers: . . . Macrobius . . . Ockham . . . Augustine . . .   (153)

Chaucer's understanding of language in the light of the realist view of language and ethics accounts very well, I believe, for what Pulsiano calls Chaucer's 'intense awareness of the moral and philosophical dimensions of language' – this is an awareness he shared with his age. However, to demonstrate that Chaucer's ideas on language are compatible with Macrobius, Ockham and Augustine would be a major feat. Ockham's nominalist views on universals are diametrically opposed to those of the two realists mentioned here, Macrobius and Augustine. Furthermore, Ockham's views on universals are matched by a theory of how language denotes universals or concepts and of how these truly relate to reality. Where is this in Chaucer? The authority for Pulsiano's assertions, and the root of the confusion, may be found in the footnote which accompanies the statement; here Pulsiano refers the reader to the articles discussed above by P.B. Taylor, Russell A. Peck, and David C. Steinmetz (107n2).

CHAUCER'S ETHICAL REALISM

Finally, there is another source of confusion about Chaucerian realism stemming from Chaucer's use of 'Plato', which can now be clarified within the context of the foregoing discussion.

'Good' and 'bad,' 'proper' and 'improper,' are not relative terms – at least for Chaucer. Chaucer's sense of ethical propriety and impropriety is revealed through and in his use of words. It was understood in the Middle Ages that, given our free will, signs may be directed or misdirected, used properly or improperly, naturally or unnaturally – a linguistic paradigm that reflects and is reflected in all spheres. Eugene Vance uses the term 'improper coupling' (205) to describe the intentional, unnatural coupling of sign and thing, which is a paradigm of other unnatural couplings, particularly sexual, that is consciously dealt with as a theme in certain works of medieval French literature. 'Improper coupling' is a very important concept that I borrow for the demonstration of Chaucerian realism in later chapters. Here it allows us to clear up a misunderstanding.

Chaucer uses a tag derived from Plato via Boethius: 'thow hast learnyd by the sentence of Plato that nedes the wordis moot be cosynes to the thinges of whiche thei speken' (Bo 3.pr.12 206–7). Similar statements are found on three occasions in *The Canterbury Tales*.

Chaucer's translation 'cosynes to the thinges' is of Boethius's 'cum Platone sanciente didiceris *cognatos de quibus loquuntur rebus oportere esse sermones*' (*Consolatio Philosophiae* 3.12.18). 'Cognatus' is a 'blood-relative,' 'related by birth,' and 'oportere' is properly rendered in modern English by the modals 'must' or 'ought to.' All words must or ought to be blood-relatives to that referent to which both the speaker and the interpreter assign them. Implicit in the concept of sign and signified as 'blood-relatives' or 'cousins' is that they are (a) not identical, but (b) that they are naturally related, and (c) that as in all relationships between blood relatives, there may be 'proper' and 'improper,' 'natural' and 'unnatural,' or 'legitimate' and 'illegitimate' relationships or couplings. This metaphor is closely linked to the Boethian and Neoplatonic concept of natural intentionality (which is really the intentionality of God, the One, Being), as well as the Stoic-Epicurean and Judeo-Christian understanding of the importance of the human will as the guiding faculty of human intentionality.[16] From the opposition between natural and human intentionality springs much of the drama of Judeo-Christian anthropology – human intentionality always has the potential to oppose natural intentionality. The metaphors of 'coupling' and 'cosyn' help us to understand that the coupling of language to thought and extramental reality is an intentional act. Like all human intentional acts, the act of speech is a willful act directed towards something. This being the case, we may bend or intend words to our own purposes, 'good' or 'bad,' 'natural' or 'unnatural,' 'proper' or 'improper.'

In his excellent discussion of the term, P.B. Taylor points out that 'cosyn' also means 'dupe' (104).[17] Since 'moot' or 'must' can have a sense of 'advisability' (a strong sense of 'should') as well as 'must' (obligation), Chaucer's statement, 'the wordes moot be cosyn to the dede,' may have ironically opposed meanings. Indeed, this statement could serve as an apt epigram to Umberto Eco's succinct definition: '*semiotics is in principle the discipline studying everything which can be used in order to lie*' (Eco, *Theory* 7, emphasis in the original) – a definition

---

[16] On the Stoic-Epicurean position here see Whitney J. Oates xix–xxi.
[17] Taylor's article was very suggestive and helpful for the present discussion of 'cosyn.'

that I shall recall on numerous occasions. Obviously, words may be used to mislead others from a subject's real intentions. 'Cosyn' is itself one of those 'double wordes slye,' 'a word with two visages' (Tr 5 898–99). Chaucer delights in playing with the various senses words may have in different contexts; P.B. Taylor's demonstration of this with the word 'cosyn' is an exceptionally apt exemplar.

Boethius's source of that which Chaucer translates as 'cosyn to the dede' and 'cosyn to the thinge' is the *Timaeus*. While the reference which Boethius translates from the *Timaeus* is not at all clearly Cratylic in its original version, it is certainly not Cratylic in Boethius's translation and in Chaucer's translation of Boethius. In the *Timaeus*, the eponymous character argues that there is a 'natural' relationship between words and things. Let us consider 'Plato's' 'cosyn to the dede' in its wider original context (Timaeus is speaking):

> And having been created in this way [by the 'artificer' looking to the 'eternal'], the world has been framed in the likeness of that which is apprehended by reason and mind . . . Now it is all-important that the beginning of everything should be according to nature. And in speaking of the copy and the original we may assume *that words are akin to the matter* which they describe.   (29 a–c, emphasis added)

The words emphasized are the only ones that find their way into *The Consolation of Philosophy*. The translation from Boethius's Latin into Chaucer's Middle English is the total of 'Plato's' words in Chaucer's *Boece*. Boethius has translated the Greek as *oportere esse*; words *ought to be* related or akin to that which they name, a nuance which Chaucer translates with the Middle English 'moot be.' The *oportere esse* translation is consistent with Boethius's sense of the two potentially conflicting spheres of intentionality, human and divine. The modal verb used in the passage by Boethius implies that words may not be cousin to that which they name, that words may lie, or, more accurately, that human beings may willfully cause words to lie. Words depend for their 'good entencioun' upon the 'good entencioun' or the good will of the human speaker. The Boethian emphasis is on the will of the speaker, not on the words themselves; this is also a late medieval emphasis; and Boethius's understanding of the function of the human will in directing the proper 'cosyning'/cousining or the improper 'cosyning'/duping of the relationship between the word and the thing, is also Chaucer's understanding. Implicit here, for Chaucer, is a linguistic intentionalist realism.

Earlier it was mentioned that a *direct* relationship between word and thing is Cratylic realism; a *directed* relationship between word and thing is intentionalist realism. In Cratylic realism the obligation – the ought to, should, 'moot' – is inherent in the relationship between the word and the 'thing'; the word partakes of the nature of that of which it is the sign. In intentionalist linguistic realism the obligation for proper or natural representation rests with the speaker. This view is nowhere more obvious than in the *Manciple's Tale*. In a tale that ironically relates a case of the sometimes dire consequences of 'tellen proprely a thing' the Manciple repeats Chaucer's favorite 'Platonic' dictum:

The wise Plato seith, as ye may rede,
The word moot nede accorde with the dede.
If men shal telle proprely a thyng,
The word moot cosyn be to the werkyng.   (IX 208–210)

The corollary of this modal phrase is that rather than 'proprely' telling a 'thyng,' it is possible for man, intentionally, to 'telle a thyng' 'improprely.' Moreover, with much irony, the tale asserts that to tell a thing improperly may often be in the teller's best interest. A crow recounts to his master, in excessively graphic detail, an encounter which he had witnessed between his master's wife and her paramour. For some time the wife, through her words and demeanor, had been 'improperly telling a thing.' In declaring herself faithful, the wife had masked her 'ententes black' with 'wordes white.' Her words and outward demeanor, signs of faithfulness, are not 'cosyn to the werkyng,' or faithful to the reality, but are used to 'cosyn' or dupe the duke. The crow's words, though unnecessarily indiscreet, are 'cosyn to the werkyng': the adulterous deed that he had witnessed. As his reward for telling 'proprely a thyng,' the crow, who was white and sang 'lyk a nyghtyngale' (IX 294), is turned black and condemned to make 'nevere sweete noyse' (IX 300) again. This corruption and inversion of propriety serves as an ironic comment on the state of 'modern,' postlapsarian man, but – and this is the point I wish to emphasize here – the 'Platonic' dictum is in no way intended to be construed as a definition of Cratylic realism: it is not the word which makes itself 'cosyn to the dede,' a direct Cratylic relationship, but rather the user of the word who makes or simulates this relationship, a directed intentionalist realist relationship. The tale deals, however ironically, with the moral imperative for the speaker to link his or her 'entente,' his or her thoughts, with the conventional 'entente,' or meaning, of the words he or she uses. This is an ethical universe where there is not only a real relationship, by convention, between words and what they conventionally signify, but where there should be or 'moot' be a real relationship between the words one uses and the thoughts one has.

So too 'Pilgrim Chaucer' in the *General Prologue* uses the 'Platonic' dictum as a rationalization for his reportorial stance. He 'must' tell tales exactly as they are told, even if they contain elements and manners of expression which may offend some ears because as 'Plato seith . . . / The wordes moote be cosyn to the dede' (I 742). Obviously here the narrator is 'playing' with this dictum, his intent being to disclaim ironically moral responsibility for the tales which are to follow, while simultaneously alerting us to our own moral responsibility in the reading of texts. Chaucer-Pilgrim tells us, then, citing Plato as an authority, that he 'moot' imitate as exactly as possible the words that he heard his fellow pilgrim tale-tellers utter so that he can fully convey the *intended* meaning or thought of his 'authors.' Given this context, there is no reason for believing that the phrase 'cosyn to the dede' is here understood in any Cratylic sense by Chaucer, that is, that he believes words somehow mimetically represent the objective realities they name. Chaucer asserts, just as the *Manciple's Tale* demonstrates, that what comes out of the speaker's mouth is governed by the speaker's will – and it is in the individual will that the source of the propriety or the impropriety of words is found.

Chaucer's ethical concern with the use of language, the implicit subject of the *Manciple's Tale*, is explicit in Chaucer's ballade, 'Lak of Stedfastnesse.' Here Chaucer expresses a conventional nostalgia for a prelapsarian time when 'the world was so stedfast and stable / That mannes word was obligacioun' (1–2). Times have changed: 'And now it [man's word] is so fals and deceivable / That word and deed . . . / Ben nothing lyk' (3–5). However, it is not language that has changed; language was and always has been conventional. Rather, it is man who has changed: '. . . for turned up-so-doun / Is al this world for mede and willfulnesse / That al is lost for lak of stedfastnesse' (5–7). Liam O. Purdon, while making the same error as many critics already discussed – thinking that 'lack of steadfastness' may reside in language itself, rather than in the will of the speaking subject – states concisely that in this poem Chaucer 'indicates that abuse of words not only distorts reality but also eventually engenders further linguistic and moral abuse' (146).

Language is only the instrument of the truth-sayer or liar who uses or abuses it. Man has a proper and ethical relationship to language, just as he has a proper and ethical relationship to all other aspects of reality. What is most important about these relationships is that they be kept in order. Augustine, in a statement that is echoed in the *Parson's Tale* (X 579), defines *peccatum* or sin as 'factum vel dictum vel concupitum aliquid contra aeternam legem' ('a deed or a word or a desirous thought which contravenes the eternal law').[18] All sin occurs when man willfully disturbs the *ordo naturalis*: 'whan man synneth, al this ordre or ordinaunce is turned up-so-doun' (ParsT X 262).[19] Lee Patterson's comment on Augustine's definition of sin in the *Contra Faustum* is equally applicable to the Parson's statement: '[Augustine] is referring to a *lex aeterna* that is known ethically in the commandments but also ontologically in the form, order, and due measure that inform reality' ('The "Parson's Tale" ' 341). Language in the Middle Ages was considered to be an integral and important part of a wider reality, and the misuse of language a serious sin. The importance of propriety in language, and the very high relative importance given to language itself in the Middle Ages, is underlined by the fact that, unlike the Greek classical tradition, there is a strict prohibition against lying in the Judeo-Christian tradition (Trentman, 'Mental Language'). From the metaphysical and ethical presuppositions which inform Chaucer's writings springs the belief that language is a gift of God which, like other gifts, may be used or abused: *mentire est abuti voce* ('lying is the abuse of words') (Scotus, Wolter 482).

In general, in the Christian tradition after St Augustine, language itself is widely understood to be imperfect, like man, and like all other created beings ('we been of o nature, roten and corrupt' [ParsT X 460]). Augustine speaks of the innate weakness of 'the corporeal matter of verbal signs' (*De ordine* 434; see Bloch 47). The mutable sign, according to Augustine's Platonism, may only imperfectly represent immutable transcendent reality. Because words may not perfectly communicate, the possibility of misunderstanding and misinterpreting was considered inevitable. Such unintentional miscommunication was not an

---

[18] *Contra Faustum* 22.27 PL 42.418; cited by Lee Patterson in his important discussion of this point in 'The "Parson's Tale" ' 341
[19] For a general discussion on the 'up-so-doun' topos see Klene 321–334; also Curtius 94–98.

abuti voce. Words were abused when they were intentionally, willfully used for improper purposes. So, Chaucer, in his 'retracciouns,' begs those who might find anything in his works displeasing 'that they arrette [attribute] it to the defaute of myn unkonnynge [ignorance, lack of skill] and nat to my wyl, that wolde ful fayn have seyd bettre if I hadde had konnynge' (Ret X 1082). While he is concerned about intentional misinterpretations that might 'sownen into synne' (Ret X 1085), it is not the unintentional misuse or misinterpretation of language that is Chaucer's primary concern. While we are responsible for careless misspeaking which may lead others into sin, our imperfect fallen nature together with the natural imperfection of language virtually guarantees that we shall all, on occasion, be imperfect language users and interpreters. Rather than such unintentional, 'natural' misuse, it is 'unnatural' misuse that is sinful: the intentional upsetting of the 'natural' relationship between word and thing that one may 'arrette' or attribute to someone's 'wyl.'

A typical medieval position on the connection between word and will, that of Aquinas, is summarized by McInerny: 'The word as conventional or arbitrary sign has the will as its source, like any other artifact. No word of human language will as such naturally relate to the thing signified by it' (51). *Language is conventional; it does not relate naturally to the things it signifies; its source is the will.* The typical position of those who gave primacy to the will, such as Augustine and Boethius, is stated as follows by Ockham: 'No act unless it be initiated by an act of the will is intrinsically virtuous or vicious.'[20] The 'proper' use of a conventional word in a conventional language is not itself a matter of convention.[21] When the deliberate 'abuse' of this 'propriety' is seen as *intrinsically* virtuous or vicious, the scare quotations around 'good' and 'bad,' 'proper' and 'improper,' 'use' and 'abuse,' must fall away and one has a linguistic realism – one which, because its source of good and bad is found in the willful intentional act of the speaking subject, is an intentionalist realism.

These 'realisms' are among those which may be attributed to Chaucer.

'WORDES WHITE' AND 'ENTENTES BLACK': CHAUCER,
ETHICS, AND LANGUAGE

The general understanding among philosophers and poets of the Middle Ages that language is conventional ensures that for them the human will is the ethical centre of the speech act.

Consider that Aquinas, a moderate realist, Walter Burley and Duns Scotus, realists both, and William of Ockham, a nominalist, all explicitly held the view that language was made up of signs imposed by the human will. Burley states the commonplace of the conventionality of language, a position that,

---

[20] Nullus actus alius ab actu voluntatis est intrinsece virtuosus vel vitiosus' (III Sent. q. 12G); see Coleman 32, and Boehner 145.
[21] Compare Gosselin 190.

with qualifications, would be accepted by nominalists, realists, and moderate realists alike: 'A word can signify whatever the speaker wants it to signify' (S.F. Brown 108). Armand Maurer notes this common ground of Scotus and Ockham: 'Ockham's guiding principle [on a particular issue] . . . is already found in Duns Scotus. Since words are conventional signs, Ockham argues, they signify primarily what the inventor and user of the words first of all intends them to signify' (800).[22] Of course, these thinkers also realized that while a word primarily signifies what the speaker intends it to signify, the comprehension of such signification is limited by the very conventionality of language.

Because language requires convention, a *con-venio* or a coming-together of a number of wills, it may be used by any willing subject to deliberately mislead. Duns Scotus states a medieval commonplace: 'ut dicit Plato in *Timaeo*: "Sunt voces institutae et impositae ut praesto fiant voluntatis indicia"' (for as Plato says in the *Timaeus*: 'Words were instituted and imposed so that they might become present indices of what we have in mind') (Wolter 482). Wolter broadly translates 'voluntatis indicia' as 'indices of what we have in mind,' but perhaps 'indices of one's will or intention' is the literal meaning. We should understand 'will' here very broadly. While, for example, Searle distinguishes between 'mental acts,' such as mental arithmetic, and 'mental states,' such as 'believing, fearing, hoping, and desiring' (*Intentionality* 3), Chaucer and the Middle Ages make no such distinction (Alexander 5). Not believing in God, fearing the devil, or hoping for salvation, and the contraries of all these, are acts of 'ought' and 'ought-not,' ethical acts and intentional acts performed by the will.

An index of the interest in this subject in the fourteenth century, beyond the circle of theologians, is its popularity as a literary theme. The role of the will is a major issue in the popular Griselda story in versions by Boccaccio, Petrarch, many French poets, and Chaucer. The function of the will is also central to the *Friar's Tale*. Also, one may consider the subjection of despairing reason to will in *The Pearl*, and the role of will as the character 'Will' in *Piers Plowman* (Bowers).

Augustine writes 'that man lies who has one thing in his mind and utters another in words, or by signs of whatever kind' (*De mendacio* 3). The ethical concern of Chaucer and his age for the willful or intentional play and mis-play with 'signs of whatever kind' is reflected in the name and actions of the character Fals-Semblant in *The Romaunt of the Rose*. Here, in what is probably Chaucer's translation, Fals-Semblant proudly confesses his masks. Clothes may present a false 'face': 'Wene ye that I nil bigile / For I am clothed mekely? / Ther-undir is al my trechery' (7316–18). Similarly, bodily expression may present a false 'face': 'Though I have chere of symplenesse, / I am not wery of shrewidnesse' (7321–22). Clothing, physical expression, and demeanor all are signs: something which can be used both to tell the truth and to lie. Fals-Semblant intermingles such signs together with the signs *par excellence* of false face, words. In a dramatic scene Fals-Semblant is portrayed kneeling before 'Love' in humble fealty, a feudal sign of pledging 'trouthe,' humility, and submission:

---

22 On some of the differences between Ockham, Burley, and Scotus see S.F. Brown (106). See McKeon (316) on the relation of ethics to philosophy in the Midddle Ages. For a specific case on the relation of ethics and language in Ockham see Clark (27).

And Fals-Semblant, the theef, anoon,
. . .
That hadde of tresoun al his face
Ryght blak withynne and whit withoute,
Thankyth hym [Love], gan on his knees loute.

(Rom 7330–33, emphasis added)

'The wordes moote be cosyn to the dede' (GP I 742), but they may also be willed *not* to be 'cosyn' to the 'dede': the real intention is in the mind of the sign-maker. If the sign-maker so intends, signs need *not* signify the real thought in the mind of the user of the word, or the thought in the mind of the wearer of the clothes as signs, or the thought in the mind of the maker of the physical expression as a sign, or the thought in the mind of the doer of the physical action. A 'face / *Ryght blak withynne and whit withoute*' is the image of the 'two-faced' sign in which the 'vox' or 'face' of the sign is literally not 'cosyn' to the thought of the sign-maker, but is intended to 'cozen' or dupe the interpreter of the sign. Consequently, the user or interpreter is involved in an economy of ethical and moral action, marked by gradations of value from extreme 'good' to extreme 'evil.' The lie, the 'blackness,' is not in the sign, it is in the thought, in the mind of the sign-maker, and the false sign-making is the *willful* evil deed of the sign-maker.

'The black' and 'the white' of words and 'ententes' are motifs in Chaucer's work,[23] and perfectly illustrate Chaucer's ethical concern with 'improper coupling,' beginning on the linguistic level and extending to all realms of willful human activity. In the *Monk's Tale* Pedro of Spain is betrayed and slain by his own brother, Bernard du Guesclin, whose treacherous duplicity, Chaucer's Monk subtly suggests, is pre-signed in Bernard's coat of arms, 'The feeld of snow, with th'egle of blak therinne' (VII 2383). The summoner of the *Friar's Tale* writes 'feyned mandement[s]' (III 1360) against adulterers and other sinners, and promises them he will 'striken hire [the wenche] out of oure letters blake' (1364) for a bribe, so making the outer sign of the sin white, while the inner blackness remains. The duplicity of the friar of the *Summoner's Tale* is demonstrated with a similar effacement of signs. Here, the names and the intentions of the poor parishioners for whom the friar promises to pray are, after payment, written by the friar's secretary on 'A peyre of tables al of yvory' (III 1741). But 'whan that he was out at dore, anon / He [the secretary] planed awey the names everichon / That he biforn had writen in his tables' (1757–58), returning the 'yvory' to its pristine white. In the *Franklin's Tale*, Dorigen wants the 'grisly rokkes blake' (859) of the Breton coast to disappear. These black rocks, which she sees threatening her absent husband's return, seem to symbolize the contingency of human existence. Aurelius, who wishes to be Dorigen's lover, creates the *illusion* that the rocks may be made to disappear, but the reality, the black rocks and the precarious contingency of our being, remains. The cheating Chanoun of the *Canon's Yeoman's Tale* is not without reason portrayed as 'A man that clothed was in clothes blake, / And undernethe

---

[23] This discussion of the 'wordes white' motif was sparked by a coversation with David Williams who pointed out to me its use in *Troilus and Criseyde*.

he hadde a whyt surplys' (CYT VIII 557–58). In the *Manciple's Tale* the *white* sweet-singing crow is turned into a *black* croaking crow for telling his master the truth about his wife's adulterous actions.[24] This is an inverted allegory on making the 'word . . . accorde with the dede' (208), or 'cosyn . . . to the werkyng' (210). In *Troilus and Criseyde*, Pandarus tells Criseyde that 'if a fool were in a jalous rage,' then he would 'feffe hym with a fewe wordes white' (3.899;901), that is, placate him with words in whose intent or meaning he does not really believe. Criseyde, in turn, charges Pandarus of using 'wordes white' (3.1567) with her. And Pandarus quite obviously does use words white or 'unthrift' (4.431), in whose intent he does not really believe, in order to aid a 'fool' of sorts, Troilus, 'lest he for sorwe deyde' (4.429) due to the absence of Criseyde.

Chaucer demonstrates an understanding that a sign may be the false or the true 'face' of the actual thought or intention of the signifying individual. This is not an uncommon metaphor. Most notably, Geoffrey of Vinsauf writes of a word having a 'face' and a 'mind' (Nims 216). There is no great distance from this image to the Saussurean notion of the verbal sign or word as being a single entity, or unified duality, composed of a sound pattern and a sense. Many other 'modern' linguistic concepts stem from long-understood notions. For example, there is the medieval linguistic axiom 'vox significat mediantibus conceptibus' (Ullmann, *Principles* 71): a conventional sound pattern, *vox*, signifies via a concept or sense for which it is a mark. This is widely known today as the 'semiotic triangle' or 'Frege's triangle' (Eco, 'Signification' 2), and goes back at least as far as Aristotle (Eco, 'Signification' 4). In the semiotic triangle, words, *voces*, are conventionally accepted sound patterns which indicate concepts, which, in turn, signify objects. But also appreciated in the Middle Ages was the fact that outside the triangle of name, sense, and thing, always stood its manipulator, the speaker.

Rabbi Bahye ibn Paquda elegantly stated in the eleventh century another metaphor that was quite common in the Middle Ages: 'Speech is the pen of the heart, the translator of the soul, and the emissary of the thoughts' (Faur xviii). One could say that while the friar of the *Summoner's Tale* sends out words that may convey truth, they do not convey the true intent he has in his heart. 'Emissaries' are notorious for exploiting the ambiguities of language to achieve the ends of those they serve. Through Diomede, in *Troilus and Criseyde*, Chaucer defines 'ambages' or ambiguities in terms reminiscent of Vinsauf's 'mind' and 'face,' and prescient of modern linguists:

> And but if Calkas lede us with ambages –
> That is to seyn, with double wordes slye.
> Swiche as men clepen a word with two visages –   (V 897–99)

It is the very nature of signs that they may be used to mislead or lie, says Diomede. However, Diomede claims that he himself is using language to tell his true thoughts. The truth of Diomede's statement to Criseyde rests on the knowledge that although thought and deed ought to be one, they need not be one, because the 'naturalness' or 'unnaturalness,' the 'propriety' or 'impropriety' of the speech-act rests with the speaker and the interpreter, not with the words.

---

[24] See also the discussion of the *Manciple's Tale* above, 24–25.

The topical interest in ambiguity, truth, and lying in Chaucer's day is revealed in a complaint the Duke of Gloucester made in 1393 regarding the perpetual perfidiousness of the French. One may wonder if the duke, who probably had the occasion to hear Chaucer recite *Troilus and Criseyde*, had Diomede in mind when, at one of the many parleys during the Hundred Years War, he complained of the French emissaries that they 'used ambiguous language, filled with "subtle cloaked words of double understanding" which they turned and twisted to their advantage – such words as Englishmen did not use, "for their speech and intent is plain" ' (Tuchman 512). Chaucer, himself a frequent emissary of the English court, reveals himself to be fully conscious of the paradoxical nature of signs: signs may be the source of untruth, but they are also necessary to reveal truth. This paradox also lies at the heart of Eco's definition of semiotics as 'the discipline studying everything which can be used in order to lie' (*Theory* 7); in fact the words of Diomede are unconsciously repeated by Eco in his elaboration of this definition: 'If something cannot be used to tell a lie, conversely it cannot be used to tell the truth: it cannot in fact be used "to tell" at all' (7). Chaucer's interest in semiotics revolves around just this issue, the nature of 'telling': telling the truth and telling lies through signs. Eco's definition of semiotics is fundamentally similar to Searle's question on the speech act which (as we shall see) is also Chaucer's question: 'What is the difference between saying something and meaning it and saying it without meaning it?' (*Speech Acts* 3). By these criteria Chaucer's writings are, in a special way, concerned with the science of semiotics as it relates to the speech act. Given this shared interest, one may next ask whether Chaucer's understanding of the 'speech act' was considerably different from our own – the answer contained in this book is that it was not.

Granting that Chaucer's interests are semiotic interests, the question remains, how good a semiotician is he? How adequate is his account of language? According to Searle: 'Any account of language must allow for the fact that it is possible to lie, and it is possible to perform a statement while lying' (*Intentionality* 168). In the *Clerk's Tale* Chaucer deals with this; we do not know if Griselda, whose 'word' is constantly being scrutinized, is always fully 'signing' what is in her heart. Walter, mistrusting her words as true indices of what she really feels and thinks, turns to another sign of that which she has in her heart, her 'cheere' or facial and other physical expressions. But, the tale subtly suggests, these signs of physical expression may be just as deliberately misdirected as linguistic signs may be. The *Clerk's Tale* leaves us grasping for interpretations of what Griselda really feels and thinks; we are forced to ask if the outward signs she gives us are 'properly' or 'improperly' directed. Ultimately, the tale suggests, the thought one has in one's heart is private; whether the emissaries of one's heart speak truly or falsely is left for the interpreter to decide or believe: signs are anything that can be used to lie, or tell the truth.

The brilliant and deliberate demonstration of the possibilities of semantical manipulations in the *Friar's Tale* offers another convincing account of Chaucer's semiotic acumen. For example, consider the incident in which a carter's words of cursing to hell his be-mired horses are shown to have no relationship to what he has 'in mind', to his real intention. The carter has no

intention of misleading anyone, but his words alone may mis-direct the
interpreter of words who is a literalist. The carter's words are not intended to be
true or false emissaries to human beings, because they are not directed towards
human beings, and they are not used conventionally. In the terms of Austin and
Searle, the carter performs an illocutionary act whose entire meaning is carried
in its perlocutionary effect (Searle, *Speech Acts* 25): his curse is a warning
intended to create fear. For the horses the words express the carter's anger; his
intent and meaning are clear: 'Get this cart out of the mud now, or next you'll
feel the lash.' This is not, however, what the words say when they are
considered as an illocutionary statement.[25]

Today, cognitive scientists say that what we believe, what we desire, what we
think, what we intend is indubitable, even though what we believe or think may
not be objectively true, for example, if we believe that the sun revolves around
the earth. Even when we doubt, that we doubt is indubitable, as Husserl and
Searle have pointed out (Dreyfus 6). This is very similar to the truth in our
hearts, as it was widely understood in the Middle Ages; one's *intentio* is true,
whether one reveals or disguises it with words. Finally, the difference between
saying something and meaning it, and saying something and not meaning it,
comes down to revealing or masking through signs the truth that is 'in our
hearts'. In revealing or masking our thoughts in and through language we are
engaged in an intentional act. In the 'thesis of intentionality,' which the next
chapter considers in detail, medieval and modern theories of language and
knowledge coincide.

[25] This and other aspects of the *Friar's Tale* are considered in great detail in Chapters Five and Six.

CHAPTER TWO

The Thesis of Intentionality:
Medieval and Modern

THE THESIS OF INTENTIONALITY: THE LINGUISTIC RETURN

Because not only language but most human activity was considered to be subject to the power of the free human will, medieval thinkers subscribed to the 'thesis of intentionality,' a classical and medieval idea which has found a remarkable new and important life in the last hundred years. For example, the thesis of intentionality, derived from Franz Brentano, who in turn derived it from scholastic philosophers, is central to the revolutionary neurobiological understanding of human consciousness developed by Gerald M. Edelman (5). It has long permeated many fields, particularly psychology, linguistics and philosophy. According to the philosopher Ingvar Johansson:

> Intentionality is the category without which people and society would have to be regarded as mere machines and natural processes. Intentional phenomena have a direction toward something outside of themselves. A statement is intentional, for it refers to something outside itself. A wish is a non-linguistic intentional phenomenon, for a wish points to a possible fulfillment lying outside itself. (196)

Language or 'linguistic expression' is but one of many intentional mental acts. For Chaucer, as for many modern thinkers, functions such as wishing, believing, hoping, speaking, perceiving, imagining, desiring, fearing, thinking of, and interpreting are all understood to be intentional mental activities.

Maurita J. Harney offers this definition of mental intentionality: 'The intentionality of the mental means the object-directedness of thought' (1). For the Christian, medieval as well as modern, not just thought and language are intentional, *everything, all being, is intentional*. Everything is 'object-directed,' in one way or another, towards what is believed to be the ultimate and only real 'object,' God, or absolute Being.

The more restricted modern version of the thesis of intentionality, that is, the belief in the object-directedness of all thought and conscious acts, including the

33

act of speech, has become as much a commonplace today in intellectual circles as the wider Christian version was in the Middle Ages. For modern philosophy and cognitive sciences 'intentionality' is usually related to the function of language, thought, mental states and acts, or 'consciousness': 'Consciousness consists in acts of intending some object. Perceiving, imagining, wishing for, thinking of, are different ways of intending some object – they are all *intentional* acts' (Harney 141–42). Referring to something by means of a 'linguistic expression is one of many possible intentional acts' (142).[1] Emmanuel Levinas expresses both the modern debt to medieval thinking on intentionality and the importance of the concept of intentionality to modern philosophy when he writes that '*indispensable to all philosophical analysis*' is an understanding of 'the obscured intentions of thought,' which understanding has been made possible by 'the new vigor given to the medieval idea of the intentionality of consciousness: all consciousness is consciousness of something, it is not describable without reference to the object it "claims"' (Levinas, *Ethics* 31, emphasis added; see also, Levinas, *Theory* 42).

Although its origin in scholastic philosophy is not always acknowledged, modern versions of 'the medieval idea of the intentionality of consciousness' appear in the writings of a wide spectrum of twentieth-century thinkers. Hans-Georg Gadamer highlights the importance of the insight into the intentionality of consciousness, as it was developed by Husserl, Dilthey, and Heidegger, for his own hermeneutical theory (198; 214ff). Paul Ricoeur assumes understanding and acceptance of the thesis of intentionality and its application to the function of language as 'discourse': the relationship of language 'to an extra-linguistic reality' ('Naming God' 217). He writes that 'language is intentional par excellence; it aims beyond itself' (*Rule* 74). And so 'the hermeneutical thesis,' based on the fact that 'Discourse [in oral and written language] consists of the fact that someone says something to someone *about something*' ('Naming God' 217), is, in a way, a restatement of the thesis of intentionality. Again, the thesis of intentionality is implicit in one of the major sources of Ricoeur's understanding of language, Emile Benveniste, who offers intentionalist axioms such as: 'parler, c'est toujours parler-de' (2: 62).

'Entencioun' and 'entente' in Middle English have a basic sense of inclining or stretching towards something and so are closely related to the modern concept of 'intentionality.' In classical Latin, *intendere*, in addition to the senses of 'to stretch' and 'to strain,' meant 'to aim weapons' such as arrows. The image of the archer nicely contains the concept of directedness: 'object-directedness' controlled by the will of the subject, the 'object-director.' While the *Concordance* to Chaucer has several hundred entries for 'entente' and its paronyms, and *The Middle English Dictionary* devotes ten columns to it, they all are connected by the concept of *directedness*. 'Directedness' is Searle's simplest definition of 'Intentionality' in reference to mental states, perception, and language ('Intentional State' 259; *Intentionality* 3), and this sense links him with

---

[1] On the relation of phenomenology and 'logistic philosophy,' and various 'semantical frameworks,' see Küng (15–26), also Harney (43; 143–178). Its source is Gottlob Frege's 'On Sense and Reference,' which is discussed in Chapter Four. For a brief history of intentionality, phenomenology and content theory from Aristotle to today, see Sajama and Kamppinen.

other major thinkers.[2] 'Directedness' is also a one-word equivalent to Aquinas's simplest definition of *intentio*: 'intentio, sicut ipsum nomen sonat, significat *in aliquid tendere*': 'Intention, as the very term denotes, signifies *to tend to something*' (ST 1–2 12.1). The medieval sense of *intentio* as 'directedness' is delivered to the twentieth century by Franz Brentano (1838–1917) in the locus classicus of modern histories of the development of theories of intentionality:

> Every mental phenomenon is characterized by what the scholastics of the Middle Ages called the intentional (or mental) in-existence of an object, what we might call, though not wholly unambiguously, reference to a content, direction upon an object (which is not to be understood here as meaning a thing) . . . Every mental phenomenon includes something as an object within itself . . . In presentation something is presented, in judgement something is affirmed or denied, in love loved, in hate hated, in desire desired and so on. (88)

Ernest Joós warns against the 'rather easy, and even superficial reconciliations of the past [i.e., scholastic views of intentionality] with the intentionality of Brentano and Husserl' (99). He notes that 'The term "Scholastics" covers a large variety of doctrines and, hence, wide variations on intentionality' (99), and argues that while the understanding of intentionality of Duns Scotus is very similar to that of Husserl, the same is not true for Aquinas and Husserl, nor is it true for Aquinas and Scotus. These are important differences; nevertheless, it is undeniable that Brentano, like other key modern thinkers on intentionality, such as Martin Heidegger and Roman Jakobson, has a keen sense of the medieval origins of the thesis of intentionality.[3] Brentano and Frege beget Husserl and, eventually, Husserl begets Searle (Dreyfus 6–9). The filiation between Brentano and the thinking of a century later is clearly evident in the following from Searle:

> Many of our mental states are in some sense directed at objects and states of affairs in the world. If, for example, I have a belief, it must be a belief that such-and-such is the case. If I have a wish or a want, it must be a wish or a want to do something, or that something should happen or should be the case. If I have an intention, it must be an intention to do something. If I have a fear, it must be a fear of something or that something will occur . . . It is this feature of directedness of our mental states that many philosophers have labelled 'Intentionality'. ('Intentional State' 259)

To appreciate the pervasiveness of the thesis of intentionality and its links with the Middle Ages and beyond, compare the close similarity of the following statement by Ramon M. Lemos with those above by Searle and Brentano:

[2] Regarding Husserl, Brentano, Frege on this common theme see Føllesdal, 'Brentano and Husserl' 34; on object-directedness see Harney 1 ff and 42; Sajama and Kamppinen 1 ff.
[3] Heidegger's doctoral dissertation was on scholastic philosophy (primarily Duns Scotus). For Roman Jakobson see 'Glosses' 297; *Six Lectures* 63. See also Faur 60.

Since it is impossible to think without thinking of something, every thought is essentially intentional. Although one can think of the concept of nothing, one cannot think of nothing except, in the sense of not thinking at all, which is identical with not thinking. Every act of thinking therefore necessarily has an intentional object, which is that of which the thinker is thinking. (Lemos 127)

Lemos elsewhere explicitly links his 'intentional object' to that of scholastic philosophers. And, wittingly or not, in his comments on the 'concept of nothing' Lemos makes the very same distinction as that made by Augustine, Avicenna, and Aquinas before him. St Augustine in *De magistro*, Chapter 2, considers nothing or *nihil* as an *intentio animae*, an intention of the soul or an intentional object. Later, Avicenna uses a similar example to argue that thought requires an intentional object, which the medieval translators of his Arabic rendered as *intentio*. John Marenbon summarizes Avicenna's position: 'our knowledge of not-being is said to be limited to an *intentio* of it in the mind' (140). Aquinas, who knew the writings of Augustine and Avicenna well, offers a similar idea, calling 'non-being,' *non ens*, a 'being of reason,' *ens rationis* (ST 1.16.3.ad2). Thoughts of nothing are thoughts of privations and negations, and these together with 'relations' are 'beings of reason,' *entia rationis*, also called *intentiones*.

For all medieval thinkers after Avicenna, those intentions which fall under the Aristotelian category of 'relations,' known as 'second intentions,' are the subject of logic: 'Real being [the subject of metaphysics] is that which exists apart from our thought. Beings of reason [the subject of logic], on the other hand, would seem by definition to depend upon our minds' (McInerny 39).[4] Lemos talks about 'thoughts,' but like everyone else cited above, his model for thought is language and thus his epistemology is linguistic. Lemos follows a tradition that goes back at least as far as Aristotle in considering thought linguistically: thought is 'natural' language which is imperfectly represented by conventional language and writing. This tradition is directly and typically referred to in the following by William of Ockham where he is discussing the meaning of terms in logical propositions:

According to Boethius . . . language is threefold: written, spoken and conceptual. The last named exists only in the intellect . . . A written term is part of a proposition written on some material, and is or can be seen with the bodily eye. A spoken term is part of a proposition uttered with the mouth and able to be heard with the bodily ear. A conceptual term is a mental content or impression (*intentio seu passio animae*) which naturally possesses signification . . . These conceptual terms and the propositions formed by them are those mental words (*verba mentalia*) which St Augustine says . . . do not belong to any language; they remain only in the mind and cannot be uttered exteriorly. (46–47)

---

[4] The category of relations and the *intentiones* of scholastic logic are crucial to the medieval, and Chaucer's, understanding of language. They are considered briefly below and in more detail in Chapter Four.

There is here a direct correlation between language and thought: *conceptus* = *passio animae* (Aristotle's impression on the soul to describe the form of something without the matter as it exists in the soul or mind) = *intentio* = *verbum mentale*. Interestingly, Boehner uses 'mental content' to translate *intentio*. 'Mental content' is a term often used in modern discussions of intentionality to distinguish the thought of something from the extramental object to which it may refer. This same distinction was habitually made in the Middle Ages.[5] In Chaucer's day, as in our own, it was quite natural to think of all mental intentionality in terms of linguistic intentionality.

Whether the motivation for considering the intentionality of language and consciousness be ethical, a prime medieval motivation, or a modern, psychological motivation; whether the context be wide (the nature of all being) or narrow (human thought), such considerations often arrive at similar conclusions and understandings. This should not be surprising, given that (a) they share the same model, language, and (b) their basic assumptions are often very similar. For example, according to Searle:

> A basic assumption behind my approach to problems of language is that the philosophy of language is a branch of the philosophy of mind. The capacity of speech acts to represent objects and states of affairs in the world is an extension of the more biologically fundamental capacities of the mind (or brain) to relate the organism to the world by way of such mental states as belief and desire, and especially through action and perception. (*Intentionality* vii)

Searle's biological assumption is, in fact, an assumption of a *natural intentionality*, for mental states are '*intrinsically* Intentional' (*Intentionality* viii, emphasis added). A medieval understanding of an intrinsic intentionality in all being is a basic assumption of Chaucer and his age.

A shared medieval and modern presupposition, and one that is due to a direct filiation, is the linguistic model of intentionality: all structures that operate intentionally may be understood to operate as language operates. For example, Searle argues: (1) 'Intentional states represent objects and states of affairs in exactly the same sense that speech acts represent objects and states of affairs . . .' ('Intentional State' 260); and (2) 'the question, 'How does language relate to reality?' is only a special case of the question 'How does mind relate to reality'' (*Intentionality* 197). Medieval understandings of the paradigm of language are the same. During the Middle Ages 'the analogy between thought and language was sometimes taken so seriously that mental propositions were thought to have a grammar like that of spoken and written propositions' (Kneale and Kneale 230; also Trentman, 'Ockham: On Mental' 288). Trentman has also

---

[5] On modern 'content theory' see Sajama and Kamppinen. For an example of its medieval equivalent see Marenbon's analysis of Radulphus Brito's (fl. 1300) distinction between 'concrete' and 'abstract' intentions, which is the distinction 'between what is thought and the thought of it' (140). The consciousness of this last distinction is comparable to what is called today the 'phenomenological attitude' which distinguishes between the object *which* is intended and the object *as* it is intended, and the 'natural attitude' which does not make this distinction. See also p. 95.

argued that 'the three basic presuppositions about language that are identified and defended [by Noam Chomsky] in *Cartesian Meditations* are philosophical doctrines that were generally held by medieval logicians and grammarians' ('Speculative Grammar' 301).[6]

Most 'medievals' would not have had any problem agreeing with the following statement from Searle, in which he expresses an assumption about the relation of the linguistic model to intentionality in general:

> By explaining Intentionality in terms of linguistic acts, I do not mean to suggest that Intentionality is somehow essentially linguistic . . . the direction of dependence is precisely the reverse. Language is derived from Intentionality, and not conversely. The direction of *pedagogy* is to explain Intentionality in terms of language. The direction of *analysis* is to explain language in terms of Intentionality. ('Intentional State' 260)

Put more briefly elsewhere: 'speech acts have a derived form of intentionality' (*Intentionality* 5), that is, derived from the more natural intentionality of intentional states. This is very close to the belief ascribed to Ockham, and typical of his century, that 'mental language has a structure similar in a certain degree to that of spoken language, so that every structural element which is in mental language is in spoken language also, but not vice versa' (Boehner 213).

Searle is simply one of the more recent thinkers to describe fundamental structure (we might call it *logos*) in terms of language. In 1929, Edward Sapir noted that the study of language was of 'strategic importance for the methodology of social science' (166): anthropology, sociology, and 'culture history' (161). He also noted its importance for philosophy, psychology, and, 'more remotely, with physics and physiology' (161). Roman Jakobson follows Sapir in arguing that phonetic language is the model of all language (*Main Trends* 32); Emile Benveniste states that music, art and society itself are based on the semiology of language: 'Toute sémiologie d'un système non-linguistique doit emprunter la truchement de la langue, ne peut donc exister que par et dans la sémiologie de la langue . . . la langue est l'interprétant de tous les autres systèmes, linguistiques et non-linguistiques' (60). Benveniste claims that ultimately 'la langue permet la société' (62). Lacan bases his psychology on the premise that the unconscious is structured like language; the premise of the sociology of Lévi-Strauss is that social structures are analysable on the linguistic model; Benveniste argues that all social discourse follows the paradigm of language.

György Márkus writes of the '*linguistic* turn' of 'mid-twentieth-century academic philosophy' (104) that it is characterized in part by 'the rejection of the earlier dominant (especially in empiricist epistemologies) quasipsychological ways of argumentation and genetic-psychological method of constitution, and their replacement by an argumentation from, or on the analogy of language.' Hence 'language and linguistic communication became considered as the

---

[6] Namely: 'first, that there is a creative aspect of language . . . secondly, that . . . there are grammatical principles that are universal in human language; and, thirdly, that one must, therefore, distinguish the surface structure of language from its deep structure' (284).

universal paradigm of all forms of human intercourse and human objectivation' (104–105). Márkus goes on to argue that, whatever their differences, Wittgenstein, Lévi-Strauss, and Gadamer share the paradigm of language as an epistemic model; what they all appreciate, as was appreciated in the Middle Ages, is that the structure of language may be used to describe other structures.

But rather than the 'linguistic turn' of the twentieth century, is it not more accurate to speak of a *linguistic return*. That language, a 'rule-governed intentional behavior' (Searle, *Speech Acts* 16), is the model of all other semiotics, was first clearly articulated by Augustine. In *De doctrina christiana* he writes of 'visible words' like 'banners and military standards'; of the sounds of 'the trumpet, the flute, and the harp which are not only pleasing but also significant'; of the odour of sacred ointment, the taste of sacraments, the touching of the hem of Christ's garment as 'signs', and then makes this concluding observation: 'And I could express the meaning of all signs of the type here touched upon in words, but I would not be able to make the meanings of words clear by these signs' (2.3.4).

That without language 'there would be neither the possibility of society, nor of humanity'[7] is a seemingly stunning assertion of Emile Benveniste. 'Seemingly stunning' because such an idea was a medieval commonplace. St Augustine says something similar (*De ordine* 2.12.36), but one of the clearest statements on this occurs in Thomas Aquinas's commentary on Aristotle's *On Interpretation* (cf. Vance, *Signals* 234):

> Now if man were by nature a solitary animal the passions of the soul by which he was conformed to things so as to have knowledge of them would be sufficient for him; but since he is by nature a political and social animal it was necessary that his conceptions be made known to others. This he does through vocal sounds. Therefore there had to be significant vocal sound in order that men might live together. (24)

From Augustine to Aquinas to Benveniste we have come full circle: the linguistic return.

'ENTENTE' AND *INTENTIO*: MEDIEVAL PSYCHOLINGUISTICS

If it is true that at the intersection of will and language we find psycholinguistics (cf. Ricoeur, *Rule* 207), then in Chaucer's works are to be found characters who are developed and revealed psycholinguistically. One can see more precisely the functioning of the intentionality of will and language in medieval psychology if the etymologies of *intentio* and 'entente,' considered above, are now examined in greater detail.

The Middle English Dictionary offers a large number of senses (distinguished with angled brackets) for 'entente': <purpose>, <intention>, <aim or

---

[7] Benveniste: 'défaut du langage, il n'y aurait ni possibilité de société, ni possibilité d'humanité' (2: 217).

object>, <reason>, <plan or design>, <will>, <wish>, <desire>, <mind>, <heart>, <spirit>, <frame of mind>, <mental or spiritual attitude>, <opinion>, <view>, <idea>, <understanding>, <meaning>, <significance>, <import>, <attention>, <heed>, <care>, <labour>, <diligence>, <a legal claim>, <a demand>, <the provisions, substance, or essence of a contract, a law, a will>. To an extraordinary degree these senses sum up many of the themes addressed in Chaucer's writings: they are about willing, wishing, and desiring; they are about understanding the meaning, import and significance of words; they are about the meaning of understanding, and the meaning of life from a Christian perspective; they are about taking care, and taking heed in the use of words, and in making verbal contracts; they are about the relation of language to one's ideas, one's frame of mind, one's opinions, understandings and views – they are about 'entente,' 'entencioun,' and 'entendynge.'

Good and bad 'entenciouns' become 'good' and 'bad' when they are willed. These 'entenciouns' are often communicated through language. This psychological understanding is as medieval as it is modern. Inasmuch as Augustinian psychology is largely concerned with good 'entente' and bad 'entente,' one could say that Chaucer's psychological concern with the function of the will is very similar to that of St Augustine. Chaucerian 'will' seems related to a Senecan or Augustinian *voluntas*. To appreciate such a *voluntas* we might well consider John M. Rist's cautionary words:

> the word *voluntas*, which we are in the habit of translating as will, does not denote for Augustine a part of the human psyche; rather it is the human *psyche* in its role as a moral agent. As in Seneca, the word *voluntas* is in Augustine almost to be translated as a 'moral self' or 'moral personality'. Quoting Luke 2:14 Augustine will describe the good as men 'of good will' (*bonae voluntatis*), where it is clear that the goodness of the 'will' is an indication of the goodness of the man. Thus *voluntas* is not a decision-making faculty of the individual, as subsequent philosophy might lead us to suppose, but the individual himself.   ('Augustine' 421–22)

One's 'ententes' are part of one's being. One's 'good entente' or 'yvel entente' is revealed or disguised by means of signs. In Chaucer's writings 'entente' is used extensively in association with the word 'will' and 'woll' both as modal verb and noun. 'Entente,' in one major sense, is the force of the 'will' of man. This identification may have been established for Chaucer while translating *The Consolation of Philosophy*: in *Boece*, 'the entencioun of the wil of mankynde' (4.pr.2 49) is also called 'the willeful moevynges of the soule' (3.pr.11 153–4). For medieval thinkers the 'strengthe' of human will is that which at the level of human consciousness 'couples' the human subject to objects beyond himself; that which at the level of grammar couples the verbal subject and verbal object; that which at the semiotic level couples the sound of a word, its *vox*, with its sense, or *intentio*; and that which at the semantic level of discourse couples the word, or *verbum*, and the extralinguistic thing, or *res*.

In brief, we are considering throughout this book a problem that Chaucer, like many thinkers before and since, addresses directly: how the intending subject relates to the world, and how the world relates to the intending subject. An idealist polarizes intentionality in the subject: the 'world' becomes a subjective 'world,' and knowledge of 'objective reality' becomes illusory. On the other hand, others, for example the materialist 'Stoycienis' (Bo 5.m.4 6), polarize intentionality in the other direction, in the material object. Such polarization can lead to the view that the cognitive faculties are passive receivers, mere extensions of the senses. This view was denounced not only by Boethius, but by some scholastics of the late thirteenth century and the fourteenth century, e.g., Peter Olivi, because it endangers the concept of free will (Tachau 40). Augustine, on the other hand, like some modern theorists, seems to have a more balanced view which suggests that there is some reciprocity between subject and object, although moral responsibility, and hence, primacy, rests with human will or intentionality.

For western Christianity 'entente' and will, or *intentio* and *voluntas*, are solidly linked for the first time not by Boethius, but by Augustine. In fact *intentio* is the factor common to descriptions not only of *voluntas*, but of *visio* and all the other sense faculties, and *libido, cupiditas, amor, passio,* and *anima* in general. The association of *intentio* and *voluntas* and all these other aspects of the human soul or psychology is thoroughly made in Book 11 of *De Trinitate.* Here, describing the image of the Trinity in the 'outer man,' Augustine uses the word *intentio* to describe the power of the mind which controls the external senses. The exemplary sense he uses is vision. In the act of sight Augustine distinguishes three things: (1) the object seen, (2) the vision (*visio*) or the form (*forma*) of the object seen, which is impressed on the organ of sight and which 'is altogether different from that body which we perceive by seeing' (11.2.2), and (3) that which controls and directs the eyes, that is, the *animi intentio* (11.2.2), the intention of the mind. The *animi intentio* is that which 'fixes the sense of sight on that thing which we see and binds both together' (11.2.2). Of the trinity involved in the act of sight, only the *intentio* is a property of the mind – it is a spiritual power which unlike the organ of sight, or the object seen, may 'neither perish nor diminish' (11.2.2). *Intentio* is this power which directs the 'rays of the eyes' (11.2.4), and so controls both seeing and looking (11.2.3). Suddenly, Augustine uses a synonym for *intentio animi*, that is, *voluntas animi*: the third element of vision is, then, also considered as 'the *will of the soul* which directs the sense to the sensible thing and keeps the vision itself fixed upon it . . . The third is proper to the soul alone because it is the will' (11.2.5, emphasis added). Moreover, we now see *intentio* linked not only with the word 'will' but with three other key words for Chaucer and the Middle Ages – the intentio-cum-will coupling or uniting (*copulandi*) the sense of sight and the thing seen can become 'so violent that it can be called love (*amor*), or desire (*cupiditas*) or passion (*libido*).'

As the sight operates, so too do the other physical senses (11.1.1), plus spiritual vision and intellectual vision: all of them are governed by the intention of the will. Under the direction of the will, the second of the three visions, spiritual vision, arrives at knowledge: 'the eye of the mind [is informed] by the various images of sensible things [fixed in the memory], just as though the sensible things themselves were actually present' (11.4.7). So 'there are two visions, one of perception (*sentientis*), the other of thought (*cogitantis*)' (11.9.16), each with their analogous trinities, but each governed by the same intention of the will: 'what the intention of the will (*intentio voluntatis*) is towards a body that is seen, and the vision to be combined with it . . . the same intention of the will is towards combining the image of the body which is in the memory, and the vision of thought (*visionem cogitatis*), that is, the form which the eye of the mind has taken into itself when it turns to the memory' (11 4.7).

As the eye of the mind, under the command of the *intentio voluntatis* unites the forms of sensible, 'temporal things' (12.13.21) in the memory with the understanding to arrive at knowledge (*scientia*), so too the *intentio voluntatis* may attach the gaze of the mind to intelligible, 'eternal things' (12.14.22) – 'intelligible and incorporeal reasons' (12.14.23) – and unite them in the memory and understanding to achieve wisdom (*sapientia*); the former is 'the rational cognition of temporal things,' the latter 'the intellectual cognition of eternal things' (12.15.24).

The net result of the focusing of the physical organ of sight on physical extramental objects, or the eye of the mind on intramental objects, images of physical extramental objects stored in the memory, or of other intelligible intramental objects also stored in the memory, is understanding or cognition: either rational cognition of temporal things, knowledge; or intellectual cognition of intelligible things, wisdom.

The *intentio* is the active principle in the mind which governs both meaningful external perception and thought, choosing that to which the organ of sight will be bound, and binding together 'objects' from the memory to the understanding, the result of which is thought (*cogitatio*) (11.3.6). The principle upon which *intentio* operates is love, desire, or passion. Will is the motor which leads to subsequent action and knowledge. Thought results from the loving, desiring, or passion of the will, not vice versa. Hannah Arendt, translating a sense of Augustinian *intentio* as 'Will qua attention' (102), nicely describes its operation: 'the Will, by virtue of *attention* first unites our sense organs with the real world in a meaningful way, and then drags, as it were, this outside world into ourselves and prepares it for mental operations: to be remembered, to be understood, to be asserted or denied' (100).

The will moves the soul towards that which will complete it. The will 'knows' that which will complete it. What love, or the will 'that does not act perversely' (15.21.41), 'knows' is the good. The heart, the seat of the will, inclines or intends towards the good. The will desires and loves that which will complete it and shuns that which will destroy it: 'For our will, which belongs to us by nature, experiences various emotions, according to whether the things which are adjacent to it or which it encounters either entice or repel us' (15.21.41). The will *naturally* intends towards the good and is repelled by the bad. It is important to consider the distinction between 'natural intention' and the intention of man's will in detail.[8] But, in brief, one may say that the will in Augustine becomes identical with love, or rather, love is a strong expression of will (15.21.41), as are desire (*cupiditas*) and passion (*libido*). The ultimate and most natural act of the will, uncorrupted by sin, is to love the greatest Good, that is, God (cf. Bourke 141).

---

[8] Natural intention: see pages 46–51.

The voyage of the will and intention from Augustine to Aquinas to Duns Scotus is a complex one. Although the functions of the will as a decision-making force become refined, the concept of will in general, though in a more sophisticated form, returns in Chaucer's century to its Augustinian roots. Whatever its developments, the Augustinian position on the prime importance of the human will never lost its currency, and, as discussed in Chapter One, attitudes towards the will in the fourteenth century were often closer to those of Augustine and Boethius than to those of Aquinas (Arendt 84–148; Alexander 141–42).

However, by the fourteenth century the word *intentio* had acquired a number of senses other than the broad Senecan and Augustinian idea of *voluntas*. Indeed, it acquires so many senses that its use becomes very confused, for example, in the works of Roger Bacon (Tachau 22). John Duns Scotus is the one scholastic philosopher who tried to sort them out:

> The noun 'intentio' . . . is used one way to mean an act of the will (*actus voluntatis intentio*); second to mean the formal reason (*ratio*) of a thing, as when [it is said that] the intention of a thing from which its genus is accepted, differs from the intention from which the thing's specific differences (*differentia*) are accepted. Third it is said to be a concept. Fourth, it is what 'intends' toward the object, as a similitude is said to be a 'reason for tending'(*ratio tendendi*) toward that thing of which it is a similitude   (2 *Ord* 13.1, Tachau 62)

Let us consider these four senses.

Intentio as 'act of the will' is the most widely used sense, and is obviously connected with the Augustinian theory of will just discussed. It is also one of the strongest senses of Chaucer's 'entente.' A homicidal example may quickly illustrate this connection between will and intent. Consider the statement: 'I *intend* to kill you.' Though more definite and assertive, the statement 'I *will* kill you' is obviously closely related to the first, and they are each an *actus voluntatis intentio*. Note also that I have a mental state, < the intention of killing you >; this form of *intent* is very much related to the mental, and so the faculty of the will. Whenever we consider the word 'entente' or 'entencioun' in a Chaucerian text we must also consider will. The conflation of the two is evident in statements such as that of the summoner of the *Friar's Tale*: 'I wol entende to wynnyng' (III 1478).

Scotus's second sense of *intentio*, 'the formal reason of a thing,' relates to the theory of first and second intentions.[9] To explain these briefly: When one looks at a particular being and thinks 'animal' (genus), one's thought or the content of one's thought is different from when one looks at the same being and thinks 'cow' (species), and the contents of both thoughts are different than they are in the situation when one looks at the same being and thinks 'Bessy' (individual). Of course one could look at this same being and think 'milk,' 'ice cream,' 'steak' or all of the foregoing at once. According to Scotus, these different ways of knowing an object occur simultaneously, intuitively as 'Bessy,' and abstractly as

[9] First and second intentions: see pages 82–84, 83n2.

'cow' and/or 'animal.' The whole point here is that, as with modern content theory, there is a distinction made by medieval philosophers between the thing *which* is intended and the thing *as* it is intended, or, in linguistic terms, a distinction between sense and reference, and in phenomenological terms, the difference between the noema of the object intended and the object itself. Today different ways of seeing something are sometimes called 'modes of presentation.' As discussed in Chapter Four, the theory of intentions is just one area in medieval thought in which the distinction between different modes of presentation is made: The 'modern' distinction between the object *which* is intended and the object *as* it is intended was common to very many medieval philosophers, thinkers, and people in general.

The third sense of *intentio*, 'a concept,' is related to considering a thought as something in itself, as having some sort of ontological status. For example, if one has the intention or thought of murdering another person this thought or *intentio* exists in the murderous thinker. An intention has the being of 'an accident informing the soul – and thereby a real entity' (Tachau 65), a notion discussed in Chapter Four under the topic of 'relations.' In brief, because of this 'being' within me, I am a different being than when I do not have such an accident, and, according to Christian theology, an intention such as this, even unfulfilled, is enough to damn the intender.

An *intentio* as a concept is also a 'natural word' which exists in the mind. An important question for many modern philosophers, for Chaucer, and for many scholastic philosophers, is the relationship between a 'natural' word (a concept or *intentio*), an 'artificial' word (a spoken or written word, a conventional sign), and the thing both concept and spoken words *intend*. A famous visual example of understanding these three from the perspective of the artificial word is Scotus's use of the statue of Hercules.[10] The statue of Hercules may be considered in three ways: (1) as a 'thing', that is, as a piece of stone, the object which is intended; (2) as the *vox* (sound or acoustic image) aspect of a *verbum* (word) that raises the *intentio* (concept) of Hercules in my mind and causes me to consider, by reflection, the *res* (object), Hercules, *as* the artist considered him to have been; and (3) as a complete *verbum*, composed of *vox* and *intentio*, functioning as a sign of the real Hercules (see *Quaestiones in I Perihermenias*, 2.1, 2.3, 2.7; cf. Tachau 65–66). Scotus makes a distinction similar to that which Gottlob Frege makes between sign, sense, and referent. We see here a fourteenth-century notion of three-level semantics, the simultaneous mind-relatedness and world-relatedness of mental states and acts, including speech acts.

The fourth sense of *intentio*, 'what 'intends' toward the object,' seems to be a modern phenomenological sense of intentionality as it is understood in three-level semantics: the *directedness* of a thought, a desire, etc., towards the object of which it is the intention. This sense also seems to be contained in Augustine's

---

[10] Such a visual metaphor for 'words' presents some obvious problems because a single word, unless it be onomatopoeic, is not a likeness of a concept. However, we see here genuine insight into the dual intentionality of language, an insight lost to those critics who claim there is an 'intentional fallacy' when one tries to determine the intention of an author. These critics, unknowingly, are involved in the discussion of a *Questio* of medieval philosophy which considered the question raised in Aristotle's *De Interpretatione*: Do spoken words signify concepts or things? (see Ashworth 30).

distinction between the will and the *intention* of the will, which names the 'strengthe' of the will, or the power of the will in act. We might think of this as similar to the distiction between a hydro-electric facility and the electricity which issues from it. So the force of the will emanates from it without diminishing its source. Tachau seems to fudge the problem of defining this sense of *intentio*, conflating it, wrongly I think, with the third sense, concept (62). Swiezawski tantalizes us with the observation that this fourth sense plays 'un rôle important dans la théorie de la connaissance' ('Les intentions' 207–8) of Scotus, but then ignores it because it is not immediately relevant to his study of first and second intentions. The interpretation of Ernest Joós supports the view hinted at by Swiezawski that this sense of *intentio* is the *directedness* of the subject (thinking of, speaking of, desiring, fearing, etc.) towards the object (82). In fact, Joós observes a dual intentionality, the intentionality *from* the object via the senses, and an intentionality *to* the object via the intellect. As Joós cautiously asks, 'Is it possible to conjecture that Duns Scotus' views were announcing the phenomenological approach to knowledge?' (82). He notes that others have done this (175n60), and he himself grants that 'we find sufficient reasons to liken his intuitive knowledge to an emerging phenomenology. This reaches its full development in the doctrines of Brentano and Husserl' (82).

If we consider the contest between two intentionalities, that of the Creator and that of man, such as it was understood in the Middle Ages, it is not surprising that such a phenomenology, that is, an appreciation of intentional structures, should emerge.

INTENTIONALITY, CREATIONISM, AND LANGUAGE

Intentionality, or directedness towards something, is a fundamental presupposition of those religious traditions that give an account of a creative Being creating other beings. As Lemos points out, speaking not of divine creation, but of creative activity in general: 'Just as it is impossible to think without thinking of something, so also it is impossible to create without creating something. Creating, like thinking, is essentially intentional . . .' (136–37). In the Judeo-Christian tradition creative Being is a person, that is, 'He' is a conscious, willing, self-directed 'Individual'. This 'Person' expresses his will or 'speaks' and in this creative act other, different and lesser beings come into existence. Among these created beings is one type, man, who because he is created in God's image is also a person: a conscious, self-directing individual with a will. So we may say that the Judeo-Christian cosmogony is creationist, personalist, and intentionalist.

We may also say that this cosmogony is existentialist – an existentialism characterized by intentionality. Given the assumption of divine creation, Christians deduce from the sensible awareness of their own existence and the existence of all other created beings around them the contingency of that existence, and the dependence of all created beings on the intentionality of the divine Creator. We may observe such a reading of the text of creation in the statement of one highly self-conscious reader, St Augustine:

Earth and the heavens are before our eyes. The very fact that they are there
proclaims that they were created . . . Earth and the heavens also proclaim
that they did not create themselves. 'We exist', they tell us, 'because we
were made . . .' (*Confessions* 11.4)

It seems obvious to Augustine that what the Christian, or any reasonable person,
should 'see' (understand) in that which is before our eyes is an ordered motion,
and this motion ought to be interpreted as a directedness from and a directedness
toward a creative Director. In Augustine's statement we also may observe a
hyper-awareness of the contingency of existence for created beings. What the
Jew or the Christian is often encouraged to feel (experience) is his or her own
existence, which is the trace of the creating being, whose name is existence, 'I
AM' (Exod. 3:14). This is a type of intentionalism and existentialism that is often
understood in terms of language because language reveals or allows one to share
perceptions of extramental reality, while simultaneously revealing the intentionality and existence of the speaker.

The presence of Being in beings (because of creative intentionality), and the
simultaneous absence of Being from beings (because of the difference between
Being and beings), is made explicable through various creationist, and, hence,
intentionalist metaphors. Examples of such metaphors include those of artist and
artwork, composer and music, and sun and light; but the most common
metaphors are those of speaker and word, or author and text.[11] These last
metaphors are the most attractive for those who hold beliefs rooted in the Judeo-
Christian tradition because they are supported by the revelation of scripture,
which makes them more than metaphors. But they are also the most powerful
metaphors because the very nature of language mimics the Judeo-Christian
existential metaphysics they describe. In the *Confessions* Augustine asks of God,
'By what means did you make heaven and earth?' He rejects the metaphor of the
'human craftsman' because such a craftsman 'imposes . . . form upon a
substance which already has being,' and God, as the scriptures tell us, created all
beings out of nothing. Finally Augustine concludes by quoting Psalm 32 (33):9:
'you spoke and they were made' (11.5).

When Augustine says that the earth and the heavens 'proclaim' that 'they did
not create themselves,' he is considering them as signs capable of being
interpreted to reveal the intentionality of the Signifier. All signs, including
spoken and written signs, are intentional because, as Rabbi Bahye ibn Paquda
(eleventh century) so succinctly and insightfully states: 'It is known that things
that are void of intentionality cannot constitute a sign . . .' (Faur 60). All created

[11] The classical source for creative intentionality is Plato: the universe is created not 'by chance' or
'by nature' but 'by art': the art of a Creator (*Laws* 889–892). For various famous quotations of
medieval metaphors of intentional creative action see Bruyne: musical (1: 360); book written by
the finger of God: a frequently developed metaphor based on Exod. 31:18 (2: 209); book,
picture, mirror (2: 287, 294). Aquinas frequently refers to God as the 'auctor naturae' (e.g. ST
1.22.2). The 'heliotrope,' the metaphor of the Sun and light, was a favourite of Platonists,
Neoplatonists (for a long list of references from Christian sources from Augustine to the twelfth
century see Javelet 2: 40n19) and Aquinas (Myles 157, 168n37). The speaker-word metaphor is
also found in non-Christian Neoplatonic usage. For copious book metaphors from the Bible to
Dante see Curtius (310–332).

reality, the word of God, is charged with the intentions, the thought, the concepts or the will of the author – all these are senses bound up in the Latin word *intentio*, and the Middle English words 'entente' and 'entencioun,' and any one of these senses or combinations of them may be released by the context in which the word is used. But how are these different notions united? The answer is suggested in Moses Maimonides' pronouncement:

> The phrase 'written by the finger of God' is therefore identical with 'written by the word of God'; and if the latter phrase had been used, it would have been equal to 'written by the will and desire of God.'
>
> (1: 66 98)

The common factor amongst these three types of 'writing' – 'by the finger,' 'by the word,' and 'by the will' – is intentionality, the concept of intentionality being expressed in terms of the will. Because in Christian belief Being causes beings to come into existence, and because Being sustains beings in existence, there is an originary or *causal intentional relationship*, and a constant *voluntary intentional relationship from* God *to* created beings. In the Judeo-Christian cosmogony beings are not the stuff of God, but they *owe* their existence to God. Existence *belongs* to God; existence is something God *lends* (because he chooses or wills to lend) to beings either on a temporary basis, or, for angels and human beings, on a permanent basis – this is the fact of which the proud human being who wishes to be like God is often forgetful: man *has* existence; God *is* existence (Myles 156–162). God gives existence to beings which he creates out of nothing. In doing this, God acts 'just like' a creating person.

There can be no doubt that in the Judeo-Christian tradition creative intentionality is an activity of will: Genesis tells of beings created *ex nihilo* by the will of God or absolute Being. Aquinas summarizes a view universally held in medieval, Christian Europe: 'We must hold that the will of God is the cause of things' (ST 1.19.4). No matter what the Christian or Jewish metaphysician may borrow from the Aristotelian or Platonic traditions, he must still take into account the act of will, both human and divine. In pagan, Greek Neoplatonism the emanation and return of beings from or to Being, or the One, is marked by necessity; in Christianity both activities are governed by acts of the will, divine and human.[12]

CHAUCER AND THE MEDIEVAL THESIS OF INTENTIONALITY

While the medieval thesis of intentionality is that 'all being is intentional, or object-directed,' for the medieval Christian, as for the Platonists and Neoplatonists before him, man is a being with a unique intentionality. The human being, like all animals, is internally governed by physical motions directing him towards the propagation and survival of self and species, but

---

[12] Many of the notions introduced here are developed in the next two chapters.

man's natural intentionality, unlike other animals', also directs him beyond mere survival of the species; man is also directed towards eternal spiritual survival in a realm beyond the physical. There is in the human being an *immanent* movement towards some spiritual, *transcendent* sphere.

The opening lines of *The Canterbury Tales* presuppose and express the unique intentionality of human beings. Come springtime in fourteenth-century England, not only does man, like the animal and vegetative realm, come to life and feel the urge to propagate, but also, 'Thanne *longen* folk to goon on pilgrimages' (GP I 12, emphasis added). Man has a *natural intentionality*, or a 'natural will,' which works like 'gravity in bodies,' as Duns Scotus typically describes it (Arendt 132). Here we see Aristotelian physics – every body seeks its natural place – adapted by Scotus, as by many others before him, most notably by Augustine (*Confessions* 13.9), to explain Christian metaphysics. There is in man a natural intentionality, or directedness, urging him to return to the source of existence, to eternal abiding Being: man's soul will 'fall' or 'rise' or return like a 'weight' to its source. This erotic, gravitational motion toward rest is, in Augustine, the motion through love to 'peace,' his equivalent to the Platonic 'rest': 'all love . . . is an analogue of the 'weight' that draws natural bodies toward the place of their repose' (Anderson, *St Augustine* 38 and n3). We have, then, in the opening lines of *The Canterbury Tales*, not only a dual ontology, an immanent reality and a transcendent reality, but also a specific human intentionality.

In Chaucer's translation of *The Consolation of Philosophy*, Lady Philosophy asks this question of Boethius: 'But sey me this, remembrestow what is the ende of thynges, and whider that the entencioun of alle kende tendeth?' (1.pr.6 37–39). The intentionality of Christian creationist cosmogony, or natural intention, is the intentionality of God, that which is according to God's will. The answer to the question, 'whider that the entencioun of alle kende tendeth,' is, of course, that 'alle kende,' all created beings, tend, or intend, back to God, who is the 'bygynnynge of al' (1.pr.6 45). This is nowhere more eloquently stated than in the famous metrum 9, Book 3 of the *Consolation*, in which God 'sowest' beings 'into hevene and into erthe. And whan thei [beings] ben convertyd to the [God] by thi benynge lawe, thou makest hem retourne ayen to the' (3.m.9 35–38). As Boethius says elsewhere 'oon ordre enbraseth alle thinges' (4.pr.6 344): natural intention expresses law and necessity; it is natural, just as the law of gravity is natural. 'Proper coupling' in all relationships – between husband and wife, a person and material goods, and word and thing – is fully realizable only if it is intended or directed towards God, the Good, or the One, as part of the process of the return to one's source.

Natural intention, or instinctive, innate directedness of the human soul is towards God, the true good. Boethius's Lady Philosophy says: 'Ad verum bonum naturalis ducit intentio.' This is translated by Chaucer as: 'And therefore natural entencioun ledeth yow to thilke verray good' (3.pr.3 6–7). Alan B. Wolter offers selections in which Duns Scotus considers natural intentionality, but under a different name, and Wolter points to the classical sources of this theory, while defining it: 'according to Aristotelian terminology, everything is said to desire or will its own perfection, where 'desire' and 'will' refer not to elicited acts, but rather to an ontological relationship or innate inclination toward what perfects the nature or agent as such' (*Duns Scotus* 42). 'Natural entencioun' is 'God's intention,' our natural instincts, tendencies, or appetites, which are essential qualities of our very beings.

In human beings, then, there is a 'natural entencioun' which, as in other animals, includes an intentionality for physical survival both as an individual and as a species, and which, unlike other animals, also includes an intentionality for personal, eternal, spiritual survival. But in addition to natural intentionality, there is in man another power, a power which man may use for his benefit, but which, as Adam demonstrated with disastrous consequences for the human race, man may also use to 'mystorneth' himself from his 'natural entencioun' towards 'thilke verray good' (3.pr.3 6–8). This power is the human will. Other animals also have a will, of sorts, that permits them to make decisions of 'wyllynge' and 'nyllynge' (Bo 3.pr.11 81–2). But this belongs to the 'entencioun' of the 'beeste' 'to lyven and to duren' (3.pr.11 83–85). This will of beasts is unlike the will of man, who is capable of 'willeful moevynges of the soule,' which Boethius distinguishes from the 'entencioun of nature' (153–55; 177–78). The scholastics would refine the faculty of the will in animals to the *vis aestimativa*, which, though it is a judgmental faculty, nevertheless is not free. So, when the sheep sees the wolf, or, thinking of Chauntecleer in the *Nun's Priest's Tale*, when the rooster sees the fox, it *must* run away. According to Aquinas, 'the sheep, seeing the wolf, judges it a thing to be shunned, from a natural, and not a free judgement, not from reason, but from natural instinct.' On the contrary, man's act of avoiding or seeking something is generally 'not from a natural instinct,' rather it is an act of the will based on a free judgment of reason (ST 1.83.1). In a less analytical manner, Boethius says the same thing; the beast's willful act is not to be confused with the 'willeful moevynges of the soule' (153–54): 'For certes in the beestis the love of hire lyvynges ne of hire beynges ne cometh not of the wilnynges of the soule, but of the bygynnynges of nature' (159–62). A sign of this difference is that, unlike the will of animals, the 'wil [of man] desireth and embraceth ful ofte tyme the deeth that nature dredeth' (163–65). Because man also has this intentionality which he possesses, rather than is possessed by, there is the possibility of conflict with that other intentionality which is governed by God's will. Man, like God, is able to incline his will this way or that. The doctrines of predestination and grace aside, the paradox is that the human being has the freedom to destroy or save himself, for his ultimate choice is either to incline towards God and be saved, or to incline away from God and be damned. If humans had made the 'right' choice, the Bible as we know it would have taken an entirely different direction at Genesis 3:5 when Eve succumbs to the devil's temptation of knowledge. There is, then, in the Judeo-Christian cosmogony an in-built potential opposition between two orders of intentionality, one superior to the other. If a being of the inferior order opposes the intentionality of the superior Being, one would expect the former to fall. Augustine's words reveal the violence immanent in the opposition of man's will and God's will: 'Before all it is necessary that we be turned by the *fear* of God toward a recognition of His will' (DDC 2.7.9, emphasis added). Adam and Eve in their pride did not recognize or fear or properly respect the superior will of God; they let the intention of *their* wills dominate their natural intention to avoid that which would be harmful to them. Natural intention *is* the intention of the will of God. For man, opposition or submission are the only possible consequences of the operations of the two orders of intentionality.

The ethics of intentionality is evident in the fact that man should will to act in accordance with the natural order. The proper order of will is God's will over man's will, and God's intention over man's intention. The definition of sin is to turn this order 'up-so-doun' (ParsT X 262). The potential for clash of intentionalities is elsewhere specifically addressed by Boethius, and glossed by Chaucer:

> 'What discordable cause hath torent and unjoyned the byndynge or the alliaunce of thingis (that is to seyn, the conjunccions of God and man)? Whiche god hath establisschid so gret bataile bytwixen these two sothfast or verreie thinges (that is to seyn, bytwyxen the purveaunce of God and fre wil) that thei ben singuler and dyvided, ne that they ne wole nat ben medled ne couplid togidre?' (5.m.3 1–9)

While the two powers, man's intention or will and God's intention or will, may be opposed, the ideal for man is to conform his will to God's will. In the *Clerk's Tale* Griselda's consistent conforming of her will to that of her seemingly cruel husband may be seen as a study of the conflict of human will and natural intention drawn to an extreme and, hence, debatable proportion.

Duns Scotus says, following Anselm, in an idea that goes back to Plato and Aristotle, that man has an 'affection for the advantageous' (*affectio commodi*) and an 'affection of justice' (*affectio iustitiae*) (Wolter 179). The former is 'natural will' (*ut natura*), that which Scotus describes as working like 'gravity in bodies,' and the latter 'free will' (*ut libera*) (Arendt 132). Natural will, or an 'affection for the advantageous,' is related to Boethius's 'natural entencioun' and the *vis aestimativa* of Aquinas and others: the inclination to achieve what is immediately good for oneself and to avoid what is harmful to oneself. This may take the appetitive form: satisfying a need or desire, or inclining away from something which may destroy a person or cause unhappiness, for example, pain; or it may involve a teleological form: such as the inclination of the acorn to become a tree or, in Christian and Platonic terms, the inclination of the soul to return to the source of being. 'Affection of justice,' according to Scotus, 'is nobler than affection for the advantageous' because the latter is oriented towards the self, while it is a 'freer act' to 'will some good not oriented to self' (Wolter 179).

These two 'affections' or intentionalities were used to explain Christ's words in the Garden of Gethsemane. With his words, 'Father . . . take away this cup from me' (Mark 14:36), praying for release from suffering, Christ manifests 'affection for the advantageous,' the 'natural entencioun' to avoid pain and death. But with the words that complete this sentence, 'nevertheless not what I will, but what thou wilt,' Christ displays 'affection of justice' and exercises an aspect of will that is unique to men, angels, and God. In his willingness to die for mankind because it is his Father's will, Christ is himself an example of where 'thurw constreynynge causes, wil desireth and embraceth ful ofte tyme the deeth that nature dredeth' (Bo 3.pr.11 162–65). Christ's words are perfectly echoed by Griselda in the *Clerk's Tale*: 'But as ye wole yourself, right so wol I' (361). As was almost surely pointed out in many of the medieval debates which followed upon the telling of Griselda's tale, Christ in the Garden of Gethsemane shows himself to be more truly human than the superhuman Griselda. Christ naturally inclines to the avoidance of suffering, he has no appetite for this 'cup,' but uses his human will to accept suffering, if that is the will of his Father (cf. Wolter 41). The example of Christ may also have been the model for Boethius, whose words in turn may have been a source of inspiration for Griselda's story: men must 'converten hem of here owene wil to the wil of here ordeynour, as thei that ben accordynge and enclynynge to here governour and here kyng' (Bo 3.pr.12 93–96).

With natural intention being an expression of the will of God immanent in created beings, and man himself having a type of will which is unique among worldly creatures, it is not surprising that the intentionality of nature and the intentionality of the human will are easily confused. The problem is further complicated by the fact that in the Middle Ages natural intentionality was also sometimes called 'voluntas naturalis': natural will. To avoid confusing this last term with the human will Scotus teaches that, properly and generally speaking, the 'voluntas naturalis' should be understood as 'appetite' (Wolter 180). Implicit in so-called natural will, or natural intention, which is possessed by all animate beings, is the *absence* of human will. Scotus makes a memorable point of this by saying that the word 'natural' in effect negates the very meaning of 'will': 'the natural will is really not will at all, nor is natural volition true volition, for the term "natural" effectively cancels or negates the sense of both "will" and "volition"' (Wolter 183). Bearing this precept in mind, the meaning of the word 'natural' in the term 'natural intention' becomes strikingly clear.

We should also note that the word 'appetite' should not be fully equated with natural intentionality. Perhaps a better synonym, and a useful one, is to call natural intentionality 'tendency,' to distinguish it from other human intentional phenomena such as acts of the will. This term used with this distinction is found in Ingvar Johansson's study *Ontological Investigations*, in which at one point he addresses the same problem that Boethius and Scotus had addressed before him. According to Johansson, following Aristotle et al., we say that an acorn has the tendency to become a tree, and that a puppy has a tendency to become a dog, or that we all have tendencies towards propagation, survival, and our 'good' in general (cf. Johansson 162). The scholastics, Duns Scotus, for example, as we have just seen, often classed the latter tendencies (propagation, survival) as 'appetites.' 'Tendencies' as a term may cover both the teleological inclinations (the acorn to become a tree, the human soul to abide with God), and the appetitive inclinations – these together make up natural intentionality.

SIGNS AND PSYCHOLOGY: THE THESIS OF INTENTIONALITY

Paul Ricoeur observes that in addition to what words say, the analysis of 'the locutionary act allows one to anchor elements in language that are considered to be psychological – belief, desire, feelings, and in general, a corresponding "mental act"' (*Rule* 73; cf. Searle, *Speech Acts* 64–71). For purposes of realistic, psychological characterization Chaucer deliberately exploits the fact that the speech act is part of an intentional phenomenon that originates in the mind of the speaking subject. Aspects of that from which language intends, the mind of an individual subject, aspects such as desires, fears, intentions, understandings, and beliefs, may be discerned through language. When we are caused or invited to discern such aspects, as we are by Chaucer, we build up a portrait of what is going on inside the mind of the subject through his or her speech acts, or other acts that indicate mental states. In carrying out such an analysis we are engaged in an interpretation of the psychological implications of the phenomenon of signs – a phenomenological psychology.

A definition of 'phenomenological psychology' which describes my own understanding and use of the term is the very broad one offered by Michael J. Apter: 'phenomenological psychology . . . is a type of psychology which makes extensive reference to subjective experience, and in this way contrasts with behaviourist psychology which systematically avoids such reference' (13). 'Phenomenological psychology [as defined here] . . . puts neither experience nor the real world, including behaviour, "in brackets" but assumes the existence of both, and is concerned with the relationship between them' (18). There are two fundamental interconnected assumptions here which I argue that Chaucer shares. Like Apter, Chaucer does not bracket experience and the real world, and like Apter he assumes that thought is intentional, and that this intentionality is that which connects the mind with extramental reality. Apter says that his definition of 'phenomenological psychology' is not idiosyncratic: 'this is the way in which the term, "phenomenological psychology," has come to be understood, at least in British and North American psychology and psychiatry' (13). This understanding contains the same assumption of British analytical philosophy that Harney describes in *Intentionality, Sense, and the Mind*:

For certain post-Wittgensteinian philosophers of the British analytical tradition, the thesis that thought is intentional is seized upon as a way of defeating the mentalistic consequences of Cartesian dualism, *viz*, that thought and its objects are private, introspectible events and items which exist in the mind. To assert that thought is intentional is to claim that *mental phenomena can succeed in achieving objective reference*. (1)

Essential to this statement is the connection and interaction between mind and world, a modern and medieval concern. In the modern notion, deriving from 'Frege's three-level semantical framework' (Harney 47), sense has a 'cognitive' or 'mind-related' aspect and simultaneously a 'semantic' or 'world-related' aspect. Such notions were also entertained in the Middle Ages. Eco asks:

Is the sign 'res, praeter speciam quam ingerit sensibus, aliud aliquid ex se faciens in cognitionem venire' (Augustine, *De Doctrina Christiani* 2.I.I) or, as is elsewhere suggested by the same Augustine, is the sign something by which we indicate objects or states of the world? Is the sign an intensional or extensional device? (Eco, *Semiotics* 18)

The answer, of course, for Augustine as for Eco, is that the sign is *both* an intensional and extensional device, a fact of which all the scholastic philosophers, as well as Frege, Searle, Chaucer, as well as the devil and the widow of the *Friar's Tale*, are acutely aware.

Three-level semantics, and its use by Chaucer, is described in detail elsewhere in this book, but here we may note that the mind-related aspects of language which this semantics reveals are identical with the 'psychological aspects' referred to by Ricoeur and which are to be 'found' in language. It is in this way that we may apply the word 'psychology' to describe one aspect of what Chaucer achieves through language in *The Canterbury Tales*: realistic psychological characterization.

The term 'realistic psychological characterization' might be a cause of concern to some. We have been told by the 'exegetical criticism' (Patterson, *Negotiating* 3–9, 26–39) of Chaucer's works that both 'psychology' and 'characterization' are 'modernisms' read into Chaucer's works by those weaned on the products of the naturalistic or realistic genres of literature of the last few centuries. It is obviously true that Chaucer's writings were not formed with a theoretical preoccupation with such 'realistic' literary concerns in mind (see Robertson, *Preface* 277; 248–57). However, if one may say that, to a greater or lesser degree, various authors and/or characters in *The Canterbury Tales*, through their own words, through the words of other authors and characters, or through various audience interpretations may be said to display such qualities as 'stupidity,' 'bad faith,' 'humility,' 'honesty,'[13] and a host of other qualities as well; and if a reader 'finds' within characters a complex of such qualities which goes far beyond monochromatic and idealistic types, then one must admit that characterization occurs for most readers of the tales. If we consider 'psychology' only in terms dictated by modern behaviourist or depth psychology, with its inclination to map pathologies, Robertson is right: 'No one thought in terms of psychology in the fourteenth century' (*Preface* 277). Applying Freud to the Wife of Bath or the Pardoner may be interesting, but, of course, it is not an exercise in which any medieval writer or critical reader could have engaged. However, if we consider the interpreting of words in order to discern a speaker's mental or spiritual condition, a meaning of psycho-logy in its Greek roots, to be an exercise in psychological discernment, then 'psychology' is as medieval as it is modern. Chaucer offers words and descriptive details intended to reveal the state of an individual's 'soul' or 'spirit' or 'intentionality,' or as Chaucer says, an individual's 'condicioun' (GP I 38), a term which includes psychological or spiritual condition.

The intentionalist approach of three-level semantics must lead any audience to attempt to formulate authorial intentions in any use of signs. Whether we call the interpretation which results a reading of spiritual 'condicioun' or a 'psychological portrait' makes little difference. *The Canterbury Tales* demands a reading of authorial intentions. David Williams describes 'the seven spheres of authorship and/or audienceship in the *Canterbury Tales*' (*Pilgrimage* 24). Williams, in a version of the hermeneutic circle, emphasizes the dynamic of 'finding the audience,' particularly ourselves while reading the tales: 'With Chaucer, we get

---

[13] I cite these from Williams, *Literary Pilgrimage*, 26, because, ironically, he has been a proponent of the Robertsonian approach.

to tell our story the moment we begin to act as audience to the other pilgrims, for interpreting another's story and creating your own are each part of the same activity' (26). But the other side of the coin of 'finding the audience,' and the literary game, is the game of 'finding the author.' For example, we are led to ask not only what the *Friar's Tale* tells of the characters of that tale, but what it tells of the Friar telling such a tale; what it tells of what the Friar thinks of the Summoner, against whom the tale is directed; what it tells of Harry Bailey, who cheers on the teller of the tale; what it tells of the motives of the narrator, Pilgrim Chaucer, who reports the tale and has given his portrait of the 'condicioun' of Friar and Summoner in the *General Prologue*, and so on. When we arrive at the *Summoner's Tale* we are invited to interpret the Summoner's intentions *vis à vis* the Friar, and to consider and reevaluate Pilgrim Chaucer's portrait of the Summoner, and our own interpretation of Pilgrim Chaucer, and so on: reading and rereading *The Canterbury Tales* is like putting our eyes to a kaleidoscope that turns with seemingly endless new patterns of authors as audiences, audiences as authors, their interpretations of each other, and our interpretations of them. Chaucer's technique calls into question both 'the intentional fallacy' as put forth by the New Critics, and the 'New Historicist refusal to specify authorial intention' (Patterson, *Negotiating* 66). I think the analysis of Chaucer's writings which follows in this book adds weight to Searle's argument that the view which considers the intentions of the author in literary criticism to be a fallacious object of study is itself an 'extraordinary' and ultimately an 'absurd' view (Searle, 'Logical Status' 325).[14] I cite Searle here because he shares the same presupposition of intentionality as Husserl (Dreyfus 7–8), a presupposition which Husserl shares with Frege, and Frege with Chaucer: that language is simultaneously mind-related and world-related, and may be a tool for interpreting the 'intentionality' or the psychology of the speaker. It is this key 'thesis of intentionality' which unites Chaucerian 'psychology' and modern phenomenological psychology.

---

[14] For a recent succinct historical review and discussion of the concept of the intentional fallacy see Charles Rosen 73–76. On the intentional fallacy see also 44n10 above.

CHAPTER THREE

Judeo-Christian Semiological Metaphysics: Chaucer's Metaphysical Option

ALL WHO BELIEVE IN the causal relationship between Being and created beings of Genesis – beings were created by Being out of nothing – operate, consciously or not, within the context of a metaphysics determined by that cosmogony. For convenience this metaphysics may be called 'Judeo-Christian.' A major distinction between Judeo-Christian metaphysics and classical Aristotelian metaphysics is a consequence of the creation myth of Genesis: because all creative acts are intentional, all that is created is charged with the intent of its creator, and so may be considered significant of that intent: Judeo-Christian metaphysics is semiological. This semiological metaphysics makes Chaucer's understanding of signs, and our understanding of Chaucer's understanding, possible.

I have already described 'Chaucer's metaphysics' – the metaphysical option implicit in the beliefs of the medieval, as well as the modern Christian and Jew – as being at once 'foundational,' 'creationist,' and 'realist.' In summary: according to Christianity, Being or God is the absolute, eternal reality which is prior to and the ground or foundation of all created beings, whose existence it wills into being and sustains – this is a foundational metaphysics. Because the realm of beings is created, and creation is an intentional act, this metaphysics is intentionalist. By definition, the belief in the real, objective existence of *a* metaphysics is a realist position. Moreover, if one believes that this metaphysics, including that aspect of it which one may call Being or God, is, *to some degree*, knowable by created human beings, one is also an epistemological realist.

This definition of Judeo-Christian (and Chaucerian) metaphysics may be further refined and understood by considering it as grounded in a 'theological cosmogony,'[1] which is at once 'creationist,' 'existentialist,' 'personalist,' and, most importantly, 'semiological.'

---

[1] The term 'theological cosmogony' I borrow from Gregory Vlastos: 'What Heraclitus had denied when he wrote, "this world, the same for all, no man or god has made," Plato makes the first principle of cosmology in the *Timaeus*.' Hence Plato establishes a 'theological cosmogony' (25).

CREATIONISM: PRESENCE AND/OR ABSENCE

In creationist metaphysics the Greek logical principle 'nothing comes from nothing' is radically modified to 'all created beings come from nothing.' In Judeo-Christian metaphysics one has two totally different kinds of being: uncreated divine Being and created beings. Stephen Gersh has pointed out that there are 'three distinct relational contexts' (283) for considering the cause or Cause in relation to that which is caused: '(i) (negative) God as totally transcendent . . . (ii) (affirmative) God as totally immanent . . . (iii) (negative and affirmative) God as transcendent and immanent' (205n9). In order to avoid future confusion of terminology I will call these: (i) the relational context of absolute absence; (ii) the relational context of absolute presence; (iii) the relational context of presence and absence. The last is obviously the Judeo-Christian 'relational context.' It may be best defined in contrast with the other two.

Let us first consider an exemplary case of the relational context of absolute presence: Stoicism. Like Christianity and Judaism, Stoicism has a 'theological cosmogony,' a history of the universe which is governed by a divine principle. Speaking of the Stoics, Philip P. Hallie says, 'There is in their physics no qualitative difference between God and the rest of the universe' (21). Going beyond physics to metaphysics, we may also say of the Stoics that ultimately for them there is no qualitative difference between Being and beings. The Stoic religion has a theological cosmos, such as the Platonic cosmos of the *Timaeus* or the cosmos of Genesis; such a cosmos may be defined as 'a crafted, composed, beauty-enhancing order' (Vlastos 3; cf. J.M. Robinson 77). However, for the Stoics the totality of nature is considered to be divine. There is no division between 'natural' and 'supernatural' because all of nature is divine. The divine 'crafting,' then, is immanent and present: this is a relational context of absolute presence. Indeed there is no relation except if it be between matter and form, and such a relationship is purely natural. Such a cosmology of absolute presence is pantheistic: 'Pantheism essentially involves two assertions: that everything that exists constitutes a unity and that this all-inclusive unity is divine' (MacIntyre 34). We might add that if the creation of new beings occurs in such a cosmogony, there is not an absolute initiatory creative process, as occurs in Genesis; there is no eschatology; no beginning, middle and end; no progress. Creation of new life evolves naturally and eternally in a circular process of birth-death-birth-death: both Being and the 'stuff' of Being out of which new beings are created are eternal: nothing comes from nothing. In the cosmogony of absolute presence there is nothing absent or transcendent – no other, no outside. The ordering principle is internal and all is eternal. In some respects the opening lines of *The Canterbury Tales* seem to express such a pantheistic cosmos:

> Whan that Aprill with his shoures soote
> The droghte of March hath perced to the roote,
> And bathed every veyne in swich licour
> Of which vertu engendred is the flour;

Whan Zephirus eek with his sweete breeth
Inspired hath in every holt and heeth
The tendre croppes . . .
And smale foweles maken melodye,
That slepen al the nyght with open ye
(So priketh hem nature in hir corages),
Thanne longen folk to goon on pilgrimages,   (GP I 1-11)

This could describe the activity of the cosmos of the *physiologoi*, 'men of nature,' Anaximander and Heraclitus, for example, who posited the infinite nature of being in time, and the mechanical transformation of that being (J.M. Robinson 23–24; 41). Some of them 'endowed their universal substance with intelligence and even thought of it as a god' (Vlastos 24). Here beings are the 'stuff' of the totality of Being, articulated in Parmenides' principle of One Being. The same is true of the 'emanated being' of Neoplatonism, which is abstracted from Plato's *Parmenides*. This process is Christianized by a number of Church Fathers, most importantly, by St Augustine and the Pseudo-Dionysius. When the Christians try to distinguish between Being and emanated being, pantheism, or hints of it, may emerge in the divinization of emanated beings. So the Christian Neoplatonist John Scotus Eriugena (fl. 860) teaches that:

So it is from Himself that God takes the occasions of his theophanies, that is, of the divine apparitions, since all things are from Him and through Him and in Him and for Him. And therefore even that matter from which it is read that He made the world is from Him and in Him, and He is in it in so far as it is understood to have being. (*Periphyseon* 679 A)

Because such statements were subsequently interpreted as identifying beings with the 'stuff' of Being, and so denying creation *ex nihilo* and the absolute difference between God and creatures, Eriugena's writings were officially condemned by a papal bull in 1225. Nevertheless, his work and less controversial writings of later medieval Christian Neoplatonists, particularly those of the poets of the School of Chartres, Alain de Lille and Bernard Silvestre, influenced later poets such as Dante and Chaucer either directly or indirectly.

The cyclical notion of the activity of being may conform to Christian orthodoxy as long as there is no suggestion either that this activity was without beginning, or that the source of the internal ordering principle is internal or natural; in other words, as long as there is no pantheism. By these criteria, Chaucer's lines are orthodox. While the first eleven lines of *The Canterbury Tales* do suggest cyclism, the twelfth line, 'Thanne longen folk to goon on pilgrimages,' states with strong rhetorical emphasis that men have a final directedness to a supernatural realm. This is also suggested by the hierarchic presentation which mimics the chronological order of creation of Genesis: first there is matter (earth, air, fire, water), then the vegetative realm, then the animal realm, and finally man, who contains all these realms plus a fourth, the spiritual.

There can be no doubt that the internal, cyclical motion of this hierarchical cosmos is directed from without. Chaucer suggests a unity of being while avoiding the second assumption of pantheism, i.e., that this unity is in itself identical with the divine.

Chaucer's words imply a classic dialectic: there is an initial unity, a subsequent motion away from unity, and a return to unity – from stasis to motion to stasis. This is suggested by the interconnected and interdependent motions of the seasons, the elements, and the vegetative and animal realms. This concept of motion and rest is embedded in primeval western cosmogonies. Fundamental to it is the idea of return to an initial primordial unity. In Hesiod's *Theogony* heaven and earth split and chaos is born. Out of chaos comes order governed by a desire for return to unity. We may see this basic dialectic translating into the typical Neoplatonic concept of emanation, remaining, return: 'All that is at rest is in some unity, while everything that is moved comes out of that unity' (Proclus, Gersh 68).

The relational context of presence is also implicit in the concept of the universe besouled: a world which is animated and divine. This soul is often conceived as a *pneuma*, a 'breath.' In Chaucer's lines, the west wind as the god Zephyrus is the breath of animation, the life-giving, soul-giving breath of air. Moreover, according to Ovid, whose works Chaucer knew well, Zephyrus is both the husband of Flora, the Goddess of flowering plants, and the father of Carpos, the god of all crops and food from the earth. The classical and Christian references are married: the words 'inspired' with his 'sweet breethe' would associate for Chaucer's more literate audience the classical conceptions of the world-soul and, even for the general audience in an age which was much more 'scripture-literate' than our own, biblical allusions to the creation, including: 'And the Lord God formed man of the dust of the ground, and breathed into his nostrils the breath of life; and man became a living soul' (Gen. 2:7). But in such associations any suggestion of a pantheistic unity of absolute presence is eliminated. It is eliminated in the difference between a breath and a breather. For the Christian 'the breather' is God. We will consider this difference below in the form of the more usual metaphor: the difference between a speaker and his words. Instead of an eternal, self-contained, self-directed absolute unity, the totality of all beings is an other-created, other-directed totality.

In the erotic movement of the pantheistic universe towards unity, such a unity may be present and materialistic. We see hints of such a universe in Chaucer's 'licour,' produced when the warm sun-soaked 'shoures' (fire-air-water) pierce and impregnate the earth. This is filiated directly or indirectly with the Stoic *logos spermaticos*, described by Diogenes Laërtius (3rd century A.D.), whom Chaucer could not have known, but whom I cite to demonstrate the common meeting grounds of Christian and non-Christian theological cosmogonies:

> God, intelligence, fate, and Zeus are all one, and many other names are applied to him. In the beginning all by himself he turned the entire substance through air into water. Just as the sperm is enveloped in the seminal fluid, so god, who is the seminal principle of the world, stays behind as such in the moisture, making matter serviceable to him for the successive stages of creation.   (Long and Sedley 1:275)

This quotation illustrates Gerard Verbeke's assertion that 'Stoicism is a kind of materialistic pantheism, and teaches that the immanent divine Spirit is corporeal' (4). As pervasive as the influences of Stoical 'materialistic pantheism' may have been in the Middle Ages (Verbeke), we can see that in Chaucer's universe, while animate beings intend only to sexual union, reproduction, and hence self-emanation, human beings also intend to the realm of the Other. This is not a pantheistic world of absolute presence, it is a Judeo-Christian and 'Platonic' world, 'Platonic' as the Middle Ages generally understood Plato, i.e., through Chalcidius's partial translation of the *Timaeus*.

We have just seen that Chaucer's world is not one in which the relational context between Being and beings is the pantheistic position of absolute presence. Nor is it one in which there is absolutely no presence of Being in the realm of beings. This latter position is either deistic (absolute Being is indifferent to the realm of created beings), or atheistic (absolute Being does not exist). Deism is maintained by a belief in "God's leaving the Universe to its own lawful devices, without any particular interventions, once the process of creation had been completed" (*A Dictionary of Philosophy* s.v. "deism"). Such a position, which maintains a belief in the existence of an ever 'hidden' Being or God, became widespread only after the turn of the seventeenth century.[2] Atheism – there is no Being or God – is the other position of absolute absence, one rebutted by Plato. The Platonic cosmogony, like that implicit in the opening lines of the *General Prologue*, is theistic. Plato condemned cosmogonies such as that of Heraclitus ("this world the same for all, no man or God has made") because, according to Plato, such cosmogonies are atheistic, holding that "the whole of the heavens . . . all animals and plants, all of the seasons [have been generated] . . . not by intelligence . . . nor by a god, nor by art, but by . . . nature and by chance."[3]

The remaining relational context between Being and beings describes Chaucer's position; it is the Platonic, Neoplatonic, and Judeo-Christian position of presence *and* absence: absence, based on the presupposition of creation *ex nihilo*, that there is an absolute 'qualitative difference between God and the rest of the universe'; presence, based on the presupposition of a personal God who intentionally creates all being including one being, which is *imago Dei*. This presupposition of presence and absence is that which is contained in the opening lines of *The Canterbury Tales*: presence in the natural intentionality of all created being towards cyclic regeneration and

---

2 The origins and consequences of such a view are described in Lucien Goldmann's interpretation of Blaise Pascal's 'hidden God' and the 'tragic worldview' of Racine. Varieties or hints of deistic, atheistic or agnostic views of absence are evident in such works as Shakespeare's *Hamlet*, Thomas Hardy's 'God Forgotten,' and Samuel Beckett's *Waiting for Godot*.

3 Quoted in Vlastos (23n2–24) where it is discussed (23–25). It is the disciples of *physiologoi* whom Plato considers heretical and impious because their position opposes his theological cosmogony: 'Regardless of many disagreements among themselves, the *physiologoi* are united in the assumption that the order which makes our world a cosmos is natural, that is to say, that it is immanent in nature; all of them would account for this order by the natures of the components of the universe without appeal to anything else, hence without appeal to a transcendent ordering intelligence' (Vlastos 241).

renewal, as well as death and decay; absence in the implication that such processes are not eternal and are motions of an inferior realm of being; absence in the realization that man is part of this inferior realm of being; presence in the fact that uniquely in man there is also a natural intentionality towards the superior, eternally abiding realm. In the context of absolute presence, beings make up the substance of Being, the parts make up the whole. This is not the case for Judeo-Christian creationism, nor of the opening lines of *The Canterbury Tales*. Augustine states what would become a commonplace Christian theological presupposition, shared here it would seem by Chaucer, as follows: 'heaven and earth are *from* God [*ex ipso*] because He made them; but they are not *of* Him [*de ipso*], since they are not of His substance' (*On the Nature of the Good* PL 42, 551; trans. Anderson, *St Augustine* 57).

Because created beings are not the 'stuff' of God or Being there is an absolute difference between Being (God) and beings. Hence there is in the Judeo-Christian cosmogony, the Chaucerian cosmogony, a dual ontology, an ontology of Being and an ontology of beings.[4] But within the ontology of beings there is a creature, man, who is *like* Being. Neoplatonism provides a theoretical base for this dual ontology. We shall now see how Neoplatonism, in being adapted to a Judeo-Christian, creationist theology of Genesis, a theology which simultaneously emphasizes existence and the creative 'word' of God, leads to a sophisticated semiological metaphysics, and how this leads in turn to an understanding of the metaphysics of language.

THE METAPHYSICS OF PRESENCE AND ABSENCE

How does one reconcile the paradox of presence and absence? The primacy of existence in a creationist metaphysics in which the Creator *is* existence and the created *has* existence provides one way. Such a metaphysics, which I have described in detail elsewhere (Myles 143–62), has been called an 'existential metaphysics.'[5] It has been argued that the elements of such a metaphysics find

---

[4] Because I posit two particular systems of being, which, nevertheless, form a wider general system of being, I generally use 'ontology' to name the particular systems, and 'metaphysics' to name the general system, while realizing that the words 'metaphysics' and 'ontology' may be synonymous. Metaphysics is considered here as an all-embracing term in the following 'wide sense': 'Speculative philosophy is commonly considered to embrace metaphysics and epistemology as its two co-ordinate branches or if the term metaphysics be extended to embrace the whole of speculative philosophy, then epistemology and ontology become the two main subdivisions in the wide sense' (*Dictionary of Philosophy* s.v. 'Epistemology').

[5] The word 'existential' should not be considered here in its recent popular senses, particularly those deriving from the philosophy of Jean-Paul Sartre. However, medieval existential metaphysics and modern existentialism are related. Heidegger's sense of 'existentialism' is deeply rooted in the medieval tradition of this concept. The filiation is most obvious perhaps in the 'theistic existentialism' of Gabriel Marcel (Keen 153). In addition to my article (Myles), for 'existential metaphysics' and the 'metaphysical revolution' of the Middle Ages, a revolution from a classical Greek essentialism to a Christian existentialism, see Anderson, 'Existential Metaphysics'; Gilson, *God and Philosophy* 67. Caputo compares Heidegger's treatment of the 'existential revolution in

their most thorough articulation in the works of Thomas Aquinas. However, the concept should not be considered to define an exclusively Thomist approach to metaphysics. I would like to show here that existential metaphysics is a useful term for: (a) distinguishing Greek from Judeo-Christian metaphysics, and (b) when used with the concept of 'presence and absence,' showing how aspects of Judeo-Christian metaphysics are equivalent to the metaphysics of speech.

Medieval thinkers as diverse as Augustine, Eriugena, Aquinas, Maimonides and the anonymous fourteenth-century English monk known as the *Cloud* author, give primacy to existence, to *thatness*. Aristotle, on the other hand, took existence for granted and so he was more interested in that which 'defines being in a primary way' (*Metaphysics* 7.1028A), that is, *whatness*. Aristotle gives primacy to essence, and his metaphysics is essentialist.

Essentialist metaphysics argues that man's soul *is* the 'stuff' of Being, or is a form or hypostasis of Being. In existentialist metaphysics man is not made up of the 'stuff' or essence of Being; rather, man participates in the existence of Being. James F. Anderson, in distinguishing between an essentialist Plotinus and an existentialist Augustine, puts his finger on this difference between their metaphysical systems:

> Now Augustine's notion of being, while significantly Platonic in an instrumental sense, was essentially existential and Biblical. It is well-known that Augustine thought he had discovered in Plotinus, in so many words, the Christian doctrine of creation. But nothing concerning the historical doctrine of Plotinus has been more clearly established than that his 'emanation' is not the communication of *esse* [existence]; on the contrary, he clearly teaches that it is the communication of an identical essence (*ousia*) to all things in varying degrees. For Augustine, on the other hand, the act of creation is expressly the communication of *esse* [existence], from nothing, by God Himself: *'facit esse quidquid aliquo modo est, in quantum est.'* (*St Augustine* 35).

In Christianity, the 'ontological difference,' that is, 'the differentiation between being and beings' (Heidegger 17) is known through revelation: *the* Being (God), who is *Esse*, or existence itself, created other beings. For the Christian, the following is a fact: 'every existing thing (*omne esse*), in whatever way it may be, is from God' (Aquinas SCG 3.7.9). While for the Christian, metaphysics is still metaphysics, the study of 'being as being' (Aristotle, *Metaphysics* 4.1 1003a), the 'doctrine of creation,' as Heidegger states, 'is bound to modify the notion of metaphysics itself in that it introduces into the realm of being a first cause to whose causality everything is subjected' (100).

In Judeo-Christian metaphysics, because Being creates beings *ex nihilo* and sustains them in existence, the existence of beings is contingent, totally dependent on the will of Being, or God. For the Greeks, on the other hand, the very idea of creation out of nothing is irrational and impossible. Aristotle used the axiom, common to the Greeks, that nothing comes from nothing in order to

Thomistic metaphysics'(8) with that of Gilson. See also Carlo for a clear and concise review of the 'revolutionary ideas'(10) of Aquinas.

prove that potentiality is real (*Physics I* 4 187a26). This is contrary to the Christian teaching that, while all things are possible in the Creator, nothing is real until 'he' creates it. If the belief that nothing comes from nothing is thought to be impossible and irrational, then the belief must follow that everything that in any way is, in some way always is. For the Greeks, then, while individual beings may be mutable, they have a common element (substratum or matter for Aristotle, the 'receptacle' for Plato, fire for the Stoics, atoms for the Epicureans), which is eternal. So while there are elaborate theories and stories of how and why individual entities come into being and what becomes of them, still they neither come from absolute nothingness nor do they pass into nothingness or non-existence; there is a constant intentionality of matter towards form.[6]

For such beliefs Aquinas chides the 'ancient philosophers,' particularly Aristotle:[7] 'Somewhat raw to begin with, they reckoned that the only realities were sensible bodies' (ST 1.44.2). Fortunately, 'others,' that is, the Neo-platonists,[8] 'climbed higher to the prospect of being as being, and observed the cause of things inasmuch as they are beings, not merely as things of such a kind or quality' (ST 1.44.2 8:13). As just mentioned, Christians (and Jews and Moslems), because of the revelation of creation, must also consider beings in the light of 'the cause of things,' something the Neoplatonists had already done by adapting Aristotelian causality to their own ends, that is, extending it to the immaterial realm.[9] Here was just the ready-made modification to Greek metaphysics that Jews, Christians, and Moslems needed to make it their own. Even 'pagan' Neoplatonism does not necessarily result in monism or pantheism. Beings may emanate from the One in such Neoplatonism but they are not necessarily identical with the One. In fact the One of Plotinus (and the first hypothesis of Plato's *Parmenides*) is totally transcendent and separate or 'beyond being.' For reasons such as this, both Plotinus and Proclus have been described as theists.[10] So in Christian Neoplatonism, we find instead of the Neoplatonic One, the Being, God, who totally transcends created beings.

Difference is not necessarily identical to opposition. The appreciation of this fact in Neoplatonism helps explain the usefulness of Neoplatonic theory both for Judeo-Christian creationism and for an understanding of the functioning of language. Because Judeo-Christian creationism is explained in linguistic terms the two areas, language and creationism, are intimately linked. Plato first argued that an ontological difference is not equivalent to ontological opposition. Differentiation is contrasted to opposition in the *Sophist*: 'When we speak of "that which is not," ' says the Stranger, 'it seems that we do not mean something contrary to what exists but only something that is different' (257b). Here, rather

---

6 The Middle Ages was widely familiar with hylomorphism. Chaucer playfully uses hylomorphism as a simile in *The Legend of Good Women* to describe the mythical Jason's appetite for women: 'As mater apetitieth forme alwey / And from forme into forme it passen may' (1582–82).

7 See ST 8:10–11 notes e and f.

8 See ST 8:13 note p.

9 Gersh: 'The Neoplatonists take over the whole of the Aristotelian doctrine of causation but subject it to two fundamental transformations. First it is extended beyond the sensible world . . . [and and secondly we see] its combination with emanation theory' (32).

10 On Plotinus as a theist see Rist, *Plotinus* 228; on Proclus as a theist see Gilson, *Being* 38. For the concept of the One or the Good above or beyond being see Plato, *Republic* 6.508e–509b, and the key elaboration of Plotinus upon this in *Enneads* 5.1.7.

than binary opposition we have a concept which has found new life today: difference. So too, in Neoplatonism, the One, which 'in no sense *is*' (Plato, *Parmenides* 141e), and the 'good' (Plato, *Republic* 6 509b) which is *hyperousia*, 'beyond being,' are related to those things which they are *not*, the realm of beings, or the realm that is not beyond being, in terms of *difference*, and not as opposition. Such terms of difference are central to Neoplatonic metaphysics. To say that the One, the Good, or God 'in no sense *is*,' is not to say that the One, the Good, or God does not exist, nor that God is a being of an opposed realm, but rather that God is anterior to, beyond, or different from the realm of beings in which we exist.

Plotinus and Proclus interpret Plato as teaching that the One, or God, is 'beyond being' (Plotinus *Enneads* 5.1.10, 5.2.1), and hence beyond the power of discursive knowledge. So while the One is somehow present in that which imitates aspects of the One (Platonism), or emanates from the One (Neoplatonism), the One is also absent from this inferior realm. The only way to know the One in this life is non-discursively in some kind of mystical encounter. Plotinus and Proclus directly and profoundly influenced, respectively, Augustine and the Pseudo-Dionysius. An index of the importance of these last two to medieval theology and philosophy is the fact that these two Church Fathers are cited more often by Thomas Aquinas than any others. The Neoplatonic precept that God may not be named – that man may not define the essence of God because God is absolute difference – is ingrained in medieval thought.

As we have seen, however, Christian Neoplatonism imports into Neoplatonism the key concept of existence. It is through existence that beings are connected with Being. When one considers the relationship between man and 'ultimate reality,' that is, God, Christian Neoplatonism is anti-essentialist, differential, and existential.[11] With Augustine this anti-essentialism becomes a staple of Christianity: the ontological gulf is bridgeable only by divine illumination and faith, not through the faculties of man (Anderson, *St Augustine* 28).

So for Jew, Christian, Moslem or anyone with a similar creationist cosmogony, there are two basic 'ways' that something is: 'the way' of God or Being, and 'the way' of created beings. These two ways we see in Augustine's words:

> Also I considered all the other things that are of a lower order than yourself [God], and I saw that they have not absolute being in themselves,

---

11 Anti-essentialism is far from being a relativist position. In the Christian Neoplatonic context anti-essentialism does not mean that one does not believe essences exist, but rather that the ultimate Essence and so the ultimate Truth, God, is unknowable. This anti-essentialism is formalized and explained by Thomas Aquinas when he centers on the issue of the *epistemological* primacy of existence over essence. Its currency in Chaucer's time and place is underlined by the absolute centrality of this doctrine to the fourteenth-century English mystic, the anonymous author of *The Cloud of Unknowing* (see Myles). For Aristotle the question of essences (the definition of a thing, a concept, a category) held primacy; for Aquinas and other Christian existentialists the question, 'Is It?', held primacy – not 'what it is,' but 'that it is,' not 'whatness,' but 'thatness,' was prime.

nor are they entirely without being. They are real in so far as they have
their being from you, but unreal in the sense that they are not what you are.
For it is only that which remains in being without change that truly is.

(Confessions 7.11)

Moses Maimonides, the great twelfth-century rabbi and philosopher, 'the most
important figure in medieval Jewry and one whose values and works constitute
the very basis of modern Judaism' (Faur 61), who exerted considerable
influence upon the Christian scholastic philosophers, says in *The Guide for the
Perplexed* that God is 'a Being of absolute existence, that has never been and
never will be without existence' (1.63 95), and elsewhere, ' "to acknowledge
that He gives existence to all that exists" is the most fundamental of all axioms
and the pillar of all sciences' (Maimonides, Faur 36). Again, the idea is restated
by the anonymous, fourteenth-century *Cloud* author: 'for that thou arte thou hast
of him and he it [existence] is' (BPC 144/10–11).

Aquinas defines 'the way' of beings other than God as *id quod habet esse* –
that which *has* existence.[12] The 'two ways' are the 'dual ontologies,' and the
difference between them is the difference between something which *is is* and
something which *has is*. The only being which is is, in Judeo-Christian
metaphysics, is God. Another way of saying that man *has* existence is to say, as
do Maimonides and the Cloud author, that existence is given. Much earlier,
Augustine had written: 'For God is existence in a supreme degree – he
supremely *is* – and he is therefore immutable. Hence he gave existence to the
creatures he made out of nothing; but it was not his own supreme existence'
(City of God 12.2 473). In this chapter of *City of God* Augustine cites from one
of the most crucial passages for Jewish, Christian and Islamic metaphysics,
Exodus 3:14: 'And God said unto Moses, I AM THAT I AM: and he said, Thus
shalt you say unto the children of Israel, I AM hath sent me unto you.' Augustine
frequently calls God *ipsum esse*, which translates 'being itself' or 'existence
itself,' whose name 'is *is*' ('Est enim est') (Anderson, *St Augustine* 5). Aquinas
equates God with Existence ('Esse . . . est Deus') (*In Lib de Causis*
12.1.12.282). And the *Cloud* author puts it this way: 'al it is hid & enstorid in
this litil worde IS' (BPC 143). Regarding Exodus 3:14 Maimonides writes:

> Then God taught Moses how to teach them [the Hebrews], and how to
> establish amongst them the belief in the existence of Himself, namely by
> saying *Ehyeh asher Ehyeh*, a name derived from the verb *hayah* in the
> sense of 'existing,' for the verb *hayah* denotes 'to be' . . . This is,
> therefore, the expression of the idea that God exists, but not in the ordinary
> sense of the term; or in other words, He is 'existing Being which is the
> existing Being,' that is to say, the Being whose existence is absolute.
>
> (1.63 94–95)

Thorlief Boman, after extensive consideration of 'hayah,' offers a similar
interpretation: 'The Israelite knows that above all others Jahveh *is*; he is the sum

---

[12] For an extended elaboration of created being as 'id quod habet esse,' see Aquinas, *In Librum de
Causis Expositio*.

of all dynamic existence and the source and creator of it. This lies in the embattled verse: *'eheyeh 'asher 'eheyeh* – 'I am who I am' (Ex. 3.14)' (48–49). For Maimonides, existence is primary because God is IS, God is absolute existence: God's essence (what he is), unlike that of any creature, is identical with God's existence (the fact that he is). Both Jew and Christian understand the difference between the existential question and the essential question, and both give primacy to existence. This primacy can be no more clearly expressed than in the *Cloud* author's exhortation to his disciple 'to thenk and fele that him-self is, not what him-self is, but that him-self is' (BPC 137 ll. 26–28).[13]

What all these different authors I have been citing share is an acute awareness of the absolute contingency of existence. Indeed, Aquinas's use of *esse*,[14] and the *Cloud* author's use of 'to be,' indicate a fundamental understanding of the Hebraic sense of 'dynamic being' which Thorlief Boman contrasts and opposes to the Greek sense of 'static being.'

Medieval existential metaphysics is characterized by both the presence and absence of absolute Being, existence, or the eternal presence 'which remains in being without change' (Augustine, *Confessions* 7.2). In man, a special being in the realm of beings, resides the knowledge that his existence is contingent, and if he wants to be always, to abide immutably, that which he *ought* to seek is IS. Augustine, Aquinas, and the Middle Ages say that while all created beings *have* existence; God *is* existence. Maimonides writes 'we say "the Lord liveth." (Ruth 3.13) and not "the life of the Lord," for His life is not a thing distinct from His essence' (1:68 100). In its directedness, Judeo-Christian existential metaphysics intends towards eternal existential presence; essence is ultimately reducible to existence (Carlo).

---

13 While in the Middle Ages, for the first time in the history of western thought, thinkers gave great emphasis to the 'thatness' half of the 'thatness'/'whatness' distinction, one should note that this distinction has been well-known all through Western philosophy. The 'thatness' (existence) and 'whatness' (essence) distinction is addressed by Aristotle (*Posterior Analytics* 2.7 92b). Aquinas says that of anything 'we cannot even ask what it is until we know that it exists' (ST 1a.2.2ad.2). Heidegger sums up the philosophical history of the insight into this distinction between essence and existence: 'In the philosophical tradition it is taken as self-evident. Everyone has this insight' (12).

14 In order to distinguish between an individual being, and the abstract notion of being, Aquinas used two words, *ens*, which refers to individual beings considered *concretely*, as essences, and *esse*, which refers to being considered *abstractly*. According to Joseph Owens, Aquinas's *esse* is best rendered in English as 'existence.' In the philosophical tradition *ens* and *esse* 'may be equally translated by "being" and "a being" in English, and express in the former way the act of being, and in the latter way the nature that exists. Both grammatical forms may signify either *in abstracto* or *in concreto*. Yet St Thomas uses the infinitive *esse* to signify only in abstracto' (Owens 15). Thomas uses *ens* in both senses, but 'For the most part throughout his works the participle *ens* is in fact used by St Thomas in the sense of "that which is" '(8) rather than in the sense of the actuality of being. St Thomas was linguistically very conservative and this 'departure from current usage' (16) was atypical. A significant verbal link between Aquinas's abstract sense *esse* as existence occurs in the *Cloud* author, who makes the same departure from common Middle and Modern English usage when he awkwardly uses the English infinitive 'to be' to indicate *esse* in the statement God 'gave thee to be' (BPC 141 l.15; *Cloud of Unknowing* 79 l.14) and when he engages in multiple play with 'to be' and 'this litil worde IS' (see: BPC 143 ll. 16–30; *Cloud of Unknowing* 80 ll. 30–43).

THE METAPHYSICS OF SPEECH

Metaphysics and language

Metaphysics and linguistic analysis became fused in the Middle Ages, a fusion that continues to this day (Henry). The recognition that the metaphysical relationship of beings to Being is comparable to the relationship of the human word to thought finds a classical expression in the analogy of Plotinus:

> Take as guide [for the ascent to union with the One] the most divine part of the soul which borders on that superior world from which she proceeds . . . the soul is no more than an image of Intelligence. As the spoken word is the image of the word in the soul, so the soul herself is the image of the word or reason in Intelligence . . . (*Enneads* 5.1.3)

Such a view is central to medieval theology. Thomas Tomasic writes:

> One of the greatest disservices of historians of philosophy has been the claim that medieval thought was God-oriented and, as a result, man was of little or no concern . . . It should be noted that *theologia* was not an objective science; there can be no *episteme* about either God or man. *Theologia* is essentially a *logos*, an attempt to disclose meaningful identity through symbol, a celebration of mystery. Entrance into this celebration is initiated by the recognition that language about God and language about the self are functionally identical, that the pivotal point of theocentric language, or *theologia*, is the fact that man is *imago* or *similitudo Dei*. (409–410)

Since 'language about God and language about the self are functionally identical,' the study of how language functions becomes a major avenue towards the understanding of God.

In the Middle Ages the nature and structure of reality as a metaphysical description became a semiological description. This may seem strange to those who hold the belief that semiological descriptions of the structure of reality and traditional ontological descriptions of reality are mutually exclusive. The semiological approach is often seen as Hebraic and the ontological approach is considered Greek. There is a tendency to make sweeping statements such as 'Christianity [unlike Judaism] . . . is bound to a Greek ontology' (Handelman 117). Following a similar line, José Faur considers the difference between Greek and Hebrew worldviews as a contrast between 'metaphysical' and 'semiological' approaches to the nature of reality (23–27). 'Semiological' describes well both the Jewish and Christian views of the realm of created entities, but there is, I believe, a serious misconception in the understanding that what is semiological is necessarily *not* metaphysical. This misconception requires rebuttal.

Faur makes the following statements which draw this false distinction between 'metaphysical' and 'semiological': 'Semiology excludes metaphysics' (38): 'In contradistinction to the Greek thinkers who conceived of the Universe in metaphysical terms, the Hebrews viewed it as a semiological system' (23). 'The most important difference between a semiological and a metaphysical entity is that the former signifies, whereas the latter *is*' (25). As we have already seen, there is no reason why something cannot simultaneously have its own being and signify. Moreover, what is metaphysics if it does not deal with the 'concepts of existence and reality' (Walsh 301)? We have also seen that interest in 'IS,' the subject of metaphysics, is a shared Jewish and Christian concern. This, I believe, is a real difference between Greek and Judeo-Christian metaphysics. In comparing 'Greek' and 'Judeo-Christian' ways of considering the nature of being, I have marked this difference by the qualifications 'essentialist' and 'existentialist,' respectively. This, I believe, is the distinction which Faur misidentifies as 'metaphysical' and 'semiotic.' Indeed we can see the Greek essentialist view in the quotation from Plotinus cited above (66). The linguistic analogy of Plotinus is Greek rather than Judeo-Christian, for it is Cratylic or essentialist: there is an essential relationship between the human 'divine' soul and that of which it is a 'word.' Judeo-Christian metaphysics of the word is keyed on existence, which also happens to reflect more closely the reality of language.

The fundamental assumption of Faur's statements, i.e., that which is semiological is not metaphysical, may be refuted by asking (a) what is a semiological system if it is not a system of signs; and (b) what do signs indicate, denote, or connote if they are not real 'things,' even if the other 'things' include not only extramental material objects, but concepts, thoughts, emotions, feelings, and even other signs? What is the Hebraic universal semiological system if it is not a sign of IS, which is the ultimate 'true reality'?

Judeo-Christian metaphysics operates on the dual ontology of the 'Speaker' (God) and of 'words.' These 'words' are of two sorts, the actual words of God in sacred scripture, and the 'book of the world,' which is created through God's word. The model for understanding this metaphysics (and so its epistemology) is obviously human and linguistic.[15] The ontology of the 'Speaker' is the ontology of Being or God; and the ontology of 'words' is the ontology of created beings. We may speak of 'dual ontologies' or dual 'orders of being' to describe the real distinction between the order of being of the 'Speaker,' God, and the order of being of 'words' or created reality. Just as we are not identical with our words, neither is God: from a Judeo-Christian perspective we are God's 'words' but we are not identical with God. However, while the ontology of the 'Speaker' is not dependent on his 'words,' 'words' are dependent on the 'speaker.' There is an order of existential dependency between the two orders of being, just as there is an existential order of dependency between us and our words. The direction of dependency is *speaker* > *words*. However, from the point of view of

---

[15] For the germinal idea of 'verbal epistemology' to describe the epistemology of the Middle Ages see Colish and p.12n9 above.

human beings, the epistemological order is in the other direction, *words* > *speaker*, just as our knowledge of another human being is dependent on his or her signs or 'words,' be they spoken or otherwise (gesture, expression, dress, actions). The Speaker, like any speaker, knows his 'words' directly. The human being knows the Speaker only by interpreting his 'words,' and the 'word' one may examine best is oneself, an image of the Speaker. Such an understanding of the order of Being and beings lends itself to self-examination, self-consciousness, and the study of the relationship of language to 'reality' on a number of levels. The difference between Being and beings may be understood as similar to the difference between you and your words which you spoke, speak, and will speak. Considering oneself as a 'word' of God may also be a humbling experience: we are before and after our words; Being is and always was before beings, and will be after most beings pass out of existence; our existence is always contingent upon the will of God.[16]

The realm of created beings is semiological because it is the creation of Being. All creative acts are intentional, and each created thing reflects, in some way, the intentionality of its creator. Both Jew and Christian, in understanding created beings as the speech of God, see or 'hear' these as signs of God's very existence and, simultaneously, as means of understanding God's intention and nature. What may be interpreted through God's speech and writing is his thought, his will, his intention. Maimonides states precisely this interpretive strategy:

> Hence you learn that in the Bible, the creation of a thing is figuratively expressed by terms denoting 'word' and 'speech.' The same thing which according to one passage has been made by the word, is represented in another passage as made by the 'finger of God' [Exod. 31.18]. The phrase 'written by the finger of God' is therefore identical with 'written by the word of God'; and if the latter phrase had been used, it would have been equal to 'written by the will and desire of God.' (1: 66 98)

Instead of the misleading distinction between 'The Ontological and Semiological Views of the Universe' (Faur 23) to describe the difference between Greek and Hebrew understandings, a more fruitful distinction is between Greek essentialism and Judeo-Christian existentialism, the former with its Cratylism of ideas and shadows, the latter with its metaphysics of speech. Judeo-Christian metaphysics is semiological, partly because it is existential.

---

[16] According to scholastic theory, God in his *potentia absoluta* could extinguish souls which he had previously created immortal. However, God has willed that some created souls should be immortal: this is a law that he has ordained and instituted and is governed by his *potentia ordinata*, and so one which he would never contradict. This distinction, which goes back at least as far as the eleventh century, was 'long-accepted' by the fourteenth (Leff 16).

Personalism: imago Dei / imago hominis

We have just seen that the key component of a linguistic or semiotic metaphysics is a speaker or sign-maker. The *theos* and Speaker of Judeo-Christian creationism is a God who is a 'conscious and moral personality' (Boman 60). This belief in a creative personality has been called 'personalism': 'the doctrine that the ultimate reality of the world is a Divine Person who sustains the universe by a continuous act of creative will' (Shepard 494). Its Christian variety, with which such eminent modern Catholic thinkers as Etienne Gilson and Jacques Maritain have been identified, has been called 'realistic personalism':

> For realistic personalists, personality is the fundamental being. That is, ultimate reality is a spiritual supernatural being. There is also, however, a natural order of nonmental being, which although created by God is not intrinsically spiritual or personal. (Lavely 108)

Man is between these two orders, for while he is natural, he is also instrinsically spiritual and personal. So man is a created being that is not just a 'which' but a 'who,' a person who, in addition to being natural and material, is also intellectual and spiritual. Unlike other beings that are created out of nothing, man is like the Person (God) because 'He' (God) created 'him' (man) in 'His' (God's) own image (Gen. 1.26; 5.1–3). Man, unique among created beings, is like *the* Person in that he is *a* person: *imago Dei*. The culmination of this personalism occurs in the man-God, Christ (cf. Javelet 2: 18). This theological anthropology has important epistemological consequences.

The medieval application of the referential structure of language to the structure of mental reference, or thought, begins with presuppositions of a Christian theological cosmogony and anthropology. The epistemological model for the relation of *human* thought, word, and referent, understood as an intentional act or 'dede,' was analogically based on an analysis of the intentional relation of created reality to God's 'thoughts' and 'words' and the 'referents' these thoughts create.[17] Man is *imago Dei*, but God, in a sense, is *imago hominis*: 'God and man are paradigms of each other,' wrote Maximus the Confessor. This was approvingly translated by John Scotus Eriugena from Greek into Latin.[18] One may define 'paradigm,' as it is understood here, as 'that through which something else may be understood, an example, an image, a form' (Moran 199). The general understanding of this belief is no better highlighted than in the statement of the pilgrim Dante, who in the climactic moments of the *La Divina Commedia*, reports on seeing in the Trinity 'nostra effige' (*Paradiso* 33.131). However, while man is an effigy or paradigm of God and God is an effigy or paradigm of man they are not identical: this would be blasphemous self-idolatry according to Judeo-Christian orthodoxy. Nevertheless, the identity was carried to the point that man was often considered as a 'God in miniature.' Such a conception, needless to say, tends towards – to use a

---

17 The paradigmatic model is developed in Book 15 of St Augustine's *De Trinitate*.
18 'Dicunt enim, inter se invicem esse paradigmata Deum et hominem' (*Versio Ambiguorum S. Maximi*) in Moran (199) and Tomasic (411). My translation.

more modern but nevertheless Dantean term – a narcissism which is a hallmark of humanism.[19]

The medieval understanding of the relationship of language, thought and reality was a historical breakthrough. This was made possible because similar but different models of human and divine thought and speech were made. The analysis of these contrasting models permitted, for the first time, an objective perspective to be formed on the nature of human consciousness and psychology. As discussed in Chapter Two, the paradigm of spoken language is the same as that for thought, or mental states. We saw that Augustine minutely analyses the similarities and differences between the speech of man and the speech of God (DT 15.11). For Augustine and the Middle Ages, the divine Word describes the communication in the Trinity (DT 15.12). This 'word' is not an utterance but a 'mental word' or thought. The divine Word is the model for human thinking, and thinking is speaking in our hearts (Psalm 13[14]:1). Based on this model it seems inevitable that the scholastics would consider thoughts to be composed of *verba mentalia*, mental words which make up propositions according to grammatical rules which are identical to those of spoken language.[20]

Many Christians (Tomasic 410n5), at least since Augustine, following Plotinus, have believed that the first step in the process of knowing God is to know oneself. Dermot Moran offers the following diagram of the relationship between man and God, such as it is expressed by Eriugena, but which contains the typical Christian understandings:

HOMO	Verbum	DEUS
MAN —————————	Paradigma	————————— GOD
	Imago (theophania)	
	Idea (notio)	

(199)

'For man to come to understand himself is to see himself as a mirror or image [or word or paradigm] of God, thus the first step towards knowledge of God is knowledge of self' (Moran 199). The Christian addition to this Platonic concept is the new emphasis on language. A by-product of pursuing what should be the goal of every Christian, that is, 'knowing' God, was a better knowledge of the functioning of human language, perception, and human consciousness generally.

The similarity between man and God also marks again the difference between man and the rest of natural creation. This human being / other beings distinction also marks Platonism and Neoplatonism, whence Christianity and Judaism draw so much theoretical support. There are also other divisions in the realm of

---

[19] On 'God in miniature' (Pico della Mirandola) and *imago Dei* see Swiezawski, 'La pensé' (14). This ancient motif of God in miniature was consistent throughout the Middle Ages and is often expressed in the idea of the 'microcosm'; see for example the series of eight articles on the subject by distinguished scholars dealing with Guillaume de Saint-Thierry, John of Salisbury, Raymondo Llull, etc., in Christian Wenin, ed., 1: 341–405. On 'theosis' or 'deificatio,' the divinization of man, see M. Lot-Borodine. On Dante's 'perception that all human instrumentality is narcissistic' (86), and this perception in general, see Shoaf.

[20] For example Ockham, *Summa Totius Logicae* 1.1. John Trentman: '[for Ockham] the analogy [between mental and spoken or written language] is so close that one can speak of the grammatical structure that characterizes mental acts' ('Ockham on Mental' 586).

beings. Within the realm of all created beings one distinguishes between inanimate and animate, and within the animate realm there is the further division between vegetative and animal classes.[21] However, finally, the dichotomy human beings / other beings is the only important division from both cosmic and human perspectives.

The basic identifying features of Judeo-Christian realistic personalism, then, are that the Divine Person (a) created the world out of nothing, (b) sustains the world in existence through a conscious act of will, and (c) created another person (man) in the image of his Person. The epistemological consequence is that knowing oneself becomes a means to knowing God.

These characteristics rule out the first two of the three 'relational contexts' of Creator to created that were outlined at the beginning of this chapter. A dual ontology, or two-world theory of Being and beings, rules out the context of absolute presence; the idea of a personal God rules out the context of absolute absence. Again, of Gersh's 'three distinct relational contexts' we are left with the third, the positive and negative: God is immanent and transcendent, present and absent.

Because of the Judeo-Christian personalist presuppositions – *imago Dei / imago hominis* – and because of the very nature of language, language provides the ideal 'metaphor' to convey the concept of the seeming paradox of simultaneous presence and absence. Indeed, as we have already discussed and shall now consider in more detail, in the Judeo-Christian tradition the linguistic 'metaphor' is no metaphor at all.

Semiological metaphysics

Chaucer's ethical realist understanding of the relationship between 'word' and 'dede,' that is, the use of language as a 'dede' was discussed in Chapter One. Now we may see in detail how this is linked to a specific metaphysical understanding of the relationship between language and reality.

Judeo-Christian metaphysics is creationist, existentialist, and personalist, and it was suggested several times above that within this metaphysics the gap between the dual ontologies of Being and beings is bridged by the metaphor of speech. In Genesis, *Being*, a personal, conscious, moral God, speaks, and *beings* are. The gospel of St John referring to Genesis starts: 'In the beginning was the Word,' defining the metaphysics of Judeo-Christianity as semiological.

As God uses speech, so too does man, God's paradigm, though in an inferior and limited manner. God's 'word' and 'deed' are one. As we saw previously, for man a 'worde' *should* be 'cosyn to the dede' (GP I 742), or 'accorde with the dede' (MansT IX 208), or be 'cosyn . . . to the werkyng' (IX 210). We may now see that Chaucer's conception of 'worde' and 'dede,' rather than being 'Platonic,' seems instead to be Judeo-Christian. In the two words 'thinge' and 'dede' we actually have one 'word' in the special Judeo-Christian sense of 'word'. 'True being for the Hebrews is the "word", *dabhar*, which comprises all Hebraic realities: word, deed, and concrete object' (Boman 56); 'the verb [*dabhar*] portrays somehow the function of speaking. *dabhar* means not only

---

[21] These divisions, of course, are commonly known in the Middle Ages as the 'Tree of Porphyry.'

"word" but also "deed" . . . "Word" and "deed" are thus not two different
meanings of *dabhar*, but the "deed" is the consequence of the basic meaning
inhering in *dabhar*' (65). As Boman points out, by the 'word' Jahveh's '*will*
comes particularly to expression' (65, emphasis added). The importance to
Chaucer of the intentional act, the act of will, in the expression of language and
other 'deeds' is discussed throughout this book; here, we see how fundamental
such intentionalism is in the Judeo-Christian understanding of the nature of
reality.

Christianity, through its appropriation of the Old Testament, also appropriates
this Hebraic sense of 'word.' 'With his *dabar* "the Heavens were made" (Ps.
33:6)' (Faur 23). John A. Alford says of the word 'Verbo' in the Latin
translation of this psalm ('Verbo Domini caeli firmati sunt') that 'Verbo':

> may be interpreted in two ways 'by the word – or by the act – of the Lord
> the heavens were made.' Both readings are correct. For medieval scholars
> . . . the Genesis account of creation was amazingly concentrated in the
> deliberate ambiguity of this single word [*dabhar*]. (744)[22]

'Ambiguity' is, I suggest, a misreading. There is *one* word, *dabhar*, which
requires the use of two or three non-Hebrew words to define it adequately.
Because the Latin *verbum* or the English 'word' are not simply equivalent to
dabhar, they must be redefined to take into account the meaning of the Hebrew
which includes 'word,' 'dede,' and 'thinge.' With these senses we can say of
verbum, as Boman says of *dabhar*, that it 'portrays somehow the function of
speaking' (65). Indeed, modern understandings of language – 'discourse is
language-event' (Ricoeur, 'Model' 92); 'a theory of language is part of a theory
of action' (Searle, *Speech Acts* 17) – may be seen to a large degree to confirm
and conform to this Judeo-Christian understanding of language.

Instead of using the abstract term 'semiological metaphysics,' we may say
more concretely that Judeo-Christian creationism and its dual ontology of Being
and being posit a semiological universe. The idea in western civilization that the
universe is a semiological system is of Semitic origin and is fundamental to
Judeo-Christian metaphysics. Although this idea is ensconced in Judaic and
Semitic traditions and is one which Semitic languages most readily translate, it is
also an idea which Platonic thinking and the Greek language attempted to
express with much difficulty (Boman 71): the sharp division between 'Hebrew'
and 'Greek' understandings of being is made more questionable by this fact.
When we say that the realm of created beings exists, as does language, we
understand that beings exist as language exists in time; beings are, and then they
are not. The realm of beings exists as a complete act of speech; each 'word'
coming into and passing out of existence is part of a larger 'sentence' which
points to a 'meaning' beyond the individual words. Being, on the other hand,
just IS.

Because the realm of beings is a sign of IS we can also say that this complete
system is metaphysical. The author/text or speaker/word relationship is more

---

[22] For expert discussions on *dabhar* or *dabar* relevant to the present discussion see Faur (23 ff.) and
Boman (56–69).

than metaphorical for the medieval Jew or Christian; it describes a real metaphysical relationship. It is an actual Judeo-Christian belief 'that the writings of God are his creations, and the words of God are his writings' (Judah ha-Levi [c. 1075–1141], Faur 59). This Jewish belief is echoed in the oft-quoted contemporaneous text of Hugh of St Victor: 'Indeed the entire sensible world is a kind of book written by the finger of God . . . and every creature a sort of figure, not invented for refined amusement but instituted by divine authority to reveal the invisible wisdom of God.'[23] This becomes a commonplace of scholastic philosophy; for example, St Bonaventure: 'the world is like a book reflecting, representing and describing its Maker . . .' (Tomasic 413). The author/writing, speaker/speech, artist/artefact, breather/breath metaphors all epitomize a dualist metaphysics in which the first term is prior to the second, and the second depends for its existence and ground on the first. The 'real reality' of the speaker precedes the speech, the writer precedes the writing and so on. This is a realistic metaphysics, a metaphysics with which Chaucer's linguistic realism is in perfect harmony.

As discussed above, the whole Judeo-Christian metaphysical system is anthropomorphic: man is a paradigm of God; God is a paradigm of man. The metaphors for the 'Other' are all anthropocentric: the 'Other' is like ourselves in our relationship to what we say, write, or create, so we know the Other in knowing ourselves. We know ourselves through our words, our thoughts. We 'know' others, human and divine 'persons,' through their 'words': language, gestures, actions, expressions, and all other external signs of an internal mental reality. God's creation is the manifestation of his word and action, it is God's created 'text.' However, the 'mind' of another human being is never totally knowable through his signs. Similarly, God is never totally knowable through his signs. Despite this, the epistemological power of this anthropocentric model of all being should also be clear. It is logical for man to consider the relationship between his own thinking, speaking, and creative processes and then to draw an analogical system in order to explain the creation around him. The examination of the functioning of the thought, word, and actions of man leads to a simultaneous understanding of those phenomena in God, or vice versa. God is a thinking, willing, conscious, and moral Being, a Being 'who' rather than a being 'which.'

Within this anthropomorphic model of Being, the paradigmatic epistemological model is language. If we consider the Creator to be a 'paradigm of man' or a conscious, willing, moral, creative being, we must understand God's creative activity, like our own, to be intentional. Moreover, the very existence of the expressive action of the speech or writing of God is dependent on his act of will, his intentional action. The existence of all 'words' is totally dependent on Divine intentionality.

That traces of the absent Author could be found in his 'work' is a commonplace of Platonic cosmology and Aristotelian causation theory as it was understood and assimilated in the Middle Ages (Klibansky 7–8; Chenu 67–68; Dolan 8), and was easily married to Christian creationism. We see this, typically, in Thomas Usk, an associate of Chaucer (Usk, Skeat xxiii). Echoing

---

[23] *Disdasc*. VII, c. 814 in Bruyne 2:209, my translation.

Rom. 1:20, 'For the invisible things of him from the creation of the world are clearly seen, being understood by the things that are made, even his eternal power and Godhead,' Usk writes in *The Testament of Love*:

> Now, principally, the mene to bringe in knowleging and loving his creatour is the consideracion of thinges made by the creatour, wherthrough, by thilke thinges that ben made understonding here to oure wittes, arn the unsene privitees of god made to us sightful and knowing, in our contemplacion and understonding.   (Prologue 54–59 2)

In the very next paragraph Usk continues the thought by citing Aristotle and paraphrasing him with: 'The crafte of a werkman is shewed in his werke' (Prologue 69 3). Writing is an analogous human 'crafte of a werkman'; in fact, it is *the* craft, for it is God's craft. So for many fourteenth-century authors and literary critics, the relationship between the divine author and his 'texts' (scriptures and natural creation) and the human author and his text is, to a degree, analogous. The distinction between the pure Being of God's silent thought and the diminished being of His speech or writing is considered in the Middle Ages to be reflected analogously in the realm of human thought and its expression in speech and writing, particularly in poetry (Freccero; Mazzotta). As God, the author of all being, creates intentionally, so too within the order of their essential limitations do humans create. Chaucer, on the other hand, is acutely aware of the power of both speaker and interpreter to manipulate and interpret words and their meanings. Language may be used and abused; it may be used 'properly' and 'improperly,' 'naturally' or 'unnaturally' – this ethical implication of linguistic realism was evident to Chaucer.

CHAPTER FOUR

Medieval and Modern Understandings of Mode of Presentation

WHEN ONE considers signs in order to determine or specify the intentional structures of a subject's thoughts, perceptions, understandings, and pre-linguistic psychological states, such as desires, fears, and wishes, one is engaged in a psychological interpretation which may be called 'phenomenological'.

The interpretation of any phenomenological psychology, medieval or modern, arises from an analysis of the difference between how an 'object' (understood very broadly) is spoken of, or thought of, and the object itself. From a person's understanding of, and attitude towards an object as revealed through signs, one may interpret, or attempt to interpret, the general psychological condition of that person. The difference between the object *which* is intended and the object *as* it is intended is the essential distinction of modern three-level semantics and of phenomenological psychology. It is also the distinction upon which Chaucer's technique of realistic psychological characterization pivots.

After defining the modern understanding of the distinction between the object *which* is intended and the object *as* it is intended, this chapter will demonstrate the pervasiveness of the appreciation of this fact in medieval thought and describe the three-level semantics arising from it.

THE MODERN UNDERSTANDING OF MODE OF PRESENTATION

The use of a word in a phrase or a statement in a particular context denotes not only that of which these words are signs, but it also reveals how the user sees or understands, or purports to see or understand, the object of which he or she is speaking. The difference between how an object is perceived and the object itself is what Husserl calls the difference between 'the object *which* is intended' and the 'object *as* it is intended' (II,i 415f; Gurwitsch 62). How an object is seen, as distinguished from the object itself, Frege calls 'the mode of presentation' of the object (*Sense* 57). Husserl calls this mode of presentation the 'noema' of perception to distinguish it from the object itself (see Gurwitsch 64). This is one of the central insights of phenomenology: 'an investigation of . . . the perceptual noema will be a description of the perceived object *as perceived*' (Harney 148). In turn, an investigation of the senses of the words a person uses tells us how that person perceives an object. The result is a psychological 'snapshot' of an aspect of the person's mind. With further snapshots a more and more complex psychological portrait begins to develop.

One of the first modern examples demonstrating and simultaneously playing with mode of presentation occurs in Lewis Carroll's *Through the Looking Glass*. Alice sees two signs, one saying 'to the house of Tweedledum,' and the other 'to the house of Tweedledee' (67). Tweedledum and Tweedledee live together and Alice learns that one object, the object *which* is intended, may have more than one sign. We may see the particular house *which* is intended *as* Tweedledum's house, *as* Tweedledee's house, or *as* Tweedledum's and Tweedledee's house. Because examples similar to Carroll's were later used by Frege to define the difference between sense and reference, P.L. Heath is correct in asserting that Alice 'is a step ahead of Frege in discovering the difference between *Sinn* and *Bedeutung*' (36). Frege's 'sense' and 'reference,' like Husserl's 'noema' and 'object,' are simply terms that may explain the difference between the two signs Alice sees, as well as the difference between the two signs and the object to which they refer. In Frege's essay 'On Sense and Reference,' rather than a particular house considered as 'the house of Tweedledum' or as 'the house of Tweedledee,' the discussion centres on the planet Venus considered as 'the morning star' or as 'the evening star.' We should point out that modes of presentation of one object are not limited to two. Indeed, the possible modes of presentation of any object are unlimited. So, for 'the planet Venus,' we may create a litany: 'second brightest celestial object,' 'second satellite of the sun,' 'the planet of love,' 'planet closest to Mercury,' 'planet between Mercury and Earth,' and so on, ad infinitum. A third classic example of mode of presentation which often crops up in Husserlian phenomenology is Napoleon considered as 'the victor of Austerlitz' or as 'the initiator of the French legal code' (Gurwitsch 62); Napoleon, like Venus, may be considered from innumerable other modes of presentation.

All these examples lead to the same type of conclusion for language use: while x may equal z, and y also may equal z, this coincidence does not imply that x equals y. Frege argues, successfully, most would agree, that the meaning of the statement, 'the morning star is Venus,' does not equal the meaning of the statement, 'the evening star is Venus.' The statements, though denoting the same object, have, in linguistic terms, different senses or values; or, using the Husserlian psychological term, different 'noemata.' One then has two different modes of presentation or two different noemata which intend towards, or are directed towards the same object. The difference between these two modes of presentation for the same object Frege calls a difference in 'cognitive values' (56). The different cognitive values of the two modes of presentation may be starkly highlighted, using Frege's example, by the fact that many people have thought, and many probably still think, that the 'morning star' and the 'evening star' are names for two different objects. Likewise, one might refer to the 'initiator of the French legal code' without knowing, and/or having it understood, that the individual this name refers to is the same individual referred to by the names 'Napoleon' and 'the victor of Austerlitz.' 'Morning star' does not equal 'evening star'; 'Napoleon' does not equal 'the initiator of the French legal code,' and neither of these are equal to 'the victor of Austerlitz.' 'Mode of presentation' is not a theory; it is a concept which helps to describe accurately the observable phenomena of perception, thinking and speaking.

FOUR MEDIEVAL UNDERSTANDINGS OF
MODE OF PRESENTATION

The theology of uti *and* frui *as mode of presentation*

The concept of mode of presentation underlies the popular, medieval doctrine of Augustinian origin, that of *uti* and *frui*, or use and enjoyment. This doctrine also provides a ground for other considerations in medieval logic, as we shall see below. According to Augustine:

> Some things are to be enjoyed, others to be used, and there are others which are to be enjoyed and used. Those things which are to be enjoyed make us blessed. Those things which are to be used help and . . . sustain us as we move toward blessedness in order that we may gain and cling to those things which make us blessed. If we who enjoy and use things . . . wish to enjoy those things which should be used, our course will be impeded, and sometimes deflected, so that we are retarded in obtaining those things which are to be enjoyed, or even prevented altogether, shackled by an inferior love.   (DDC 1.3.3)

Fundamental here is how one considers an object: as a means or as an end. This requires that one distinguish between the object itself, or the object *which* is intended, and the object *as* it relates to us or to other things. According to Augustine we should will to use and/or enjoy an object:

> For to use, is to take up something into the power of the will; and to enjoy, is to use with joy . . . Accordingly, every one who enjoys uses; for he takes up something into the power of the will, wherein he is also satisfied as with an end. But not every one who uses, enjoys, if he has sought after that, which he takes up into the power of the will, not on account of the thing itself, but on account of something else.   (DT 10.11.17)

So, things which on their own 'make us blessed' may be simultaneously used and enjoyed, while those things which 'move [us] toward blessedness in order that

we may gain and cling to those things which make us blessed' are only to be
used. Augustine offers examples of both in *On the Good of Marriage*:

> Truly we must consider, that God gives us some goods, which are to be
> sought for their own sake, such as wisdom, health, friendship: but others,
> which are necessary for the sake of somewhat, such as learning [for
> wisdom], meat, drink, sleep [for health], marriage, sexual intercourse [for
> friendship].   (Chap. 9)

But even permissible ends, such as wisdom, friendship, and health, finally,
according to Augustine, should not be used and enjoyed only for themselves, for
they are further means to an ultimate end, as means of attaining presence with
the only 'thing' that may be ultimately enjoyed eternally, the Trinity: 'The things
which are to be enjoyed are the Father, the Son, and the Holy Spirit, a single
Trinity' (DDC 1.5.5).

Whatever one may think of the Augustinian doctrine, what cannot be denied is
that it introduces a distinction between the object *which* is intended and the
object *as* it is intended into the human consideration of various 'objects;'
Augustine's aim, in other words, is to make every Christian aware of what we
call today 'mode of presentation.' The wide acceptance and understanding of
this doctrine implies a wide acceptance and understanding of mode of
presentation under a theological guise. That this is true is supported by St
Thomas Aquinas's Augustinian-inspired considerations of the use and/or
enjoyment of God. In the *Summa Theologica* (1.2 16.3), Aquinas argues that
God may be enjoyed but not used. While we need not consider his argument, in
formulating it Aquinas observes that 'the last end may be taken in two ways:
first, absolutely; secondly, in relation to an individual.' This is a distinction
between the object *which* is considered, that is, 'absolutely,' and the object *as* it
is considered, that is, 'in relation to an individual.' To make the distinction clear
Aquinas uses the example of money considered as the object which is intended,
'the thing in itself . . . good only as there is some good in money,' and money as
it is intended by a miser, as his 'last end.' The difference, for Augustine and
Aquinas, between intending to enjoy things as ends, such things as meat, drink,
sleep, sexual intercourse, and money, rather than to use these same things as
means, is measurable in the effect these different cognitive values have upon the
intending subject. Here, the cognitive value happens to be measured in moral
currency, while the 'morning star' / 'evening star' difference is measured in the
currency of perception and/or knowledge.

What is most interesting is that we take on the 'cognitive value' of how we
evaluate or intend objects, something appreciated by both medieval and modern
thinkers. If I have enjoyed viewing Venus as the morning star, that innocent
pleasure and knowledge is part of my being, my experience. So we often express
such experiences in the present perfect tense, 'I have seen the morning star,'
even if such experiences occurred many years in the past. The medieval
theologians, of course, are interested not only in how the pursuit of wisdom,
health, and friendship affects one's being, but also in how the pursuit of less
innocent pleasures, or outright evil intentions, affects one's being. Central here
is the idea that the will through the 'mouth of the heart' (Augustine, *On*

Continence Chap. 2 379) speaks its 'word,' which is at once its 'deed,' and its 'consent': 'if he hath consented, he hath already spoken in his heart, although he has not uttered sound by the mouth' (Chap. 3 380). 'The inner man hath an inner mouth, and this the inner ear discerns: what things go forth from this mouth go out of the heart, and they defile the man' (Chap. 4 380). Any mental act or experience affects man's *relation* to the world, a term which has recurred in this chapter and which, as a metaphysical category, will be studied in more detail below. For now we may say that a change in relation, as both Augustine and Aquinas have implied in their discussion of use and enjoyment, changes a person. There is an understanding here that is not exclusive to Augustinian theology; it is the view of Aristotelian metaphysics, medieval logic, and modern thinking as well.

The doctrine of use and enjoyment has serious implications when applied to literary theory. The literary artefact, like any human artefact or natural object, should, in strict Augustinian terms, be used with good intention, primarily as a means, rather than an end. In any relationship between a subject and most objects, all the intentionality, and hence, all the moral responsibility lies with the subject. For example, one cannot consider an object such as the food that one eats as having any moral force; the same is true of most man-made or processed objects. But the literary artefact is different from most artefacts because it is crafted of those objects which are charged with intention and meaning, namely, words. Determining authorial intentionality, and so authorial moral responsibility, was a primary concern of medieval textual analysis and was a Chaucerian concern. In the creation of the work of art, there is also a creation of a relation between the author and the readers, actual and potential: this is not a subject-object relationship, but a subject-subject relationship. It is possible, because of the ontological status and capabilities of the intending subjects, that one's words as writings, which are intentional artefacts, may effect a change in the person or persons who hear or read them, just as one's spoken words may effect change in a subject who hears them. There is an authorial responsibility to speak or to write properly.

An ironic demonstration of how and why this may occur is found in Chaucer's *Merchant's Tale*. May advises her husband, January, that 'He that mysconceyveth, he mysdemeth' (IV 2410). May uses these very words as part of an argument that demonstrates that one subject's words (her own!) may cause another subject (January) to question the validity of a perception. January had correctly perceived May copulating in a pear tree with her lover Damian, but May's words lead him to believe that he had 'misconceived.' While January had originally neither misconceived nor misdeemed what he had seen, May's words cause him to *believe* that he had misconceived and so misdeemed what he had seen: he believes that her 'improper' copulation had not occurred at all. Ironically, of course, the real *mis*-conceiver, because of her illicit act of potential conception, and so the one who has truly 'misdeemed' in this particular action, is May. Chaucer demonstrates here that one's words may affect how an individual might see the world, and, implicitly, he also demonstrates that the use of words contains an ethical component; they may be used properly or improperly.

The listener or reader is also responsible for 'proper' or 'improper' reception of a text. Negative exemplary readers *par excellence* are Dante's Paolo and

Francesca, whose improper love and subsequent fall is occasioned by the
reading of a romance of another pair of improper lovers, Guinevere and
Lancelot. In reading, Paolo and Francesca come to see themselves as a pair like
Guinevere and Lancelot. Indeed, Dante gives an overt Augustinian cast to the
whole episode by setting up counter, positive 'exemplary readers,' including St
Augustine himself (Patterson, *Negotiating* 141; see also Hollander 106–14;
Dronke 113–35). The paradoxical line between authorial responsibility and
reader responsibility is often difficult to draw. Of the *Roman de la rose* Lee
Patterson points out:

> Andreas Capellanus may have meant his treatise [on courtly love]
> ironically, but Bishop Tempier missed the point or feared that others
> would, and so condemned it. And he was right to do so: the thirteenth-
> century translation by Drouart la Vache suppresses Andreas' ironies and
> renders the treatise an unambiguous handbook of *fine amor*.   (141)

With the ironies and the allegories of the treatise either missed in the original,
and/or 'suppressed' in translation, the text might and did serve unintended
purposes. For some it became a handbook of *fine amor*; one that also confirmed
and inculcated misogynist points of view. Whether or not they intended such
readings, from a medieval perspective, the authors bear some moral
responsibility for such negative receptions.

There is evidence that Chaucer had a concern with such 'improper' receptions
for his own work. In *Troilus and Criseyde* the narrator demands of his readers
that they 'herkneth with a good entencioun' (1.52). Chaucer seems to be
concerned simultaneously with authorial and reader/listener responsibility. An
example of a use of 'good entencioun,' or a proper mode of presentation, from
which to consider Chaucer's rendering of this classic love story has been
presented to us by Lee Patterson in his study (*Negotiating* 115–53) of the
fifteenth-century work of spiritual guidance for nuns known as the *Disce mori*.
This work extensively and approvingly cites Chaucer's *Troilus and Criseyde* as
an exemplum of how ' "flesshly love"(*amor*) undermines "love spiritual"
(*amicitia*)' (119). Such a 'proper' reading strongly supports a view that
Chaucer's reasons for including *Troilus and Criseyde* among his 'retracciouns'
(Ret X 1085) was not because of any 'bad entente' on his part in its writing,
which he expressly denies for all of his works (1082–83), but because of his
concern for how his readers might use and enjoy his love poem: 'properly' or
'improperly.' Chaucer was aware that different readers could see his poem *as*
different poems. By missing or suppressing the ironies of the poem, by reading it
cynically, by ignoring, or not reaching its conclusion, a reader of *Troilus and
Criseyde* could, following the path of Paolo and Francesca, experience it, too,
only as a titillating romance, or like *La Roman de la rose*, as a handbook on
'Th'olde daunce,' 'th'amorouse daunce' (Tr 3.695; 4.1431), *fine amor*.
Chaucer's 'retracciouns' suggests and the *Friar's Tale* demonstrates that
Chaucer understood and believed that the way we relate or direct ourselves
towards objects and other subjects in this world may have serious consequences
for both other subjects and for ourselves.

The category of relation

While similarities between Fregean interests and scholastic interests have been remarked upon (Moody, 'Buridan'), the same has not been true for Chaucer. Chaucer, like some of his contemporaries who were teaching and studying at Oxford and Paris, would not be surprised by the revelation that 'the morning star' does not equal 'the evening star,' even though these terms refer to the same object. We can be sure of this for Chaucer because, as is demonstrated in detail in the next two chapters, the *Friar's Tale* pivots on an equation of exactly the same type: a 'rente,' a legal income, does not equal a 'briberye,' an illegal income, even when these terms are used to refer to the same object, a frying pan. In other words, Chaucer clearly distinguishes between the object *which* is intended and the object *as* it is intended. Such understandings of mode of presentation, centuries before Alice and Frege, were widely appreciated, in part because of the treatment of the category of relation by classical and scholastic philosophy.

While in 'the thirteenth and early fourteenth century many thinkers argued for different theories concerning the ontological status of relations' (Henninger 1), no one doubted that relations did have some kind of ontological status. According to the Aristotelian category of relation, because a relation is an accident which may exist in a subject, any relationship with any object affects the intending subject. If, like Aquinas's miser, one focuses one's attention on acquiring wealth, one has a relationship with those things which are considered wealth, even if one does not possess them. Most importantly, such a relationship becomes part of that which makes up one's being. If the person focused on wealth drops or changes that focus, that person also changes himself or herself. So in the *Friar's Tale*, seeking a 'panne' or 'twelf pens' *as* a 'briberye,' and seeking a 'panne' or 'twelf pens' *as* a 'rente,' does not change the pan or twelve pence, but it does change the 'value' of the seeker or the intending subject, because he or she then has a different *relationship* to the object. The different cognitive value of twelve pence taken, or even intended to be taken, as a bribe, and twelve pence taken as a legal 'rente' changes the moral value of the taker. If one changes one's relationship to an object, one changes oneself because 'there is a real relation in the knower to the known' (Henninger 8).

Whether the object of one's intending is (a) an inanimate object, such as coins, or (b) an object which is also a subject, such as a person, or (c) an object that is charged with the intention of a person, such as a work of art, all these relationships affect and change the intending subject. Also in (b) the other subject could be changed by the relationship; and in (c), as we discussed above, the author of a work of art, because of his moral responsibility, could be changed, even unknowingly, by the relationship of another subject to the work he created. In case (a), whether or not one has a relationship with the coins does not usually change the coins, unless one is doing something to them physically, because in such a relationship 'there can be no real relation to the knower in the thing known' (Henninger 8). This is the knower-known relationship, or subject-object relationship, 'subject' and 'object' being distinguished by the fact that subjects have intentionality or will, and objects in themselves are totally lacking in intentionality (cf. Johansson 197). In a subject-subject relationship, case (b), a relationship usually between two people, because both terms may be directed towards each other, the relationship may change both subjects.[1] Case (c), subject-to-work-of-art, is a special case of a subject-subject relationship.

In brief, for the category of relation, as with the doctrine of use and enjoyment, *how* a subject intends towards an object, that is, the kind of noema one has of an object, as distinguished from the object itself, affects the being of the intending subject. What is usually considered in phenomenology to be a psychological entity, in medieval thought was part of a metaphysical entity, a human being. Indeed the medieval conception is the same as the phenomenological one.

Faculty psychology, logic, and first and second intentions

I have argued that considering 'twelf pens' *as* a 'briberye,' and 'twelf pens' *as* a 'rente' is an example of the distinction between an object *which* is intended, twelve pence, and an object *as* it is intended, understood today as 'mode of presentation.' We may go elsewhere than the category of relation and the moral doctrine of use and enjoyment to demonstrate the widespread understanding of this phenomenon. In Chapter Two the distinction between first and second intentions in scholastic logic was described briefly. Now we may add that this distinction rests precisely on the distinction between object *which*, and object *as* it is intended. The objects which are intended, say some particular circular metal objects, are first intentions; and these objects as they are intended, as money, as a bribe, or as a rent, are second intentions.

First intentions begin with the perception of individual things, say, a formed piece of gold metal. This occurs through the senses, or in fourteenth-century English, the 'wits.' According to Boethius, in Chaucer's translation: 'the wit comprehendith withoute-forth the figure [form] of the body of the man that is establisschid in the matere subgett' (Bo 5.pr 4 154–57). This 'figure' of an individual formed piece of gold metal is stored in the 'ymaginacioun': 'the ymaginacioun comprehendith oonly the figure withoute the matere' (157–59). This 'figure' is what the scholastic philosophers called an *intentio*, and, in this case, a first intention. First intentions reside in the *imaginatio*: '*Imaginatio* is the last resting place of sensible forms; it is simply a treasury or storehouse, and it does not discern or judge in any way' (Harvey 44). With a first intention there is

---

[1] As further explanation of the different ontological status of subject and object in the subject-object relationship in the context of the distinction between the object *which* is intended and the object *as* it is intended, consider a person 'intending' or considering twelve pence. As one may know the planet Venus in many ways, so too may one know/intend twelve pence. But the twelve pence cannot know/intend me. I can hold out my hand to you with the same twelve circular objects in it and say: 'Here is/are the x,' and substitute for 'x' such words as 'twelve pence,' 'twelve round objects,' 'rent,' 'bribe,' 'coins,' 'money,' 'investment,' 'fee,' 'bet,' 'legal tender,' 'pieces of precious metal,' 'a certain weight of atoms, of a certain molecular structure,' and they all *intend* the same objects, and so *relate* the names to the objects. When I say the words I have put in quotation marks in the previous sentence I also *present* the 'coins' in different ways. Because of the ontological status of the coins as pieces of metal of a certain molecular structure, they may be changed accidentally in relationship to me but they are usually not changed substantially by my relationship to them. However, the same is not necessarily true of relationships between people: the intending-subject-to-intending subject relationship.

no judging, no comparing, combining or dividing of thoughts; there are no
'adjudicative acts of the intellect' (Tachau 63), nor is there any active work of
the intellect. First intentions occur, as Duns Scotus says, 'sine opere vel actu
intellectus' ('without the operation or movement of the understanding') (Tachau
63n30). But another faculty, reason, discerns and judges first intentions, and the
result is second intentions: 'resoun surmountith ymaginacioun and comprehendith by an universel lokynge the comune spece that is in the singuler
peces' (Bo 5.pr 4 159–162). When one begins rationally relating the form of this
particular individual gold piece of metal to similar other pieces, and considering
the use which has been assigned them, one may conceive the concept of the
'comune spece,' in this case, 'money,' or 'coins.' A concept such as these is a
second intention, something which is not immediately known, but which is
rather a relation I make in my mind. By the process of mental judging the reason
may also consider this particular first intention, a piece of formed gold, as
numerous second intentions other than as 'money' or as 'coins,' for example, it
may be considered as a bribe, or as a rent. Such activity, as Avicenna first put it, is

> That which is most proper to man . . . to form universal intelligible
> intentions, entirely abstracted from matter . . . and to proceed from
> known intelligibles to the knowledge of unknown ones, by a process of
> forming and affirming.   (Harvey 47)

This is the stuff of medieval logic, which was concerned with second intentions.[2]
But did Chaucer understand the distinction between first and second intentions? The
theory of intentions was widely known and, given the Oxford company Chaucer
kept, it is unlikely that he was not aware of it. Furthermore, there is an article that
attempts to demonstrate that Chaucer in fact played with the distinction between
first and second intentions in the *Friar's Tale* (Williams, 'Grammar's Pan').
Whether or not one fully accepts this particular reading, my own reading of the
Friar's Tale lends support to the view that Chaucer understood the distinction
which underlies the theory of first and second intentions, the distinction between the
object *which* is intended and the object *as* it is intended.

Negative and positive theology and analogical thinking

In addition to 'mode of presentation,' the distinction between the object which is
intended and the object as it is intended is sometimes known today as the

---

[2] The 'mental beings' which become second intentions in medieval logic are found in 'the Stoic
distinction between words as *lekta* and words as natural signs of real beings,' which Augustine
uses 'to underline the differences between language and logic' (Colish 38–39). That relations are
second intentions and that second intentions are the subject of logic was the view of all major
medieval scholastic philosophers, starting with Aquinas, who adopted the principle from Avicenna
(see Kneale and Kneale 229–30). On the history of first and second intentions, and an exemplary
outline of them from Radulphus Brito (late thirteenth century) see Marenbon 139–143. John Duns
Scotus, following Henry of Ghent, most fully explained second intentions (Tachau
64). For a lucid explanation of second intentions as 'relations' see Swiezawski ('Les intentions'),
who gives a classic outline of the definitions and arguments of John Duns Scotus. My own
discussion owes much to Swiezawski. The relation of second intentions themselves to extramental
reality is central to the nominalist-realist debate, but is not an issue in the present discussion.

difference between the content of thought and the object of thought. In the Middle Ages Radulphos Brito makes the same distinction when he speaks of ' "concrete" first and second intentions (*in concreto*) and "abstract" ones (*in abstracto*) . . . between what is thought of and the thought of it' (Marenbon 140). John Duns Scotus also makes this same distinction between the thought itself, be it a first or second intention, and the object of that thought (Swiezawski, 'Les intentions' 225). But these logical investigations by scholastic philosophers into the nature of relations, of first and second intentions, and so of mode of presentation and the object and content of thought, actually begin with attempts to understand how one can name God, know God, and be known by God. Here is a fourth avenue through which the distinction between the object which is intended and the object as it is intended enters medieval thought.

According to many scholastic thinkers (Ashworth), our thoughts of God *in abstracto* will all be different and will never adequately describe God, but when we say or think 'God,' our words still denote God *in concreto*. The approaches to naming God are two, and they are considered by many of the major Church Fathers and scholastic philosophers. These two 'ways' are the Christian Neoplatonic consideration of the *via positiva* and the *via negativa*. As discussed in previous chapters, the Middle Ages understood there to be an absolute difference between God and man. Implicit in this ontological difference is an epistemological difference. God simply cannot be adequately known or understood through the means usually available to the realm of created beings. This meant that language, in its ordinary use, was inadequate for the naming of God. Alain de Lille, in a statement that is typical of medieval theology, writes: 'As it has been proved that God is incomprehensible, thus it is evident that He is innominable' (Ziolkowski 125). Once this presupposition was acknowledged, however, one could begin understanding God, although inadequately, by naming Him. In *The Mystical Theology* the Pseudo-Dionysius writes: 'In *The Divine Names* I have shown the sense in which God is described as good, existent, life, wisdom, power and whatever other things pertain to the conceptual names for God' (1033A). But in this treatise he declares of the 'supreme Cause' that 'It has no power, it is not power, nor is it light. It does not live nor is it life' (1048A). These statements do not mean that God is the logical opposites of these names; that He is 'powerless,' 'darkness,' or 'lifeless,' but that God is, for example, *neither* 'power' *nor* 'not power': 'Darkness and light, error and truth – it [the supreme Cause] is none of these. It is beyond assertion and denial' (1048A–1048B). Here again, the question is one of difference, not opposition. We may name God as 'good,' as 'beautiful,' as 'wisdom,' or as 'truth,' and with dozens of other attributes, but they all refer metaphorically, or, more precisely, analogically, to a single, unnameable referent, a referent beyond or transcendent to human concepts. At the same time that God is *neither* darkness *nor* light, He is also *both* darkness *and* light: 'The divine darkness is that "unapproachable light" where God is said to live' (Pseudo-Dionysius, 'Letter Five' 1073A).

Elaborate and accurate semantic theories of analogy were developed to explain how the ordinary language of human experience could, in a way, describe God (Ross; Ziolkowski 125–30; Ashworth). When one hears or uses one of the many names of God one is caused to consider God from that particular mode of presentation. A principal point of positive and negative theology was to make one aware that each particular name of God was only one of an infinite number of modes of presentation through which the nature of God could be considered. The value of these many names, or modes of presentation, was to give one a sense or senses of God or the realm of Being, without ever presupposing that these senses fully or accurately named that which was beyond human experience, and so beyond human language. Thus, for example, a litany invokes many names of God and causes the listener/speaker to consider the 'object' from many different modes of presentation. One is to contemplate in the potentially infinite variety of names at once the wondrous nature of God as well as his unnameability.

Among the many illustrations of naming that which cannot be named, a particularly helpful example is the motif of 'Christ as a Gardener' that occurs in medieval art and drama. I say 'particularly helpful,' because I think it illustrates that what has lately been called 'mode of presentation' was manifest in medieval plastic and dramatic arts and so goes well beyond monastery or school.

According to Christian Scripture, Christ appears to Mary Magdalen after his resurrection. At first she does not recognize him, 'supposing him to be the gardener' (John 20:15). V.A. Kolve has gathered a number of examples in medieval art and drama of this meeting in which Christ is represented as simultaneously holding a shovel while maintaining a '*nolle me tangere*' pose.[3] Kolve offers plausible interpretations for the simultaneous do-not-touch-me attitude of Christ, such as the relationship which must obtain between God and man, or Christ-as-second-Adam and Magdalen-as-second-Eve. While not using the language of phenomenology or Fregean semantics that I employ here, Kolve argues that the representation of Christ with the shovel would cause the informed medieval viewer to consider Christ *as* the second Adam and *as* the gardener of the soul. The second-Adam interpretation is particularly convincing because Kolve offers examples from medieval art not only of Christ holding a shovel, but of Adam holding a shovel; a sign of the latter's punishment to dig and delve, to gain nourishment through the sweat of his face (Gen. 3:17–19). Considering Christ as a second Adam leads one to see Mary Magdalen as a second Eve, as a bride of the second Adam, and the two of them may be seen as representing the relationship of Christ with his Church, and with the individual Christian soul, Church and soul both being 'brides' of Christ. The typological symbolism is intended to reach right out to the faithful viewers who would make these same linkages, with Christ, Magdalen, Adam, Eve, for themselves; the viewers may see themselves from many different modes of presentation: *as* types and heirs of Adam and Eve redeemed by the second Adam, *as* 'gardens' which Christ through his grace and mercy cultivates, *as* 'brides' of Christ because they are members of his church. The pose of Christ may also be intended to represent his warning,

---

[3] That which I attribute to V.A. Kolve here is filtered through my own notes from, and interpretation of, his Maxwell Cummings Lectures given at McGill University, Feb. 7 and 8, 1991: 'Christ as Gardener in Medieval Art and Drama' and 'Christ as Pilgrim in Medieval Drama,' which I attended. Professor Kolve characterized these lectures as 'essays towards' a forthcoming book on this subject.

made shortly before his Ascension into heaven, that soon man would no longer be able to know him in the flesh. This interpretation is strengthened by the fact that two of the illustrations of Christ as gardener that Kolve presents have a companion illustration of doubting Thomas touching Christ's wounds. The combination seems to suggest that Thomas's way of knowing Christ would soon no longer be possible: after the Ascension the relationship which must obtain between God and ordinary mortals would only be one of faith. 'Thomas, because thou hast seen me thou hast believed: blessed are they that have not seen, and yet have believed' (John 20:19). Before Christ's Ascension, experiential knowledge was possible for those who were his disciples; but, just as before the birth of Christ, so after the Ascension, God is not to be known through sensible experience. The pair of illustrations suggests that after Christ's passing from this world he may be known *as* this or *as* that, as a second Adam, as a gardener, but that all these names are ultimately inadequate for really knowing God, and that finally our belief in Him must be based on faith, not on knowledge. So we know Christ or God *as* a gardener, *as* a second Adam, and so on, while simultaneously recognizing that God is *not* a gardener, *not* a second Adam, and so on. God is known through these names only metaphorically or by analogy. We may move to understanding how God is simultaneously 'good' and 'not-good.' To me the 'Christ as Gardener' representation becomes a concrete and graphic exemplar of what seems initially to be a very abstract and difficult theology, the theology of the *via positiva* and the *via negativa*.

Such a view that man is unable to know God absolutely in this life, and hence to know absolute Truth, might be called anti-essentialism.[4] But this anti-essentialism does not suggest that one cannot know to a degree the Divine Essence, or Truth. In naming God one does know God in a way, but not essentially. This view lies at the heart of Christian Neoplatonism. What the medieval Neoplatonist posited of God and of other beings, Frege posits of the 'referent' and Husserl posits of the 'transcendent object.' Frege has his sense / referent dichotomy; Husserl his noema / transcendent object dichotomy, and these are the same (Harney 144). The object which language describes, or which perception grasps, is ' "transcendent" insofar as it is "intendable" under a multiplicity of perspectives, none of which, individually, "exhausts" the object' (Harney 144). Medieval thinkers came to exactly the same conclusion as Frege and Husserl by considering the problem of naming what was for them the ultimate 'transcendent' object: God.

The anti-essentialist or perspectivist habit of thought encouraged by the double dialectic of positive and negative theology, the theology of *uti* and *frui*, the understanding of the category of relation, and the understanding of first and second intentions, are all intimately linked with a distinction between the object *which* and the object *as* intended, and so supply a rich context for understanding why Chaucer so obviously appreciated this 'modern' distinction.

---

[4] On anti-essentialism see pages 19, 63n11.

THREE-LEVEL SEMANTICS

Having introduced 'three-level semantics,' the understanding of the simultaneous mind-relatedness and world-relatedness of language, in Chapter Two, I would now like to consider how such a semantics may successfully describe how signs behave according to mode of presentation.

'Three-level semantics' (Kung 15; Harney 3) finds its modern origins in structural description of the semantics of language based on the consideration of the three elements Frege called '*Zeichen* (sign, expression), *Sinn* (sense, meaning), and *Bedeutung* (reference, denotation)' (Kung 15). It would be tangential here to consider the similarities and differences between Frege's 'expression' and 'sense,' Saussure's 'sound pattern' and 'concept,' and Ullmann's 'name' and 'sense.' For our present purposes the important distinction between Frege's logistic philosophy and the linguistics of Saussure and Ullmann is Frege's interest in the third element, reference, that is, the bi-directional relationships of language to the elements it expresses: on one hand cognitive or psychological aspects of the speaking subject, such as belief, fear, desire, understanding, and, on the other hand, extramental 'things' (concepts as well as material things). The three-level semantics which arises from these considerations is not immediately related, then, to the structuralist linguistics of Saussure and his followers which tackles a narrower area, the internal structural relationships within language itself. As far as the composition of the sign is concerned, in such structural linguistics the interest is limited to relationship between the 'sound pattern' and the 'concept,' and broader internal relations, rather than to the extralinguistic 'things' such linguistic relations attempt to denote. Typical of this linguistic school, Ullmann writes: 'Since the "thing" is non-linguistic, it has no place in a purely linguistic analysis. The linguist can confine himself . . . [to the analysis of name and sense]' (*Meaning* 6). Paul Ricoeur, following Emile Benveniste and others, distinguishes between a 'linguistics of language,' which he sees Saussure and Ullmann practising, the study of the internal structure of language, and a 'linguistics of discourse,' which, unlike the linguistics of language, considers constantly the relationship of language to the speaking subject and to the world (see Ricoeur, 'Model'). It is the semantics of this last linguistics, a linguistics of discourse, that is three-leveled.

We have seen that while including reference in his linguistic equation, Frege does not lose sight of the psychological import of sense. 'Sense' has a 'cognitive value' which reveals how the 'thing' is perceived, thought of, and spoken about. At the same time Frege allows for language to refer to 'things' which do not exist in the real world, like a pegasus, or 'things' which have an abstract but real relationship to things in the world, like 'justice' or 'hunger.' All these interests of Frege, as we have just seen, were also scholastic interests.

Basically, three-level semantics describes the operation of the simultaneously mind-related and world-related intentionality of language. In considering this phenomenon one may interpret the 'intentionality' or the psychology of the speaker. Three-level semantics does not imply, however, that the sense of a word intends towards another locus. Sense is in the mind and contains the 'cognitive value' of the sign. At the same time the sign is world-related, denoting objects or relations between objects in the world and between the speaker and the world.

To say that spoken words are mind-related and world-related is to say that words, like all signs, are bi-directional. Words are directed to two 'positions,' the mind and the world – to one, either one, primarily, and to the other secondarily. Words that are primarily world-related do not just signify objective material or immaterial entities, they secondarily signify mental entities, which we usually call concepts. If I say 'that is a table,' my words signify the specific extramental entity known as a table, but they also signify that I know the concept 'table.' If I say 'there is the morning star,' my words primarily denote a particular object in the sky, and secondarily signify my 'concept' or understanding of that class of objects. If I say 'that was a just decision,' my words refer not only to a just act, but to the fact that I know a concept, 'justice.' If my words happen to be primarily mind-related they will also be world-related. For example, if I attempt to define the concept 'table,' or the concept 'justice,' I will attempt to show to myself or others that particular tables, or particular acts of justice, have independent extramental existence. Even words which name entities which have no independent extramental existence, for example, 'pegasus,' while being primarily mind-related, are also, secondarily, world-related: 'pegasus' points to a combination of an equine and a flying creature, and both horses and flying creatures exist independently of the mind.

In summary, three-level semantics argues that a word is an entity composed of a sound (or acoustic image, or sound pattern) and one or more senses, the sense often being determined by the context or use of the word. The sense in which a speaker uses a word within a significative expression constitutes in that instance the word's meaning. Meaning is mind-related and world-related: this is a fundamental insight appreciated by Chaucer. For example, I will demonstrate that in the *Friar's Tale* Chaucer's art deliberately causes the audience to consider how the devil, in certain senses, *is* a yeoman, and *is* a bailiff, even while we are fully aware that he also *is not* either of these. Similarly, the audience is invited to consider the summoner of the tale *as* a bailiff, *as* a devil, and *as* a yeoman, although he too is simultaneously *not* any of these. Chaucer's art functions on articular movement, back and forth, between the mind-related and world-related functioning of verbal signification, an understanding of mode of presentation which we in turn may appreciate in the terms of the three-level semantics which describes it.

THREE-LEVEL SEMANTICS FROM AUGUSTINE TO FREGE

The definition of a sign 'destined to become classical throughout the Middle Ages' (R.A. Markus 73) is Augustine's: 'a sign is a thing, which in addition to what it is perceived to be by the senses also causes something else to come into thought' (DDC 2.1.1). Markus paraphrases and comments on this definition:

A sign . . . is an element in a situation in which three terms are related. These we may call the object or *significatum* for which the sign stands, the

sign itself, and the subject to whom the sign stands for the object signified
. . . Augustine appears to be the first to have stressed this triadic nature of
the relation of 'signifying': it had been noticed before that signs belong to
the category of relation . . . but in all previous discussions the relation of
sign to *significatum* is conceived as a straightforward dyadic relation.

(74)

When Umberto Eco remarks on Augustine's insight into the bi-directional nature
of the sign (Eco, *Semiotics* 18), his observation is similar to that of Markus.
Eugene Vance also notes that in *De Trinitate* 'Augustine's semiotics becomes
distinctly triadic, in the sense that he speculates actively on the relationship
between signifier, referent, and concept, or between what Peirce called sign,
object, and interpretant' (*Augustine*, 64). We may describe Augustine's
understanding as an appreciation that the sign is simultaneously mind-related and
world-related: the basic principle of three-level semantics.

Both Augustine and Frege take pains to point out that signs not only denote
extramental things, they also reveal, articulate or formulate intramental,
subjective ideas, understandings, and attitudes. Augustine writes:

> Conventional signs are those which living creatures show to one another
> for the purpose of conveying, in so far as they are able, the motion of their
> spirits (*motus animi sui*) or something which they have sensed or
> understood. Nor is there any other reason for signifying, or for giving
> signs, except for bringing forth and transferring to another mind the action
> of the mind (*id quod animo gerit*) in the person who makes the sign.
>
> (DDC 2.2.3)

'Motions of their spirits' are what we would call today 'mental states' such as
fears, desires, beliefs; and the 'action of the mind' seems to consider 'mental
acts.' Augustine argues that all conventional signs, particularly language, have a
prime function of attempting to express or articulate subjective mental states,
acts, or ideas. Similarly, Frege sees words as sounds with objective senses,
senses shared by a number of people, which we use to reveal, or articulate,
subjective ideas: 'the idea is subjective' while 'the sign's sense . . . may be the
common property of many' ('Sense' 59).

In addition to Augustine, how similar are the medieval and modern interests in
and understandings of language? My answer is 'very similar.' John Marenbon
writes of a group of thinkers who were very much interested in 'the differences
between how things are and how they are thought and spoken about by humans'
(136). This description could characterize the project of Husserl and Harney but
in fact Marenbon is describing a number of major late medieval thinkers. While
Marenbon is not unaware of the parallel between medieval and modern thinkers,
he minimizes their similarity. Of the *modistae*, a school of late medieval
grammarians, Marenbon writes:

> A modern reader might also believe that they are interesting philosophi-
> cally because – so he imagines – the *modistae* engaged in linguistic

analysis, similar in character, though not in terminology, to that pursued by some modern philosophers. But they are not.   (137)

I do not agree with Marenbon. According to him one of the 'fundamental differences' between *modistae* and 'modern linguistic philosophers' is that 'the *modistae* hold the view of the *De Interpretatione* [Aristotle] that thoughts are what words primarily signify, not things' (137). But in some cases of signification this is a view with which, I think, Frege and Husserl would agree. Moreover, Marenbon fails to point out in this discussion that there was another medieval school that thought words primarily signified things not thoughts. Those who thought that words primarily signify concepts included Aristotle, Boethius, and Aquinas; those who thought that words primarily signify things included Roger Bacon, Henry of Ghent, Walter Burley, John Duns Scotus, and William of Ockham (see Ashworth 30; S.F. Brown 108–109; Eco, 'Significa-tion'). The disagreement then was on whether thoughts or things were *primarily* signified by the sign. What they all agreed upon, and where they are in agreement with 'modern' three-level semantics, is the understanding that words signify *both* thoughts and things.

The modern formula, 'a word has sense which determines meaning' (Ullmann), finds its equivalent and its source in a 'medieval' maxim oft-quoted approvingly by modern linguists: 'vox significat mediantibus conceptibus' (Ullmann, *Principles* 71). Medieval thinkers generally, like modern thinkers generally, believed that 'concepts' are signified either primarily or secondarily in all significative acts. This is not surprising, given that both medieval and modern thinkers share an area of common concern and investigation: the distinction between the object *which* is intended and the object *as* it is intended. Three-level semantics describes the semantic functioning of the semiotics of mode of presentation, be it in its medieval or modern forms.

The crucial distinction in modern phenomenology between the object *which* is intended and the object *as* it is intended is also the distinction crucial to the theology of *uti* and *frui*, the understanding of the category of relation, the appreciation of the difference between first and second intentions, and the insight underlying the dialectic of negative and positive theology. It is beyond doubt that the understandings of perception, cognition, and language we describe today with the terms mode of presentation and three-level semantics were available to Chaucer, and, as we shall now see, both the subject and the object of his art.

CHAPTER FIVE

Chaucerian Entencioun:
Mode of Presentation and
Three-level Semantics in
the *Friar's Tale*

WHEN THE MORAL IMPLICATIONS of the 'proper' and 'improper' use of words in relation to the the things that they denote becomes the subject of a poem one is moving in a world of linguistic and ethical realism, and in Chaucer's case, intentionalist realism. It is in such a world that one finds oneself in the *Friar's Tale*, one of Chaucer's most mature and highly-regarded works,[1] in which there is a conscious focus on the semantic play of the word 'entente,'[2] a play

---

[1] V.A. Kolve, in one of the most recent articles on the *Friar's Tale*, sums up the general critical opinion: 'widely celebrated as one of Chaucer's most brilliant achievements in short fiction' (5). Murtaugh sees the *Friar's Tale* as 'an exceptionally pure example of Chaucer's mature art' (107). The reviews 'brilliant presentation of character' (F.N. Robinson 705) and 'masterful characterization' (RC 875) occur in the explanatory notes of two highly respected critical editions of the works of Geoffrey Chaucer. For further critical consensus on this view see Murtaugh 107n1.

[2] The *Friar's Tale* is one of Chaucer's shortest (363 lines), yet he uses the noun 'entente' or its paronyms seven times. Each of the five times 'entente' is used, it is used as an end-rhyme, more than any other word in the poem. On three of these occasions 'entente' is rhymed with 'rente,' more than any other pair. Only four other pairs of end-rhymes occur more than once; he/duetee (1351–52; 1391–92), live/yive (1429–30; 1530–31), brother/another (1395–96; 1567–8) wynne/synne (1420–21; 1605–6) occur twice. Moreover, all three rente/entente pairs occur within the space of 75 lines of each other – once every 25 lines. The four other pairs of end-rhymes which are repeated twice occur respectively within 50 lines, 98 lines, 169 lines, and 183 lines of each other. The frequent repetition of the 'rente'/'entente' pair is but one index of a poetic strategy aimed at developing an associative field of meaning. The associative field of 'rente'/'entente' is given wider reference by the fact that on each occasion that it is uttered it is by a different voice – the narrator, the summoner, and the devil, respectively. On each of these occasions the word 'rente' is intentionally coupled by the speaker with an unconventional sense or 'entente' of the word 'rente.' Moreover, with the initial use of 'rente,' a game of playing with the various senses or 'ententes' of many other verbal and visual expressions becomes firmly established. The word 'entente' in its other two occurrences rhymes once with 'repente' and once with 'hente.' As we shall see below, the 'ententes' of 'hente' and 'repente' are also

which demands of the readers an interpretation of intentionality as good or bad, proper or improper.

We have seen that the medieval articulation of Judeo-Christian semiological metaphysics made posible the awareness of psychological and semiotic facts – intentionality, mode of presentation, three-level semantics, the category of relation as it was understood in the Middle Ages; facts that, because they are exploited and made actual themes of the *Friar's Tale*, make the poem an ideal candidate for a demonstration of Chaucerian realism.

I will begin by indicating Chaucer's deliberate play in this tale with what structural semantics today refers to as 'fields of association.' Saussure first described these as resulting from the 'associative' and 'syntagmatic' relations of words (171–75). The former relations are supposed to develop between words which share senses, and the latter from the alteration or shifting of meaning of words through their contiguity with other words and the changing contexts in which they operate. The boundary between associative and syntagmatic fields of association is not clear because syntagmatic relations often contain fields of associative relations and vice versa. With some success, other terms, such as 'metaphorical' and 'metonymical' have been developed to try to sort out these relations.[3] For the present purposes, lengthy discussions of the definitions of such terms are not necessary; they serve simply as basic taxonomy. Therefore, I will use 'associative fields' here to describe the field of senses and words that are primarily built up in texts through play with homonymy, synonymy, polysemy, rhyme, as well as those fields developed through the potential that words have to denote multiple referents (Ullmann *Meaning* 24 ff.; *Principles* 78–79). We will start with the associative field which begins with the word 'rente' in the *Friar's Tale* and extends out to include a large number of words, beginning with the rhyme words 'entente' and 'repente.' In playing with such fields the text reveals the complex intentional structures of signs, and invites an equally complex and entertaining interpretation of the intentionality of their users, and their users interpretation of the intentionality of other users.

---

key players in the tale. Fittingly, 'hente'/'repente' is itself the end-rhyme for the last couplet of a poem in which the devil has 'hente' a 'rente' which has refused to 'repente.'

The extensive use of 'entente' in the *Friar's Tale* has formed the basis for several articles (Williams, 'Grammar's Pan'; Passon; Murtaugh). However, the full significance of the play with many senses of 'entente' has not been explored. While David Williams' study of intentionality is seminal to the present study, there are important differences which I discuss in Chapter One and below.

[3] Following Jakobson, signs in 'metaphoric' relationships are substituted for each other on the basis of an 'associative relationship' (Saussure Chap. 6) founded on a 'similarity' (Jakobson 75) between senses of the signs. Implicit in such 'similarity' is 'difference.' In 'metonymic' relationships, there is also an associative relationship, but one in which words refer to each other on the basis of 'linear sequentiality,' or 'contiguity' (Jakobson, 'Two Aspects' 75). Below I consider the medieval definition of metonymy or *denominatio* which was well-known to Chaucer. Jakobson's theory has survived remarkably well. For a refinement see Johnson; for a critical review see Bredin.

THE 'ENTENTES' OF 'RENTE'

In fourteenth-century terms, because the word 'entente' has a number of meanings or senses including <meaning> and <sense>,[4] instead of speaking of 'fields of associations' of words, one could speak of the 'ententes of wordes.'

'Rentes' and 'brybes'

> Seyde this yeman [the devil in disguise], 'Wiltow fer to day?'
> This somnour hym answerde and seyde, 'Nay;
> Heere faste by,' quod he, 'is myn *entente*
> To ryden, for to reysen up a *rente*
> That longeth to my lordes *duetee*.'   (1387–91)[5]

Considering a 'rente' as something that belongs to someone's 'duetee' allows us entry into the rich fields of associations of 'rente.' Etymologically, the modern word 'rent' and the Middle English word 'rente' are derived from the Old French 'rente,' whose Latin root is the verb *reddo*: to give back, restore, to give something as due.

A 'rente,' then, is something one legally owes someone else for some kind of service, because of a legal obligation or because of a relationship of servitude: it is one's 'duetee' or <obligation> to pay one's rent. This was often called 'rente servise' <a service due to a feudal lord>. The serf paid for the use of his master's land and for his master's protection through his servile labour, the service of his labour, working his lord's private lands – plowing, planting, harvesting. By Chaucer's day, this type of 'rente' <harvesting the crop of one's lord> had been widely, although not universally, supplanted by the commuting of labour 'rentes' into money 'rentes' (Strohm 15; Tuchman 375, 172). Because it was one's 'duetee' to pay one's lord or master for the use of his land through service or money, we can see how such 'rente' comes to have a sense <duetee>. These words, then, have overlapping senses, <rente> for 'duetee,' and <duetee> for 'rente.' Simultaneously, senses of 'duetee' other than <rente> are put into play.

While in the *Friar's Tale* numerous fields of association are put into play simultaneously, at some point they all interconnect. For example, before he meets the 'yeoman' the narrator of the *Friar's Tale* has already brought the connected senses of 'rente' and 'duetee' into play; he tells us that the summoner's 'maister [the archdeacon] hadde [from the summoner] but half his duetee' (1352), thus connecting two senses of 'duetee,' <rente> and <obligation>. It is typical of Chaucer's poetic technique to create such play

---

[4] For example, <meaning> or <numerous senses> is the meaning of 'ententcion' in the following from *The Testament of Love*: ' "necessary" and "necessite" ben wordes of mokel entencion' (Usk 3.2.139–49 110). I deal with the etymology and use of 'entente' as derived from *intentio* in Chapter Two.

[5] All cases of emphasis in this and subsequent quotations from the works of Chaucer are added.

with overlapping senses and so develop an association. By extending such play to other senses, and other words, constantly expanding fields of association are created.

The field of association that can be mapped around the word 'rente,' is the largest in the *Friar's Tale*. Among the senses of 'rente' offered by the *Middle English Dictionary* which come into play in the *Friar's Tale* are the following: <a revenue from a property>, <income>, <a source or item of revenue>, <property yielding revenue>, <wealth>, <the produce of a crop>, <fruit>, <a profit>, <a dwelling place for which rent is paid>, <a payment made periodically to a landlord>, <a tribute>, <tax>, <toll>, <a payment due to somebody by right>, <a reward>, <a recompense>, <a salary>, <a right>, and, as we have already seen, <a duty>. However, the most general sense which passes through all these senses of 'rente' is <legal income>.

In lines 1389-90 the reader or listener is deliberately caused to consider the *misuse* of the word 'rente' as <legal income>, because, of course, when the summoner says that he is out to raise a <legal income> he is lying; his 'entente' is to obtain an <illegal income>, a sense of the word 'brybe.' However, already for the reader, and now for the summoner, the word 'rente' carries this special inverted sense <brybe>; it was earlier introduced by the narrator through the play of the words 'briberyes' and 'brybe' with 'rente' and 'entente':

> Certeyn he [the summoner] knew of *briberyes* mo
> Than possible is to telle in yeres two.
> For in this world nys dogge for the bowe [a hunting dog]
> That kan an hurt deer from an hool yknowe
> Bet than this somnour knew a sly lecchour,
> Or an avowtier, or a paramour.
> And for that was the fruyt of al his *rente*,
> Therefore on it he sette al his *entente*.
> And so bifel that ones on a day
> This somnour, evere waityng on his pray,
> Rood for to somne an old wydwe, a ribibe,
> Feynynge a cause, for he wolde *brybe*.   (1367-78)

Here fields of association between the emphasized words are being developed. When, eleven lines later, the summoner lies to the 'yeoman' that his 'entente' is to raise a 'rente,' the word 'rente' with the sense <brybe> is firmly set in the mind of the reader-listener. But just as important, from the viewpoint of characterization, the reader realizes that this sense is one that is also set in the mind of the summoner. Obviously 'rente' also relates to some object in the world which may be considered *as* a <legal income> or *as* an <illegal income>. We see here an exploitation of the mind-related and world-related nature of signs that is described by three-level semantics. Both 'subjects,' the audience and the summoner, share a special sense of 'rente' for the duration of the poem. This special sense of 'rente' is 'improper,' in that the <bryberye>

or < illegal income > does not *properly* (as defined by convention) *belong* to the word 'rente': this is what I mean when I say that Chaucer's linguistic and ethical realism is the very subject of this poem. The audience is caused to reflect on the *proper* meaning of the word 'rente,' to consider it apart from the objects it may denote. This is facilitated by the fact that the *improper* sense of 'rente,' < illegal income >, defines negatively the proper sense of the word; it tells us not what 'rente' is, but what 'rente' is not. This semantic play also allows the audience to characterize the summoner; moreover, the summoner unwittingly characterizes himself by revealing the nature of his relationship to certain extra-mental objects. In the discussion of various medieval understandings of mode of presentation we saw that for medieval man it was widely understood and believed that such subject-object and subject-subject relationships have meta-physical consequences affecting the very being of intending subjects. In masking what the audience knows to be a 'brybe' as a 'rente,' the summoner is not only masking his 'entente' from the 'yeoman', he is masking his very being. The masking, of course, has the exact opposite effect for the audience: it unmasks an aspect of the very being of the summoner that he intends to hide.

The difference in cognitive value between the two senses, or modes of presentation, of 'rente,' its conventional sense and its special sense here of 'brybe,' may be expressed as a difference in moral value between someone who pursues a certain object *as* a 'rente' and someone who pursues the same object *as* a 'brybe.' In making evident the summoner's lie, 'Heere fast by . . . is myn entente / To ryden, for to reysen up a rente' (1389–90), the author has contrasted modes of presentation or noemata, and in the difference between these the narrator has caused the summoner to characterize himself as a liar and a hypocrite. An index of moral propriety is linguistic propriety.

One might argue, with reason, that such character-revealing play occurs in any use of words; that one may consider any character in any work to be characterized through the mind-related aspects of his or her own words, by the words of the author, by the words of other characters, and through the senses the audience on its own interpret these words to have. But here, and throughout the *Friar's Tale*, attention is called again and again to the semantic process itself, and *we are led* to consider different modes of presentation. In the case just discussed, one is caused to adopt what today is called by some the 'reflective phenomenological attitude,' the conscious attitude which one adopts in considering *how* someone sees something. This is unlike the usual 'natural attitude' one normally has in which one does not consider *how* someone sees something (cf. Føllesdal, 'Husserl's Theory of Perception' 96; see also p. 37n5 above). Unlike just any play with words, the *Friar's Tale* repeatedly forces the audience to consider objects in the world as they are considered by the minds of various characters, while simultaneously causing the reader to consider the psychological, moral, and other implications of different characters intending towards identical objects in different manners, and perceiving identical objects from different perspectives. In effect, by deliberately causing his audience to shift from a 'natural attitude' to a 'reflective phenomenological attitude', Chaucer forces his audience to make what phenomenology calls the 'phenomenological reduction' (see Sajama and Kamppinen 90–92).

Yeoman, 'yeoman', and the Liar paradox

The 'word' with which the devil meets the summoner, that is, his disguise as a hunting yeoman, indicates that one lying hypocrite has met another. Like all 'good lies', however, both lies contain elements of truth. The devil is a 'gay yeman,' with 'arwes brighte and kene,' with a jacket of 'grene,' and a hat with 'frenges blake' (1380–83); these and many other signs would cause a fourteenth-century audience to consider the 'yeoman' *as* a devil.[6] For such an audience, there are two objects *which* can be intended by someone dressed as a yeoman: a yeoman and a *diabolus venator* or hunting devil. The former is the conventional sense and the latter is a special sense; the referent of the former is a yeoman, the referent of the latter is a devil or, more precisely, a devil considered *as* a yeoman, *as* a <hunter of prey>. Unlike the example of 'rente' and 'brybe,' which are two *different* ways of seeing the *same* object, the yeoman/devil play revolves upon a *similar* way of seeing two *different* 'objects,' namely, a yeoman and a devil. A yeoman was usually an armed retainer of a noble, who might, as in the case of the 'Yeman' accompanying Chaucer's Knight, serve a military role or, in more pacific times, act as his lord's forester. His duties sometimes included collecting 'rentes.' Such yeomen were renowned for their skill with the longbow and also had a reputation for hunting and poaching. In numerous senses the 'yeoman' of this tale is comparable to many a yeoman: he hunts and poaches game (souls) on his master's (God's) property (Earth).

The devil's visual rather than verbal presentation of himself as a 'yeoman' also shows Chaucer's broad sense of semiotics in which words are just one of many kinds of sign. In addition, the play with the sign here is of still another sort than the 'rente'/'brybe' play. In the latter case, the audience is informed of the play. But with the iconography of the *diabolus venator* the audience is expected to be in on the joke, a more subtle type of play. The *Friar's Tale* is a virtuoso performance of the art of manipulating modes of presentation.

Consideration of the deliberate play in the poem with mode of presentation lends support to a reading that considers the summoner as having believed the devil's yeoman-lie, that is, as believing that the devil is truly a yeoman.[7] This approach complements perfectly the general semantic play with mode of presentation. Considering the 'yeoman' to be a yeoman, the summoner sees the devil as a yeoman rather than as a hunting devil. The summoner is one of those who 'Professing themselves wise . . . became fools' (Rom. 1:22). Paul says of such fools that they 'changed the truth of God into a lie' (Rom. 1:25). It is

[6] The devil-in-disguise, any disguise, was a widely appreciated medieval topos, but the hunting devil, or *diabolus venator*, as Mroczkowski has pointed out, was in the Middle Ages 'a fairly well-known figure . . . found in manuscript illuminations and in spiritual treatises' (111). Moreover, black is the devil's colour (Cawley 178), so we have the devil-yeoman's 'frenges blake,' and widow's curse,'Unto the devel blak' (1622). Also, the colour green, as in the coat and hat of the yeoman, is often associated with underworld creatures in general and the devil in particular (Robertson, 'Why' 470–72). For those who rightly view suspiciously the smooth-talking yeoman's swearing of 'brother-hood,' and promise of gold and silver, or who pick up the reference to the devil's dwelling place 'fer in the north contree' (1413), the 'yeman' is obviously a devil. See notes to FrT III 1380–83, and 1413 in RC written by Janette Richardson; also Birney 21–26; Cawley 178; Mroczkowski 111–15; Richardson, 'Hunter' 159–61.
[7] I will consider the critics on this in the next chapter.

consistent with the summoner's 'up-so-doun' understanding of reality that in believing the devil to be a yeoman he 'changes the lie of the devil into the truth.' When the devil tells the truth with the assertion, 'I am a feend' (1448), the summoner in turn 'changes the truth of the devil into a lie.' Once the initial lie, 'yeoman', is considered to be the truth, all subsequent claims of the devil become suspect.

Many in Chaucer's audience would have discovered a delightful bonus in the semantic play of the summoner and the devil, for they would have seen in such play a perfect inversion of the Liar paradox: 'A man says, "I am lying." Is what he says true or false? "I am lying" is true only if it is false, and false only if it is true.' In the *Friar's Tale* the devil tells the truth; the summoner thinks that he is lying; therefore everything he says that is true is taken as a lie. This is a type of conundrum which delighted thinkers of Chaucer's century.[8] The evaluation of the truth-value of signs is not only a modern preoccupation (Frege, Eco, Searle), it is also a scholastic one (e.g., Buridan) and, as we now see in the *Friar's Tale*, a Chaucerian one as well.

'Rentes,' 'lords,' 'maisters,' 'yemen,' 'baillyves,' 'develes,' 'somonours,' and 'theves'

The summoner is outsmarted by the very one he thinks he is outsmarting, for the devil continually outlies him. The devil's disguise, while playful, is also serious; it is intended to achieve a particular end, one that is achieved by the devil's 'wynnyng' of the summoner's soul. Devils, he tells us, 'wol us swiche formes make / As moost able is oure preyes for to take' (1471–72). The 'prey' or 'rente' that the devil is poaching on the Lord's land is the summoner's soul.

Ironically, the devil, who knows this summoner well because of his life of sin, leads the summoner into believing the lie of his yeoman disguise by pretending to believe the summoner's own lie about riding forth to collect a 'rente.' With feigned credulity he 'innocently' responds to this information by asking 'Artow thanne a bailly?' (1392). A 'bailly' is a 'bailiff, an agent for a lord's estate who collected revenues and administered justice' (RC gloss to 1392). The summoner lies, 'Ye' (1392) he is a bailiff, and the devil lies in return, 'Thou art a bailly, and I am another' (1396). This line has a delightful twist because many in Chaucer's audience would have been aware that in popular literature of the period a 'bailly' is another disguise for a devil. For example, in Chaucer's translation of *The Romaunt of the Rose* Love twice identifies Fals-Semblaunt as a 'devel' 6223; 6797), and Fals-Semblaunt brags, 'Full wel I can my clothis chaunge' (6325), and lists among his disguises those of a 'forster' (6329), that is, a hunting yeoman, and a 'baily' (6331). Irony is compounded when in this last disguise both summoner and devil find a common identity.[9]

At the same time, the devil's claim to be a 'bailly' is reasonable, for yeoman-retainers often collected rents and administered justice on their masters' estates.

---

[8] I thank David Williams for pointing out to me that my reading of the *Friar's Tale* reveals a perfect inversion of the Liar paradox. The Liar paradox, which dates back to the Megarians (fifth century B.C.), 'engaged the minds of medieval logicians for two centuries or more' (Moody 'Logic' 534), and has been a major consideration of logicians in our own century.

[9] All this suggests, of course, that Chaucer's choice of name for his host, Harry *Bailey*, is far from casual. In the tale-telling contest Harry *is* a bailey who collects revenues and administers justice.

However, whether or not one believes that the 'yeoman's' claim to be a 'bailly' has been accepted by the summoner, the summoner is led to think he has encountered a naive, credulous yeoman who has accepted both of his lies, 'rente' and 'bailly,' as 'trothe.' The 'yeoman's' 'naivety' is reinforced by his too-quick confession that, because of his master's miserliness and cruelty, he must resort to 'extorcions' (1429) in order to live. The summoner now knows that this 'yeoman' is, like himself, an extortionist, and hence every word the 'yeoman' speaks is, like every word the summoner speaks, a potential lie, even if he considers this liar naive and stupid. A few lines later when the 'yeoman' makes his claim, 'I am a feend' (1448), the summoner could interpret this as the ridiculous attempt of a fool who dares to play with him, the sly summoner.

If at any time the summoner had believed that the yeoman was a bailiff, he might now question this claim as well. From the summoner's perspective, what he now sees is a lying-yeoman who first says he is a bailiff and then says he is a devil: he sees a devil *as* a yeoman. The summoner's later ironic lie, 'I am a yeman' (1524), the irony of which he expects the stupid 'yeoman' to miss, reveals his misunderstanding: 'If you are a devil and a bailiff as well as a yeoman,' he is saying, 'then I am a yeoman as well as a bailiff.'[10] If the summoner could borrow the Nun's Priest's words, he might say that the devil's claim that he is really a devil is as 'trewe . . . As is the book of Launcelot de Lake' (NPT VII 3211-12). Whatever one's interpretation may be, the continual lying back and forth serves to strengthen the relationship between the summoner and the devil, showing them to be 'two of a kind'; they are 'brothers' even without swearing brotherhood.

We have, then, the 'entente' of 'bailiff' < collector of legal rents > entering into the play with the 'ententes' of 'yeomen,' 'summoner,' and 'devil'; in one capacity or another all these may be seen from the mode of presentation of 'rente'-collector. This common mode of presentation may lead us to consider how they differ, or should differ, as collectors of rents; that is, we are caused to consider a rent-collector *as* a summoner, *as* a yeoman, *as* a bailiff, and as a devil. To use the phenomenological term, the play with the noemata of summoner, devil, bailiff, and yeoman is possible because they all may have a sense or 'entente' in common, < collector of rents >. Since both a 'summoner' and 'a devil' are, *in a sense*, < 'rente'-collectors > or < collector of revenues due one's lord >, then, *in a sense*, not only is a summoner a devil, but this common association allows the devil to be identified as a summoner.

What a summoner, a devil, a bailiff, and a yeoman have in common, in addition to being collectors of 'rentes' and 'administrators of justice,' are 'lordes' or 'maisters' for whose intentions they are the servants or instruments. The various referents that the name 'lorde' or 'maister' may point to in the poem are four: (1) archdeacon, whom the summoner names as both 'maister' (1352) and 'lorde' ('lordes duetee' [1391]); (2) Satan, or the arch-devil, and (3) God,

---

10 We may also consider that the summoner can claim to be a yeoman despite his dress; not all yeomen are of the green-clad variety. The term 'yeman' covers many occupations: 'any sort of countryman of the middling classes usually a farmer but sometimes a servant or an armed retainer (like the Knight's Yeoman and the Canon's Yeoman in *The Canterbury Tales*)' (Trevelyan 24n1).

the latter two both referred to in the devil's statement, 'My lord [Satan and God] is hard to me and dangerous' (1427); and (4) Jesus, whom the widow invokes: 'Now, Lord . . . Crist Jhesu, kyng of kynges' (1590). This widened sense of feudal lord-servant relationship, with its 'rente-servise,' 'fief-rent' obligations (see Strohm 15), is reinforced, and the field of association extended from one tale to another by the pilgrim Summoner, who in his tale which follows the *Friar's Tale*, has his corrupt friar name those 'duetees' with which he should be coupled, but with which, of course, he is not:

> I walke and fisshe Cristen mennes *soules*,
> To yelden Jhesus Crist his propre *rente*;
> To sprede his word is set al myn entente.   (SumT III 1820–22)

We see here <soules> considered *as* Lord's 'rente,' a sense carried, I suggest, to the *Summoner's Tale* from the *Friar's Tale*. In the *Friar's Tale*, the devil and summoner are, as the devil recognizes in his own case, 'Goddes instrumentz' (1483). Through their attempts at the collection of various 'rentes,' summoner and devil, either directly or indirectly, aid in the expedition of a particularly important 'rente,' <soules>, to the appropriate 'lorde,' either God or Satan. Of course, their success as 'Goddes instrumentz' is dependent upon their failure as the instrument of that other 'lord,' Satan. In the summoner's case his success should be God's success. Because it is not, the relation between the summoner and the 'yeoman' is consolidated even further.

From the perspective of the 'soules' whom the summoner attempts to extort, or whose souls the devil attempts to poach, the ultimate 'rentes' or <items of revenue> which they might acquire, and do acquire according to their just desserts, are either <salvation> or <damnation>. We return full circle to an original feudal sense of 'rente' mentioned above: <harvesting the crop of one's lord>. From the 'entente' of 'rente' we are led to the 'entente' of a large number of collectors of rents (yeomen, bailiffs, devils, summoners) and to a consideration of the masters and lords whom they serve or whom they should be serving. This gives us a rapidly expanding associative field of proper and improper couplings of names and senses: the improper couplings always suggesting by their very impropriety the nature of propriety.

'Theef' is a major player in this expanding field of association. A thief, <collector of illegal income>, is the contrary of what yeomen-bailiffs and summoners are supposed to be, <collectors of legal incomes>. In pursuing souls that rightly belong to the ultimate Lord, the devil is a thief of Christ's 'rentes,' while the summoner, through the abuse of his office, is able to lighten his victims of their worldly goods, and is thus also a thief in its usual sense. Two of Satan's most famous 'rentes' are Judas and the false thief of Calvary, both of whom serve the wrong masters, and both of whom fail to repent. Both of these 'rentes' of Satan, the false thief and Judas, are explicitly associated with the summoner at the outset of the tale. So we have the apposition, 'This false theef, this somonour' (1338), and shortly thereafter an association of both the false thief of scriptures and the summoner with Judas, who is very pointedly defined as a 'theef' through the *conduplicatio*, or quick repetition of the word 'theef':

> And right as Judas hadde purses smale,
> And was a *theef*, right swich a *theef* was he;
> His maister hadde but half his duetee.   (1350–52)

As we can see from the last line, the poem very quickly further associates 'theef' and 'maister,' and suggests the pattern of considering someone *as* serving more than one master or the wrong master: the 'someones' being the false thief, Judas, the summoner, and the devil, all of whom may also be considered *as* 'Goddes instrumentz.' At the same time we see in the poem that the summoner himself, just like Judas and the false thief, becomes a real object of 'rente' for the devil, who is the master-thief. Like Fals-Semblant in *The Romaunt of the Rose*, our devil 'Robbe(s) both robbed and robbours' (6823). Moreover, the summoner becomes a 'rente' of the master-robber for exactly the same reason as his two more famous predecessors, the false thief and Judas: he fails to repent. We shall return to 'repente' and its knitting with 'rente' and 'entente' below, but we may note now how the pattern of the summoner, Judas, and the false thief is exquisitely completed in the final lines of the poem. The devil's last words to the summoner, an unrepentant 'false thief,' 'Thou shalt with me to helle yet tonyght' (1636), perversely mimic Christ's words on the cross to the good thief, 'Today shalt thou be with me in paradise' (Luke 23:43).[11] Following the master-servant structure, Chaucer completes a symmetry of Christ/good-thief, Satan/false-thief, devil/summoner.

The field expands: 'rente,' 'profit,' 'fruyt,' 'purchas,' 'wynnyng'

Let us now consider some of the other signs in the proliferating galaxy of association around 'rente' in the *Friar's Tale*. After he has demanded 'twelf pens' (1599) as a bribe, his 'rente' from the widow, the summoner lies:

> I shal no *profit* han therby but lite;
> My maister hath the *profit* and nat I.   (1600–01)

By means of one sense of the word 'profit,' <item of revenue>, this word is associated with 'rente.' Taken literally, the summoner's claim, 'I shal no profit han therby but lite,' is a boldfaced lie. There is the unlikely possibility that his immediate master, the archdeacon, would get half the bribe, for we are told that the summoner gives his 'maister . . . but half his duetee' (1352). But this particular 'rente,' the bribe from the widow, seems more like a freelance effort, putting it among the 'what' of 'His maister knew nat alwey what he wan' (1345). But even as a percentage, the summoner's relative profit in the twelve pence would be anything but 'lite.' However, the quick repetition, or *conduplicatio*, of 'profit' would trigger in many among his audience an association with Mark 8:36: 'For what shall it profit a man if he shall gain the whole world, and lose his soul,' and many other similar biblical references to 'profit.'[12] Particularly appropriate in the summoner's case is 1 Sam 12:21: 'And turn ye not aside [from following the Lord]: for then should ye go after vain things, which cannot profit

---

[11] On the good thief/bad thief theme in medieval literature and Chaucer see Lenaghan 291.
[12] See especially Matt. 16:26; Prov. 11:4; 1 Sam. 12:21; Isa. 44:9; Jer. 2:8; Gal. 5:2.

nor deliver for they are vain.' The association with Mark 8:36 is reinforced by the allusion to it by Chaucer, if not by the widow, in her avowal that she could not put her hands on the twelve pence even if 'This wyde world thogh that I sholde wynne' (1606). So, in the sense of compensation for the loss of his soul, the statement, 'I shal no profit han therby but lite' is indeed true: the profit of twelve pence is extremely 'lite.' Likewise, the statement of the next line, 'My maister has the profit but nat I,' is a lie at the literal level of meaning, where 'maister' refers to the archdeacon and 'profit' to the twelve pence, but it is also the truth, for at a more profound level the summoner's 'maister' is the devil and the 'profit' which the summoner will render to this 'maister' is his own soul.

The bond between summoner and devil is increasingly revealed to be a master-servant relationship. The summoner through his extortions and pimping (he is a 'baude' [1354]) has long been to the devil like a 'dogge for the bowe' (1369), a dog who fetches the prey of his master (a hunting bowman, a yeoman). The master-servant, master-dog relationship is thus suggested at the outset of the poem, the hunting 'yeoman'-devil being joined by his efficient and successful 'dogge for the bowe.' In a sense, then, the summoner does sniff out or hunt out 'profit' for the devil, and the devil speaks the truth – as he so often does in this poem in which his truth is considered by the summoner to be a lie – when he comments to the summoner that 'thou rydest for the same entente' (1452). Of course, the devil gets the meat, and his dog-summoner gets the bones of their prey; the devil the souls, and the summoner the material profit of his extortions. On one level, as already suggested, the 'profit' is the summoner's own soul. So what this self-cannibalizing 'dog' ultimately fetches for his master is his own soul, and his profit is not 'lite' but heavy, damnation. The summoner's profit, relative to the devil's, truly is 'lite' – just as he says, but not as he means. On still another level, the 'maister' is God, and God's 'profit' is the soul of the good widow who all her life has resisted the temptations of 'Goddes instrumentz,' such as the summoner and the devil. In the poem she proves herself to be a true servant to her true master, the 'Lord.' The summoner's profit (and the devil's) here is 'lite' only in the most ironic sense.

Beyond 'profit,' the associative field of 'rente' includes 'fruyt,' in an extended sense, as in the '*fruyt* of al his [the summoner's] rente' (1373). This alludes to Matt. 3:8 (in Chaucer's Parson's words): 'By the *fruyt* of hem shul ye knowen hem' (ParsT X 115). For the *Friar's Tale* this could be restated as: 'by their "rentes" shall you know them.' 'Fruyt' can also allude to John the Baptist's rejection of the Pharisees and Sadducees as candidates for baptism with 'Bring forth therefore *fruits* meet for repentance' (Matt. 3:8), linking the 'rente' field of association with the 'repente' field of association – a field considered below. Simultaneously, 'fruyt' links the 'rente' and 'repente' fields of association with the 'entente' field. 'Fruyt,' such as the accumulation of gold and silver, is the outward sign of secret inner 'entente': ' "Dooth digne *fruyt* of Penitence"; for by this *fruyt* may men knowe this tree, and nat by the roote that is hyd in the herte of man' (ParsT X 114).

Yet a final association of 'rente' that we will consider here is with 'purchas,' a 'coseyn' of 'rente,' but with independent being. The devil states:

> And heere I ryde aboute my *purchasyng*,
> To wite wher men wol yeve me any thyng.
> My *purchas* is th'effect of al my *rente*.
> Looke how thou rydest for the same *entente*.   (1449–52).

The summoner sees this as a further point confirming his brotherhood with the devil, for later he notes 'both we goon about oure *purchas*' (1530). Interestingly, for it suggests a strong connection with the Friar as described in the *General Prologue*, the only other immediate association of 'purchas' and 'rente' in Chaucer's work occurs in the description of the narrator of our tale, the Friar, in the *General Prologue*: 'His *purchas* was wel bettre than his *rente*' (I 256). The Friar should be an expert on the distinction between the two words. The distinction is that a 'purchas' is usually something one has in hand, as opposed to a 'rente,' which may be something that is owed. Moreover, a 'purchas' may be won through trickery or acquired by force, and is not necessarily a legal income such as is a 'rente.'

The *Medieval English Dictionary* indicates three main groups of senses for 'purchas.' The first two have a positive or neutral moral value and the last a morally negative one: (1) <acquisition>, <gain>, <something acquired or received>, <a possession>, <wealth>, <property>, <goods>; (2) <begging>, <entreaty>, <proceeds from charity>, <alms>; and (3) <illegal gain>, <graft>, <extortion>, <booty>, <spoil>, <plunder>. The first two groups of senses would associate 'purchas' with 'rente,' while the third group would associate 'purchas' with 'briberye.' Chaucer's statement in the *General Prologue* that the Friar's 'purchas' was better than his 'rente' may mean simply that he received more income from begging than he did as a return for services, but it more 'sleyly' suggests that the greatest part of his income came from <graft> or <extortion>. This would make the tale-teller more of a 'brother' of the summoner and devil of his own tale, as well as of the pilgrim Summoner, than he might like to admit. For the devil and the summoner 'purchas' is obviously intended in negative senses which are disguised behind neutral or positive values.

Interestingly, an isolated sense of 'purchas' in the MED is <deserved torment> for sins, which, given both the devil's and the summoner's final permanent address, may lend the devil's statement, 'My purchas is th'effect of al my rente,' even another painful twist!

A final member of the 'rente' field of association to be considered here is 'wynnyng.' Chaucer's early fondness for associating this word with both 'rente' and 'purchas' occurs in the *The Romaunt of the Rose*. There, that 'devel,' Fals-Semblant, says, 'To *wynnen* is alwey myn *entente*; / My purchace is bettir than my rente' (6837–38). Here we see an early association of 'wynnen' not only with '*rente*' but with 'entente' and 'purchace.' Given the 'sermon' (6136) delivered up to this point by Fals-Semblant, there can be little doubt that 'purchas' has here a negative sense. Another devil-like character, the Pardoner, in his 'confession' brags likewise, 'For myn *entente* is nat but for to *wynne*' (PardT VI 403). Both the devil ('And yet ne *wan* I nothyng in this day. / I wol *entende* to *wynnyng*, if I may' [1477–78]) and the summoner (who at least pretends to ask the 'yeoman' to teach him 'how that I may moost *wynne*' [1421]) adumbrate this sense of 'wynnyng.'

'Wynning' suggests a game, and a game suggests willing participants. The stakes in the game played by the summoner and his victims or would-be victims, or the stakes set by the devil with those whom he tempts, are high, but the whole process suggests the winner takes ('hente') spoils that the loser gives ('yeves') *willingly* because of the original assent to play the game. This brings us to a further expansion of the associative field. The devil says he shares with the summoner 'the same entente' (1452), namely, that he will 'hente' that which 'men *wol* yeve me' (1450), repeating what he has said before and will say again, 'I take al that men *wol* me yive' (1430). People give the devil what might be called 'billes' (1586) to their souls which they play with when they engage in the devil's or summoner's game and willfully give in to their temptations. This 'bille' may be repurchased through repentance: repenting is another willful act which, if properly done, may reverse the effects of a previous willful act. But with these words, 'entente' and 'repente,' our field of association is growing so large that it will be easier to deal with it by shifting its centre to another word.

THE 'ENTENTES' OF 'ENTENTE'

Telling confessions: the 'entente' of 'repente'

What makes a confession good or bad is 'entente.' In the *Friar's Tale* we witness a panoply of confessions made with bad or wrong 'entente.' The 'yeoman' confesses a 'feithful tale' (1425), that 'by extorcions I lyve' (1429). The summoner in turn also confesses that he lives by 'extorcioun' (1439), a true meaning of 'rente' for both the devil and the summoner. The summoner also brags that he would never confess to a priest: 'Ne of swiche japes wol I nat be shryven' (1440), and 'I shrewe thise shrifte-fadres everychoon' (1442). Finally, he damns himself near the end of the tale with the confirmation that it 'is nat myn entente' (1630) to 'repente' (1629).

Besides these overt references to 'confessions,' there are numerous metonymic associations.[13] One of these is the cumulative effect of the twenty uses of 'telle' or 'tolde' in the tale. The narrating Friar promises at the outset 'to telle' the sins the summoner of his tale *should* tell: 'To *telle* his [the summoner's] harlotrye I wol nat spare' (1328). Implicitly, but not very subtly, the suggestion is that the types of sins the Friar is about to recount are also those of the pilgrim Summoner. The Host urges on the Friar in his project of tattle tale: 'Now *telleth* forth, thogh that the Somonour gale' (1336). The secrecy of confession is associated with telling of the 'bawdes' or pimps (1339) who '*tolde* hym [the summoner] al the secree that they knewe' (1341). So too there is the association of whispering secrets in the ear and confession with the 'wenches' or prostitutes who '*tolde* it [their information of others' and hence in many cases their own sins] in his [the summoner's] ere' (1358). 'Harlotry,' 'secrets,' 'telling,' 'ear,' 'al,' without 'sparing' – all these are metonymically associated with the

[13] See 92n3 above.

sacrament of penance. Indeed, the association by a scripturally literate audience of the phrase 'tolde it in his ere' (1358) with Proverbs 23:9, 'speak not in the ears of a fool' would further strengthen the consideration of the summoner *as* a type of fool. And this is not the end of 'eres': the image of confessing, and the question of 'How many fools are we really encountering here?,' are raised by the spectacle of the summoner in a confessional tableau: 'And neer the feend he drough, as nought ne were, / Ful prively, and *rowned* [whispered] in his ere' (1549–50). These perverse confessions, confessional attitudes and relationships, would call to mind for Chaucer's audience how one should 'telle' one's sins according to the Christian faith. To encourage the audience to make such associations the words 'telle' and 'faith' or 'faithfully' are collocated within a single line no less than four times, three of these occurring within thirteen lines of each other during a single exchange between the summoner and devil.[14]

In the confession of the sacrament of Penance, one is supposed to tell not only a 'true tale,' but also a 'feithful tale' (1425). To 'tell faithfully' in 'Confessioun,' we are told in the *Parson's Tale*, a sinner 'moste [must] confessen hym of *alle* the condiciouns that bilongen to his synne . . . / *Al* moot be seyd, and no thyng excused ne hyd' (X 319–320). When the summoner 'hears' the devil's 'confession' he acts like a model father confessor: he demands that the devil tell all. The devil resists, saying he would 'nat *entende* our wittes to declare' (1479), ironically indicating that his confession has not been, and will not be, 'good.' Although telling, he does not tell all. Furthermore, according to the Parson's faithful formula for 'Confessioun,' one must manifest 'Contricoun of Herte, Confessioun of Mouth, and Satisfaccioun' (X 108). Only the middle condition is met. The words of the 'up-so-doun' confessions of the devil and the summoner have world-related and mind-related (or heart-related) aspects. Their words are 'cosyns to their dedes.' They do tell some of the sins, or the types of sins, they have committed. But the mind-related aspects of their words reveal that rather than having sorrow and contrition for their sins, they take pride in them; rather than the firm intention never to sin again, their words show the contrary intention. From a Christian perspective, their words are not empty of intention, but contain perverse intentions.

We also see the 'repente'/'entente' fields here unite. That which 'is hyd in the herte ' (ParsT X 115) of the summoner and devil is not 'contricioun' but the 'pride of their hearts' (Isa. 9:9).[15] The pride manifest in the confessions of the summoner and the devil reveals them to be fools: 'the foolish is a rod of pride' (Prov. 14:3). And, of course, as the tale demonstrates, 'pride goeth before destruction' (Prov. 16:18). The semantic reversal here, good confession/bad confession, nicely parallels the semantic reversal of good thief/bad thief discussed above.

Willing and nilling: prayers meet preyers

'To pray' and 'to prey' are homonyms with totally different etymological roots. While the homonyms are distinguished in modern written forms by their

---

[14] This occurs between lines 1420 and 1433; the other simultaneous use is in line 1504.
[15] See also Jer. 49:16; Obad. 3; Mark 7:22.

different vowels, the two spellings seem to be used indiscriminately in the Middle Ages. However, one may wonder if either Chaucer or his scribes played intentionally with the spellings: the summoner is 'evere waityng on his *pray*' (1376), and the devil says he would ride 'Unto the worldes ende for a *preye*' (1455); the devil says to the summoner, 'Of thyn aqueyntance, I wolde *praye* thee' (1398), and the summoner requests of the devil, 'Now, brother, . . . I yow *preye*, / Teche me' (1417–18). We see here a visual word-play which mimics a play that occurs on the oral/aural level. This play highlights the difference in intentionalities between a subject preying and a subject praying. Praying is what the widow and, possibly, the carter of the tale do; preying is what the summoner and the devil do. The difference in the cognitive values of the two intentionalities is measured in ethical terms: when used to evaluate the summoner there is a contrast of what ought to be done against what is done.

Even before the 'yeoman' says to the corrupt summoner, 'I wolde *praye* thee' (1398), the audience has been prepared for a play on 'prey' and 'pray.' The narrator has used the latter sense in 'I *praye* that noon of you be yvele apayd' (1282) and the former sense in 'This somnour, evere waityng on his *pray*' (1376). The devil's conscious play of 'prey' and 'pray' is made fully evident by his continued use of them. Part of the pleasure of the game for the reader may be the appreciation of the irony when 'This somnour, evere waityng on his *pray*' makes *his* statement, ' "Now, brother . . . I yow *preye*" ' (1417). This is parallel to the devil's earlier 'I wolde *praye* thee.' The summoner, then, seems to be indulging in the same pray-prey wordplay as the devil-in-disguise, without appreciating, however, that the individual whom he considers to be a foolish, lying, and ignorant yeoman has already 'played' the word in exactly this way. In any case, the listener, or the reader, may delight in the multiple irony that the devil is actually 'preying' on the summoner, while, simultaneously, the summoner is under the illusion that it is he who is doing the 'preying.'

Beyond the delight in the irony, such an elaboration of word-play not only renders the audience highly aware of the very device of word-play, but also causes it to become focused on the 'entente' or intentionality behind the words of the speaker. An audience, once made conscious of and sensitive to the intentionality of words, is also rendered receptive to the general semantic play of modes of presentation. Many would become aware, for example, that 'prey' also belongs to the associative field of 'rente' as < income > for both summoner and devil: 'This somnour, evere waityng on his pray' (1376). The specific 'preys' also name specific 'rentes': the 'bawdes' (1339), the 'lecchours' (1310; 1371), the 'avowtier' (1373), the 'wenches' (1355), and the 'paramour' (1372), as well as their 'gold and silver' (1400). In causing us to consider these various 'objects' both *as* 'preys' and *as* 'rentes,' Chaucer demonstrates how the two expressions 'rente' and 'prey' have different mind-related senses for the two different intending subjects. For example, the cognitive value of 'lecchour,' seen as 'rente,' is different for the summoner than it is for the devil. The former sees a 'lecchour' *as* a source of a material 'rente,' while the latter sees the 'lecchour' *as* a soul which could be an eternal 'rente' for Satan. The similarity and difference between these two modes of presentation also indicate what a proper mode of presentation for a proper summoner towards a 'lecchour' should be. A proper summoner should view the 'lecchour' *as* a soul who is part of the 'rente' which

Christ purchased with his death. A summoner should see his function *as* an agent of Christ seeking to secure Christ's proper 'rente.' Instead, in seeking the lechers' goods rather than their souls, the summoner has become an agent of the devil, helping him win what rightfully belongs to one's ultimate Lord and Master.

In all this play of hunters and preys, we are emphatically led as an audience to notice that the 'preys' or the 'rentes' of the summoner and the devil are always *willing* victims: their ultimate, eternal predicament is a consequence of their own 'entente.' This is what distinguishes them from the ordinary prey of the ordinary hunter. In the perspective presented by this poem, human beings are all, from vicious summoner to holy widow, potential prey of the devil and his agents. All of us as prey are in a position to 'will' or 'nill' certain courses of action which determine our fate as prey. We see with the 'prey-pray' play what we saw with the play with 'rente' above: the importance of the category of relation. When one relates in thought or deed towards another 'thing,' another person or material object, such intentions, good or bad, become part of what one is. Intending, be it away from something, towards something, or intending some object or another subject in one way rather than another, e.g., as a means rather than an end, changes a person. But the person who wills the changes is the willing subject, not the object or the other human subject which is intended, nor the agent, good or bad, who encourages one to intend one way or the other. Although Christians are not without help when being preyed upon by the tempting devil, still, because they are willing victims or victors, all preys of the devil or his agents are ultimately responsible for the changes, positive or negative, that their encounters with the hunters of souls cause in them.

The ideal conscious action of the Christian, the action which will make the soul worthy of salvation, is to intend always in accordance with God's will. This ideal state of 'entente,' intentionality, or directedness is an attitude we have already considered in its epitome in the *Clerk's Tale*, in which Griselda, as the ideal human being, swears the submission of her will to her husband's (God's) will with the words: 'I *wol* no thyng, ne *nyl* no thyng, certayn, / But as yow list' (IV 646–47). Willing and nilling are both conscious acts, the two possible acts of a free will: 'Wherfore in alle thingis that resoun is, in hem also is liberte of willynge and of nillynge' (Bo 5.p2, 18–20). In the *Friar's Tale*, the devil, in order to obtain his 'rente' or < income >, the soul of his prey, must determine his prey's 'entente': how they have willed or nilled regardless of whether the willing subject has taken external action. Because, according to orthodox angelology, the roving devil of the *Friar's Tale* cannot read minds,[16] he must rely on the various signs which reveal the subject's intent. These signs may include the obvious overt deed or act of a 'bawde' or 'theef.' However, since the intentional deed or act in itself, for example, the thought of committing a crime, accepted or rejected, is also an act which changes the intending subject, it is important for the devil to interpret various signs in order to determine such 'ententes.' In such a case the devil must attempt to determine what Frege would call the 'cognitive value' of his prey's 'expression' or signs: what they reveal of the 'idea' (Frege, 'Sense' 59) of the intending subject rather

---

[16] A power that God reserves for himself. Unfallen angles, however, and so guardian angels, may see into the minds of human beings by seeing them reflected in the 'face' of God which they, unlike fallen angels, may contemplate.

than what they may denote in the world. Repenting is a 'willynge' action; not repenting is a 'nillynge' action. Each action changes the intending subject, and each action makes more probable for the intending subject the securing of one of two possible ultimate 'rentes': salvation or damnation. The tale presents a number of cases in which the issue is the determination of such intentionality.

In the case of the widow, good prayers, those of the widow, meet good preyers, the summoner and the devil. Because the good prayer, the widow, is also someone who nills to sin, she is an unbeatable nilling victim. One will not have to 'repente' if one does not sin, and one will not sin if one avoids the occasion of sin and resists temptation, as the poor widow of the tale claims to have done all her life. Confronted by temptation or danger one must 'nill' it, a negative action. But in such a situation the Christian may also pray for assistance, a positive action. The widow in her encounter with the summoner makes both of these willing and nilling actions.

According to medieval Christian doctrine and belief, the summoner would be legally, properly and consciously 'Goddes instrument'; an instrument whereby wayfaring Christians are 'hente' to the sacrament of penance. In his office as God's agent, the summoner could demand and expect assistance, cooperation and submission wherever and whenever he needed them. The widow, always behaving with propriety, greets 'Goddes instrument' as he should be greeted, with a prayer and a respectful submission of will, 'God save you, sire, what is youre sweet wille?' (1585); with these words, in a poem about agents of Satan and Christ, the widow submits her will, 'thy will be done,' through the agency of the summoner, to her ultimate Lord. In a spectacular, but at the same time subtle fashion, a Chaucerian hallmark, the horrendous degree of the summoner's perversion of his office is revealed.[17]

The widow comprehends very quickly that the immediate lord and master whom this summoner serves is not their mutual proper master. Realizing that she is being preyed upon, she does what she should do in such a situation; she prays to the ultimate 'lorde' and 'maister': ' "Now, Lord," quod she, "Crist Jhesu, kyng of kynges, / So wisly helpe me, as I ne may" ' (1590–91). In the widow's prayerful humility we see the contrary of the preying pride of the summoner and the devil. Here, as well, the whole 'lord' and 'master' word-play discussed above is further knit into the fabric of the poem. Pressed by the summoner, the widow prays again,

---

17 'Will,' and the submission of will to one's legitimate master, alludes to the submission of will in the Lord's Prayer, the submission of Christ's will to that of his Father, the submission by Job and by Abraham of their wills to God. As for 'sweet,' Chaucer uses the word extensively to allude, often ironically, as in the *Miller's Tale* and the *Merchant's Tale*, to the Song of Songs: 'his mouth is most sweet' (Song Sol. 16). The Song of Songs was very widely alluded to in both religious and secular medieval poetry, most significantly by Dante (Chydenius, *Dante* 137–149). The relationship between Solomon and the bride was read allegorically by both Christian and Jew on as many as four levels, considered either individually or in combination: the 'bridegroom,' and 'bride,' were variously husband and wife in the sacrament of marriage (e.g., by Aquinas), Christ and the Church (by Christians in general), God and the soul (by Christians and Jews in general), and God and the Church Triumphant (e.g., by Aquinas) (Chydenius, *Dante* 121–137). The sweetness of the bridegroom's words suggests their 'Truth' and 'Beauty,' the ironic opposite of the summoner's use of words. Moreover, a key to the nature of the relationship between the 'bride' and 'groom' was considered to be the relationship of their *wills*. The widow's act of submission is similar to Griselda's 'I wol no thyng, ne nil no thyng, certayn / But as yow list' (ClT IV 646–47), and both are adumbrations of the proper attitude of will prescribed in the Christian prayer of prayers, 'Thy will be done.'

this time appealing not to Christ directly, but to Christ's primary intermediary, agent, or instrument, his mother: 'Now, lady Seinte Marie / So wisly help me out of care and synne' (1604–5). The good 'entente' of the widow's prayer is marked in part by the bad 'entente' of the summoner's mocking oath and parody of the widow's praying as he invokes the name of the Mother's mother: ' "Pay me," quod he, "or by the sweete Seinte Anne, / As I wol bere awey thy newe panne" ' (1613–14). The inversion of swearing and praying is brought to the direct attention of the audience. A further irony, one that would hardly have been missed by Chaucer's audience, is that Anne, as the patron saint of widows, might well enter the fray in response to the summoner's 'prayer,' but in an appropriately inverted manner, on the widow's behalf.

THE 'ENTENTE' OF CURSES

As in the scene with the widow, oaths, swearing and prayers also mark the words of the carter. The carter's scene is, in fact, a study in intentionality that the later encounter with the widow closely parallels; the two incidents are directly linked by the parallel use of the word 'al' in the second curse of each. The carter makes an initial curse against his horses stuck in the mud, 'The feend . . . yow fecche, body and bones' (1544), which he rephrases: 'The devel have *al*, bothe hors and cart and hey!' (1547). The widow makes an initial curse against the bribe-seeking summoner, 'Unto the devel blak and rough of hewe / Yeve I thy body and my panne also!' (1622–23), and rephrases it upon the demand of the devil: 'The devel . . . so fecche hym er he deye, / And panne and *al*, but he wol hym repente!' (1628–29). Some of the importance of the word 'al' to the widow's curse has been argued by David Williams ('Grammar's Pan' 87), but he does not note its use in the carter's curse. In a poem replete with carefully crafted thematic patterns, verbal associations and adumbrations, the fact that the widow with her use of 'al' repeats a pattern in a parallel scene of cursing makes it highly unlikely that its first use in the carter's curse is insignificant. Moreover, the legalistic cast of the entire poem – its emphasis on the legal consequences of 'signing' one's intent with certain words – should cause the reader/listener, like the devil, to pay attention to the 'fine print' in any character's statements. I believe that with the introduction of 'al' into the curses, the audience is invited to examine the fine print of such verbal expressions. A bonus of such an examination is that it will allow us to solve what I call 'the mystery of the widow's panne.' As we shall see, the word 'panne' becomes the ultimate instrument in Chaucer's game with words and 'entente' in the *Friar's Tale*.

The carter's curse

When the devil and the summoner happen upon the carter cursing his horses and cart of hay stuck in the mud the summoner purports to see the objects of cursing as potential 'rente.' The 'entente' of the carter seems to have been signalled. As we have seen, the major limitation for both devil and summoner is that they may take or 'hente' only what someone willingly 'yeves.' The carter's curse seems to fulfil this criterion: the carter in his verbal expression seems to have willed his 'rente' or

< sources of income > to the devil. Of course, the devil knows that the carter's words are empty of their conventional 'entente'; he advises the summoner, 'It is nat his entente, trust me weel' (1556). The 'yeoman' advises the summoner that what the carter says is not what he means: 'The carl spak oo thing, but he thoghte another' (1568). The devil knows he may not 'hente' anything because the carter has not 'yeven' anything. Whether or not the summoner has considered this important legal requirement is, to a degree, irrelevant for him at this point, for with his aside to the carter's curse, 'Heere shal we have a pley' (1548), the summoner reveals that in his demand to the yeoman-devil, 'Hent it anon, for he hath yeve it thee' (1553), he is toying with what he believes to be a yeoman pretending to be a devil.[18]

The incident with the carter also reveals some important differences in how the summoner and the devil view reality. The carter's curse is another illustration of the importance of the appreciation of modes of presentation in the poem; how differently the summoner and the devil consider their common 'preys' and 'rentes.' As with the 'bawdes,' 'wenches,' and 'lecchours,' the summoner and the devil 'see' different aspects of the same thing. Whatever the 'entente' of the carter, the horses which are mere 'body and bones' (1544), without immortal souls, would not interest the devil, whose interests are only in the eternally substantial. For this reason, the 'al' of the carter's curse, 'The devel have al,' could have interest for the devil in a tale that plays with crucial legal niceties. The devil's only interest in the carter would be his eternal substance, his soul. Unlike the devil, the summoner, when considering souls, reminds us of the 'cookes' who the Pardoner says 'turnen substaunce into accident' (PardT VI 539), in that he reverses the process, turning accidents into substance. The summoner is both perceptually and morally a materialist, perceiving the outer physical appearance of the yeoman as constituting his real identity and desiring the material goods of the carter. In general, he seeks or intends towards accidental material 'rentes,' anything that may further his materialistic self-indulgence either directly or through conversion, such as the 'panne' which he attempts to extort from the widow. In the encounter with the carter he sees a horse and cart and hay which could be sold for gold and silver or exchanged for other goods. The summoner also turns substance into accidents when he mistakes the 'yeoman's' accidental appearance for the substantial reality. The carter's soul is not the 'what' or the essence that the summoner seeks to 'wynne' or intends towards, though as 'Goddes instrument' this is precisely what he ought to be intending towards. The devil's intending is towards what is really the 'al' of the carter or any other human being, his or her immortal soul. The devil, on the other hand, through bitter experience, has learned to consider things from the viewpoint of eternal reality. Such a view does correctly turn some substances into accidents because all things that are not eternal, such as the carter's horses, cart and hay, are ultimately accidental.

David Williams has presented technical evidence for support of his argument for the importance of the use of the word 'al' in the widow's curse. The same evidence holds for the carter's curse. According to medieval grammar, 'al' is among those syncategoramic terms which 'signify nothing until added to another term'

---

[18] I will fully develop this interpretation in the present and the next chapters.

('Grammar's Pan' 87). In other words, the meaning of 'al,' as with other syncategoramic terms, is totally dependent on its metonymical relationship to other words. In metonymical rather than syncategoramic terms, we may say that the carter (including his soul) is associated with the horse and cart and hay. The carter's soul is combined with the series; there is a contiguity between the elements. The 'al' of the carter's curse, 'The devel have al, both hors and cart and hey!' metonymically and superficially, if unintentionally, adds the carter and his soul to the package of horse and cart and hay. Of course, the devil realizes that the carter does not have this intent for the word 'al.' He is so certain that this is not the carter's intent that he does not seek to verify his interpretation, an omission he does not repeat with the wary widow's 'curse,' as we shall soon see.

As we have noted, to the summoner's ironic suggestion that the devil claim what the carter has cursed to him, the devil replies that the carter's words do not carry the carter's 'entente,' that is, the words are not intended to express their conventional meanings. The carter's subsequent blessing of the horses, after they succeed in extricating the cart from the mire, proves, as the devil says, that 'The carl spak oo thing, but he thoghte another' (1568). But this clearly does not mean that the carter 'spak' one thing and thought *nothing*, or that the words carry no 'entente.' It means simply that his audible words or, in Saussurean terms, his sound patterns are not 'cosyns' to their usual 'mental words' or concepts. The carter's words do indeed indicate both mind-related and world-related aspects of the carter's intentions. How do we know? Because the devil, the horses, and probably the summoner all understand what the carter is saying; they understand his intentions.

The carter's words are not empty, windy sounds of words: the word as *flatus vocis*. In more recent, but equivalent terminology the carter's curse is not a mere 'utterance act': 'Utterance acts consist simply in uttering strings of words' (Searle, *Speech Acts* 24). Instead, his curse is indeed an 'illocutionary act': 'uttering words in sentences in certain contexts, under certain conditions and with certain intentions' (24–25). The proof of this is that in response to the carter's words the horses increase their efforts and pull the cart out of the mud: they understand. Most obviously, the carter's words contain and express a mind-related *intentio* of the carter: they express a warning or anger or encouragement, and a combination of these. The context in which the carter's words are expressed – 'context' including a whole range of factors centred on the not uncommon experience for a carter and his horses of being mired in mud, and such elements as tone of voice, and gestures – gives his words a certain meaning for the horses: at the very least, a sense of what would come next if they did not pull the cart from the mud. The carter's anger, expressed through signs, some of which happen also to be words, results in the horses' fear of his intent (probably of a lashing or a beating). The intention of creating this fear with the words that express his anger is what Austin and Searle call a 'perlocutionary act.' The fear that he succeeds in creating is the 'perlocutionary effect' of that speech act.

'Modern' semiotics considers signs through which animals, not just human animals, communicate. In this it has retrieved a medieval understanding, the understanding of the difference between *voces significativae ad placitum* and *voces significativae naturaliter.*[19] Many animals, not just men, use signs. Augustine first analysed the differences between the signs animals, including man, use and the signs which are peculiar to man. In this, thinkers such as Roger Bacon were to follow him. They recognized that man shares with other animals certain mental states – fear, anger, affection, happiness, sadness – and that these animals have signs to indicate such states. The statement that the carter utters is not intended to express the conventional meaning of the words he forms. As Augustine would put it, the carter's words are among the signs of fear, anger, warning, happiness, affection, lust and so on, 'which living creatures show to one another for the purpose of conveying, in so far as they are able, the motion of their spirits [i.e., their feelings, their thoughts, their *intentiones*] or something which they have sensed or understood' (DDC 2.2.3). The carter is, quite sensibly, speaking to the horses in a language they understand, a language that has been spoken by any human being who has ever shouted at an animal in fear or anger or murmured to an animal with tones of pleasure or affection. The carter's words are like the barking of a dog, the 'entente' or aim of which is to get the horses moving.

The carter's 'blessing' of the horses after their success at extricating the bemired cart, 'ther Jhesu Crist yow blesse, / And al his handwerk' (1561–62), is interesting within the context of the theme of good and bad 'prayers,' as well as the theme of 'preyers meeting prayers' already discussed in the context of the exchange between the summoner, devil and widow. The blessing may or may not be a 'good' blessing or prayer, 'good' in the sense that his words are necessarily 'cosyn' to the mental deed of blessing the horses and thanking God. Like the curse, the words of the blessing may not carry their conventional senses, they may only be expressing the carter's happiness and relief. On the other hand, they may be expressing such emotions while also signifying the proper intent for a blessing. A point here is that while we may often attempt with success to interpret the 'entente' in the heart of a speaker, ultimately we are all like Walter in the *Clerk's Tale*: we may believe or disbelieve someone's inner 'entente' as expressed through signs, but we cannot know with absolute certainty anyone's 'privitee.' Interestingly, within this context, if the carter's prayer and blessing are good (and there is no evidence that they are or are not), with the 'al' of the phrase 'And *al* his handwerk,' the carter is also praying for those who are, unknown to him, preying upon him: the summoner and the devil. Let us turn now and examine the quality of the cursing of that accomplished prayer, the preyed-upon and prayerful widow.

---

[19] On *voces significativae ad placitum* and *voces significativae naturaliter* and the later medieval development of the Augustinian concept see Pinborg (407).

Metonymic multiplicity or the mystery of the widow's 'panne'

When the summoner demands a bribe of 'twelf pens,' the widow says she does not have it. Seemingly out of the blue, the summoner then demands instead her 'new panne' (1614). The widow's first curse includes this item: 'Unto the devel blak and rough of hewe / Yeve I thy body and my panne also!' (1622–23), as does her second curse. Here we have a wise and cunning widow who is no fool, and who out-lawyers both summoner and devil in their legalistic manipulation of curses.

Let us first consider the 'panne' of both curses. There has been no prior reference to a 'panne.' Why a 'panne'? Indeed, what is a 'panne'? Is it a frying pan or a bolt of cloth? Both meanings are found in the *Middle English Dictionary*: 'a metal or earthenware vessel, usually used for heating; a caldron, a pot, or pan,' and bolt of 'fabric.' David Williams points out that these homonyms have entirely different etymological roots: ' "panne" as derived from French "pan," Latin "pannus," indicates a bolt of cloth or piece of cloth; "panne" as derived from Old English "panne," or "ponne" signifies a container, and as applied domestically, a pot or pan' ('Grammar's Pan' 62). Robert E. Pratt, through his gloss to 'panne' in line 1614 of the *Friar's Tale*, opts for 'panne' with the single sense of 'cloth; garment.'

Responding to Pratt's gloss, Thomas Hahn ('The Devil and His Panne') reviews the arguments for considering 'panne' as a cooking utensil and pan as 'cloth; garment.' He introduces new evidence to support the view that Chaucer intended his 'panne' to be a frying pan: in medieval art devils were often portrayed as holding frying pans. This fact suggests a very plausible explanation of why Chaucer would introduce this particular item into the tale. After hefting this solid iconographic evidence, Hahn concludes that the 'weight of evidence' indicates that frying 'panne' should be '*the* reading' (emphasis added) rather than 'Pratt's ingenious and plausible suggestion' (352). However, David Williams has argued that Chaucer intended *both* meanings; to this last and, until now, unique view, I will now lend support.

The meaning of 'panne' as 'a cooking instrument' is one shared by Old, Middle, and modern English. This 'panne' is used a number of times by Chaucer in other tales. If in the *Friar's Tale* Chaucer intended the Middle English meaning of 'panne' as cloth, then it is the single use of this word with this meaning in Chaucer's writings. However, this absence of use may only suggest that the foreign borrowing of 'panne' as 'cloth' was already falling into disuse: Chaucer had more usual English words, such as 'clooth,' to name this item and used them. But does not this very point in the *Friar's Tale* offer Chaucer an ideal occasion to play with the homonyms of 'panne'? And, given the wide and clever play with meanings and senses of words in the *Friar's Tale*, is he not likely to exploit it?

One of the strongest associations to support panne as cloth (which, curiously, Hahn points out but then does not account for, and which, presumably, Pratt expected readers to make, and so justify his gloss) is the summoner's response to the widow's suggestion that he repent:

'Nay, olde stot, that is nat myn entente,'
Quod this somonour, 'for to repente me
For any thyng that I have had of thee.
I wolde hadde thy smok and every clooth!' (1630–33)

The summoner has no intention to repent of taking a 'panne' from the widow. Indeed, he says that if he could he would take from her every piece of cloth that she has, including the very dress that she is wearing. 'Panne' as 'bolt of cloth' works in perfectly with this comment. And one can add here previously ignored evidence from the *Medieval English Dictionary* which solidifies this association: s.v., 'Also . . . panne . . .': '1. (a) a garment, esp. a cloak or mantle.' Not only is a 'clooth' a 'panne,' but a panne is also a large containing garment such as a cloak or, quite possibly, a 'smok,' such as the widow is wearing and which the summoner evinces a desire to take – this reprobate summoner would literally take the shirt off a poor old widow's back.

Further evidence that a meaning of 'panne' as 'clooth' is intended in the *Friar's Tale* is that such a reading also helps associate the Friar's widow with that most famous widow of *The Canterbury Tales*, the 'clooth-makyng' (GP I 447) Wife of Bath. The Wife had worked a negative characterization of friars into her tale as requital for an intervention of the Friar at the end of her Prologue. The Friar's play with 'panne,' all by itself, makes a brilliant, pointed, and wonderfully simple return volley aimed at the Wife of Bath, whose attitude towards the estate of widowhood contrasts sharply with that of the ideal widow of the *Friar's Tale*.[20]

---

[20] A respectable and profitable way for a widow to support herself in Chaucer's England was through 'clooth-making,' an occupation traditionally associated with the estates of wife and widow (Mann 121–22). If the Friar's widow has a 'new panne,' it is likely that she has just finished making it. This also makes such an item reasonable for the summoner to demand as a bribe. Indeed, considering the use of 'panne' out of the blue, this second meaning is more reasonable than 'cooking instrument.' That the Friar's 'clooth-making' widow is very different from the Wife of Bath is precisely why the Friar would be moved to introduce such an association. In contrast to the lusty Wife, who frankly admits that the ideal life of chastity is not for her, and so is actively seeking a sixth husband, the Friar's widow is a 'proper' widow, fulfilling the ideals of her estate, innocent of the improper sexual liaisons of which she is falsely accused.

One attains in such an association of the two widows a nice symmetry of clever and, in the Friar's case, subtle, estates satire compounded by individual attack. The Friar, of course, has considerable motivation to fashion such an attack, for he had been the victim of an identical assault. In her tale, the Wife, as a 'reward' to the Friar for his rude interruption of her prologue, describes friars as latter-day imitators of incubi, *devils* (another association between the two tales) who in a former age were preoccupied with seeking sexual union with women. For the mendicants who had vowed chastity this is an unfavourable comparison, to say the least. To this injury, an instance of the running estates satire in the tales, the Wife had added the insult that not only were friars imitators of incubi, they were *inept* imitators. It is interesting that in the final analysis the foolish summoner of the *Friar's Tale* is at once an inept imitator of devils, for he does not recognize one when he sees one, and, as a successful tempter, an excellent imitator.

The wife's insult has been seen as one reason to justify a reading of the *Friar's Tale* as a parody of the *Wife of Bath's Tale* (Szittya). While one may reasonably take issue with such a reading (C. Brown and Egge), this interpretation of 'panne' may also add to the renown of the *Friar's Tale* as being readable as part of the 'roadside drama' of *The Canterbury Tales* (Leicester, 'No Vileyns Word'). The central focus of this drama is the mutual flyting of the Friar and the

More importantly for the tale itself, there is simultaneously a metonymical association of the *other* sense of 'panne,' a cooking instrument. The following example of metonymy, the third from the *Rhetorica ad Herennium*, would connect a frying pan with the person who has it in hand, as occurs in medieval art: 'substituting the instrument for the possessor' (Murphy 370). This adds a widely understood medieval rhetorical technique to Hahn's iconic evidence that the widow's 'panne' as 'frying pan' should be associated with the devil.

Another metonymical play of 'panne,' that argued by David Williams, is the subtlest, cleverest, and perhaps the most enjoyable, because it associates the two different meanings of 'panne.' Williams points to the sixth and seventh examples of metonymy in the *Rhetorica ad Herennium*, 'substituting the container for the content' and 'substituting the content for the container,' to argue that 'both of those things which it [panne] can mean are clearly containers – a length of cloth to wrap up a subject, or a pan to cook one in' ('Grammar's Pan' 84). Williams sees the summoner 'contained' by both of them in the widow's curse, in which she calls on the devil to fetch the summoner 'panne and al' (1629).[21]

Curiosity over the meaning of 'panne' is not only heightened but made necessary and so deliberately invoked by the importance that the word attains in the widow's first curse. The summoner, master abuser of bodies of people, of words, and of 'things' in general, accuses the widow of misuse, or miscoupling of her body, adultery. This evokes the widow's curse:

> 'Thou lixt!' quod she, 'by my savacioun,
> Ne was I nevere er now, wydwe ne wyf,
> Somoned unto youre court in al my lyf;
> Ne nevere I nas but of my body trewe!
> Unto the devel blak and rough of hewe
> Yeve I thy body and my panne also!'   (1618–23)

The summoner and devil have been swearing empty oaths to each other continually throughout the poem, '*Depardieux*,' 'by my faith,' 'by God and by St Jame,' 'benedicte,' and so on. As we have seen above, the summoner has just sworn an oath 'by the sweete Seinte Anne' (1613). But now we see for the first time an honestly made oath, and a very pointed one for both the widow and the summoner: '*by my savacioun*' (1618). Ironically, the summoner's very salvation is at stake in his response to the widow's subsequent 'curse.'

Summoner. The contention between the Friar and the Wife of Bath adds an amusing side-battle in which the Friar has the last shot by slinging his 'panne' at her.

The use of 'panne' to connect the two widows is also an example of what was appreciated in the Middle Ages as metonymy or *denominatio*, which David Williams has already argued to be at work with the use of 'panne' in connection with the widow's curse in the *Friar's Tale*. According to the *Rhetorica ad Herennium*, which Chaucer knew well, metonymy is defined as 'a figure which draws from an object closely akin or associated with an expression suggesting this object meant, but not called by its own name' (Murphy 370). Then, in the *Rhetorica*, follow seven examples of such association. The first, 'substituting the name of the greater for that of the lesser' could relate the generic term 'widow' to other specific widows, such as the Wife of Bath. The second and fifth types of metonymy, 'substituting the name of the thing invented for the inventor,' and 'substituting the effect for the cause,' could describe an association of 'panne' with 'Wife of Bath.'

21 For other uses of metonymy in this scene see the last paragraph of the previous note.

Importantly, that which the widow's oath is attached to is her body. A proper relationship between her body and soul helps to assure her salvation. In the 'curse' which follows, the widow 'yeves' the devil the summoner's *body*, not his *soul*, the accident, not the substance. By simultaneously giving the devil her 'panne' along with the summoner's 'body,' the widow herself suggests such a reading; whether the 'panne' is considered to be a frying pan, a bolt of cloth, a 'smok,' or all of these, the widow is giving the devil the container, not the contents. What we have here is a cunning and wise widow who simultaneously outsmarts both devil and summoner, a fitting performance for someone who has successfully resisted the temptations of the devil and his agents all her life. According to orthodox theology (which the analogues to the *Friar's Tale* ignore) no one should curse anyone to hell: 'Vengeance is mine; I will repay saith the Lord' (Rom. 12:19) writes St. Paul, echoing numerous verses in the Old Testament. If the widow outrightly and with heartfelt intent curses the summoner to hell, she is committing a sin, a victory for the devil. Unlike the case of the carter, whose true intention anyone could easily interpret correctly, the widow's intention requires careful analysis by the devil. The devil, as with the carter, considers the widow's intent, but this time he misses the fine print. If by 'body,' in 'Yeve I thy *body*,' the widow means just that, *just the body*, not including the main prize, *the soul*, then this body alone, this container, would not have had much interest for an ordinary devil, nor would the widow herself be a potential prize due to the sin of cursing. When one knows that the body alone, as a container without the contents, like a 'panne' without contents, was of no use to devils, her curse becomes empty of the serious intent of cursing the summoner's soul to eternal damnation. So her first 'curse' is not a curse at all; the widow is playing with words, outplaying the two other master wordplayers. The widow, whom the summoner treats with such contempt, is wise, and the summoner, who thinks himself wise, is a fool (cf. Rom. 1:22). Indeed the widow also fools the devil who, unsure of the widow's 'entente,' asks the widow to repeat and clarify:

> 'Now, Mabely, myn owene mooder deere,
> Is this youre wyl in ernest that ye seye?'
> 'The devel,' quod she, '*so* fecche *hym* er he deye,
> And panne and *al*, but he wol hym repente!'   (1626–1629)

But this 'clarification' has a number of twists. First of all, the widow does not simply reply 'yes.' Instead she rephrases a questionable 'curse.' The 'so' and the 'hym' of the phrase 'so fecche hym' may still refer to just the body of the first curse, 'just "*so*," ' 'just *that*,' 'as I have already said' – she still has not sinned by cursing the summoner's soul to hell. Moreover, when one recalls the iconographic reference of 'devil and frying pan,' 'panne and *al*' may refer metonymically to the devil! She is cursing the devil to hell, which since he has already been eternally damned and cursed to hell, presents no moral transgression on her part. The widow is not fooled; she shows that she, unlike the summoner, knows how to recognize the devil and his representatives, regardless of their 'container.'

I have shown that the widow's 'curse' is much more subtle than the usual reading, i.e., that it is acceptable for her to curse because 'she makes her curse conditional' (Beichner 374) upon the summoner's 'entente' not to 'repente.' In the very next line the summoner accommodates her by appropriating the curse and altering it with the crucial assertion that to repent 'is nat myn entente' (1630). Indeed, this reading would, I believe, strengthen my argument. One has a widow who does not really curse a fellow human soul to hell; a widow who recognizes the devil and curses him back to the hell from whence he came and to which he is already damned by God; and, deliciously, we have a vicious, proud and foolish summoner, master word-monger, who 'flubs' the final test, and like a fool curses himself to hell.

CHAPTER SIX

Intentionality: The Couplings of a Fool

IF *'semiotics is in principle the discipline studying everything which can be used in order to lie'* (Eco, *Theory* 7, emphasis in original), then the *Friar's Tale* is a practical demonstration in semiotics. It assumes and shows that signs – words, clothing, posture, expression – are anything that can be used to lie, or tell the truth. 'Wordes,' an ideal paradigm of all other signs, are, of course, those considered most closely by Chaucer. In particular, he considers 'wordes' as 'deedes': in modern parlance, 'speech acts.' Chaucer, like Searle, six centuries later, is intrigued by the question: 'What is the difference between saying something and meaning it and saying it without meaning it?' (*Speech Acts* 3). In the *Friar's Tale* this question is answered by revealing a structural relationship between signs and those 'things' which they signify. The structural relationship between verbal signs and thoughts and other things is understood to describe the relationship between signs in general. This paradigm of language is also understood to describe the relationships between all beings in general. The difference in values between different relationships, for example, the difference in value between a relationship towards money which sees it as an end, and a relationship towards money which sees it as a means, was measured in ethical terms of good and bad, or proper and improper.

This chapter will deal with the general medieval understanding of the semantic structure of signs based on the paradigm of language as it is extended to all areas of human activity. In doing so we see that the 'modern' understanding of signs as it occurs in the *Friar's Tale* does not operate in a vacuum; it is not a freak anomaly. The first section below shows that the *Friar's Tale* shares with other medieval texts an interest in the paradigmatic structure of language as a means for evaluating the ethical value of all relationships based on intentional acts. The final section demonstrates the rich reading of the tale that can be achieved by considering the deliberate play with the intentional structure of signs.

THE *FRIAR'S TALE* AND THE GRAMMAR OF SEX

I have already discussed the metaphysical and ethical groundings of medieval interest in sign theory, and indicated that these are all aspects of a general medieval realism. To recap: Because the human subject may willfully exploit signs to tell the truth, mislead, or lie, signs may be considered to be used 'properly' or 'improperly'. In considering signs, or any other beings, to be properly and improperly directed, one enters an ethical world of ought and ought-not; this world is a function of a belief that the directedness, or natural intentionality, of all human beings is towards Being or God, a form of intentionalist realism. The evaluation of the proper and improper coupling of sign and 'thing' ('thing' being considered in a very wide sense) is a means used extensively in medieval literature for evaluating the spiritual-psychological condition of an individual. In a few cases, and the *Friar's Tale* is one of these, this means of spiritual-psychological evaluation is an issue considered directly in the text itself. In short, Chaucer's *Friar's Tale* studies the propriety and impropriety of the directedness of human beings in terms of their couplings.

The word 'coupling' is ideal to describe intentional activities. In willfully tending towards something, one has already chosen to couple with it, and in the very choosing one is changed by the intentional act which establishes, in medieval terms, a real relation between subject and object. On an ethical scale all such willed couplings always have some degree of propriety or impropriety. In Chaucer's translation and glossing of Meter 3 of Book Five of *The Consolation of Philosophy*, Lady Philosophy laments that things which have been or should be bound together 'ne wole nat ben medled ne *couplid togidre*' because of the action of the 'fre will' of man (Bo 5.m.3 1–8). The word, 'couplid' or 'coupled' may be extended to all human relationships, for example, marriage. So the Merchant says of his wife that 'For thogh the feend to hire *ycoupled* were, / She wolde hym overmacche' (MerT IV 1219–20). Ironically, because according to orthodox doctrine he is wrong, January in the *Merchant's Tale* thinks that the absolutely proper coupling of the marriage vows extends propriety to every possible relationship with his wife:

> In trewe wedlock coupled be we tweye,
> And blessed be the yok we been inne,
> For in oure actes we mowe do no synne.
> A man may do no synne with his wyf,
> Ne hurte hymselven with his owene knyf,
>
> (MerT IV 1836–1841)

Here is an extension of 'coupling' beyond its sexual and marital implications. The point of January's argument is an ethical one, and one which, according to Christian orthodoxy, is wrong, as the Parson would point out:

And for that many man weneth that he may nat synne for no
likerousnesse that he dooth with his wyf, certes, that opinion is fals.
God woot, a man may sleen hymself with his owene knyf, and make
hymselve dronken of his owene tonne.   (ParsT X 858)

In the previous chapters the metaphysical implications of the category of
relationship were discussed. Here we see, on a very practical level, that
Chaucer understands that the relationships subject-subject (husband-wife)
and subject-object (person-knife, person-wine) are willfully directed
by every subject. Chaucer, like his contemporaries, considered subject-
object relationships and subject-subject relationships generally as couplings
of an individual with any other created being, what a fourteenth-century
author calls 'beyng thinges' (*Cloud* author, *Hid Divinity* 121). While the
object in such relationships may be food, drink, material property and goods,
power, fame, and relationships, sexual and otherwise, with other human
beings, the 'goodness' or 'badness' of these couplings, their ethical value, is
determined by the degree to which they promote the ideal and ultimate
coupling of that special created being, man, to that uncreated Being, God. All
coupling, or lack of it, has 'ontological consequences,' that is, the very being
of a subject is changed in the act of willing or nilling a relationship with any
other being. This general sense of intentional coupling and its ontological
consequences are considered in great detail in the clearly didactic *Friar's
Tale*: while man may and in some cases must 'couple' with created 'beyng
thinges,' he ought to intend these couplings properly. This propriety is
determinable by the subject through the acute awareness of the various modes
of presentation by which one may consider an object; for example, as we saw
in the last chapters, *as* means rather than as ends, or in the case of the *Friar's
Tale*, *as* 'briberyes' rather than *as* 'rentes,' and vice versa. Man, according to
this understanding of the nature of reality, is responsible through the exercise
of his will for judging how he perceives something and intends towards it;
man should govern himself according to an ethical imperative; he ought to
intend himself properly towards all things; he ought to have 'good
entenciouns.'
    Central to our present discussion is how such coupling relationships were
understood in the Middle Ages. The paradigm of language and the paradigm
of sex were two ways they were understood, and these two merged, creating a
single 'grammar of sex' (Ziokowlski). Some of the relationships which mimic
the paradigm of the improper coupling of sign and thing in the *Friar's Tale* are
the following: the improper couplings of the summoner with other subjects,
both living (bawds, fornicators) and dead (Judas, the false thief), and both
human and non-human (the devil and God); the improper couplings of the
summoner with objects (gold and silver, food and drink); and the improper
coupling of the summoner with his office (he is a simoniac). Against such
improprieties are set the widow's proper couplings of her words and thoughts,
of her being with her estate (widow), and ultimately of her being with God.
This last is the model by which all coupling should be judged. The widow is a
proper widow 'married' to Christ; she is an exemplar of the 'clene wydewe'
described by the Parson, as one who 'eschue[s] the embracynges of man, and

desiren the embracynge of Jhesu Crist' (ParsT X 943). This last notion was one widely appreciated in the Middle Ages.[1]

The model of the linguistic paradigm of the impropriety of the summoner and propriety of the widow is sharply delineated in the tale by the morally neutral example of the carter. As I demonstrated in the last chapter, the carter, while yelling at his horses to encourage them to pull his mud-bemired cart, appears to be cursing, but he uses curses with no thought of the intentions or senses their conventional uses contain; as the devil notes, 'The carl spak oo thing, but he thoghte another' (III 1568). The carter, as we have seen, performs an illocutionary act in which the perlocutionary act and the perlocutionary effect have nothing to do with the conventional couplings of the words he utters and their usual senses. Chaucer clearly and accurately appreciates and demonstrates a 'modern' understanding of language.

The analogy of proper and improper linguistic coupling with proper and improper sexual coupling, the 'grammar of sex,' was widely exploited in the Middle Ages. This is important to appreciate for it demonstrates that Chaucer's understanding of language, and his literary play with such an understanding, were not anomalous. In the Middle Ages linguistic abuse was a symptom and barometer of spiritual illness; there was a 'tight relationship between grammatical and moral rectitude' (Ziokowlski 139).[2] Chaucer's oft-repeated variations of Boethius's rendering of Plato, 'the wordis moot be cosynes to the thinges of whiche thei speken' (Bo 3.pr.12 206–7), may be well appreciated from the grammatical-sexual perspective of moral rectitude. The word 'cosyn' signifies a relationship. Relationships between cousins have strict guidelines of propriety. We may recall that Chaucer asserts that the relationships of 'wordes,' 'werkyngs' 'thinges,' and 'dedes,' like all other relationships, have a 'natural' or 'proper' order. Sin is the willful displacement of this *ordo naturalis*; the Parson expresses this: 'whan man synneth, al this [natural] ordre or ordinaunce is turned up-so-doun' (ParsT X 262). We should not be surprised, then, when in the *Friar's Tale* the linguistic model of natural order, which applies to 'word as in thoght and in dede' (ParsT X 579), serves as a paradigm for the natural order of all 'relating' or 'coupling,' for use, for enjoyment, or for any other intention which is subject to the human will.

When it came to the sexual act, however, even a good intention, such as procreation, was not enough to make it proper. While vaginal intercourse between male and female was, of course, considered natural, it was also frequently considered to be improper to some degree, even between husband and wife. Here, the position of Chaucer's Parson is typical: the 'Trewe effect of mariage [is that it] clenseth fornicacioun . . . and it chaungeth deedly [mortal] synne into venial synne bitwixe hem that been ywedded . . .' (ParsT X 919). Indeed, if the object of the 'assemblynge' of a husband and wife is 'oonly to hire

---

[1] Widely known because of the common medieval typological interpretations of the Song of Songs which included the nuptial metaphor of coupling, the concept of the human soul, and/or the Christian church as 'the bride of Christ' (Chydenius, *Symbolism* 57–60).

[2] For Dante and other continental writers on this see Vance, including his references, *Signals* 184–255. For Chaucer, the closest approach to my own is that of Vance in his chapter 'Mervelous Signals: Chaucer's "Troilus and Criseyde".' This should corroborate my own approach, which I came to independently, using many different sources.

flesshly delit' such a coupling may be a 'spece of avowtrie' (903). If the 'natural' sexual act was widely considered to be improper to some degree, it is not difficult to imagine the horrendous degree of impropriety medieval Christianity would ascribe to 'unnatural' sexual acts – and the act of greatest impropriety was sodomy.

Sodomy, in the Middle Ages as today, is a term usually applied to sexual coupling between males. The Parson cannot bring himself to name 'thilke abhomynable synne, of which that no man unnethe oghte speke ne write' (ParsT X 901), and the author of the early fourteenth-century poem *Cursor Mundi* can only define it in terms of what it is not: 'Unkindli [unnatural] sin and sodomite, Austin [Augustine] cals al swilk delit, that es not twix womman and man' (27966). In *Jacob's Well*, a fifteenth-century manual for the penitent, of the same lineage as the *Parson's Tale*, the anonymous author lists degrees of lechery based on the status of the individuals. Taken into consideration in determining the seriousness of the sin were questions of whether or not the 'lecchours' were single, married or widowed, and then whether there were blood relationships, and, if so, the closeness of those relationships. Most sinful were sexual relationships between people in the clerical or religious estate; the higher the degree of the cleric, the more serious the sin. The first degree, or 'firste fote [foot] depth' in the 'well' of the sin of lechery, is a sexual relationship between a 'syngle man and syngle womman' (160); the last and worst: the 'xiiij [fourteenth] fote depth is sodyme, that is synne agens kynde [nature]' (162). This is glossed in the unique manuscript margin: 'peccatum sodome contra naturam' (162n2). There is an implication that such sins *contra naturam* include all sexual acts not named in the first thirteen categories: all same sex relationships plus bestiality. But the relationship of greatest concern to the Christian Church was sexual relationships between men.

Sodomy, in its usual sense, is the issue of one of the first great humanistic works of the Middle Ages, the primary source of the 'grammar of sex,' Alain de Lille's *De planctu Naturae* (*The Complaint of Nature*). There, the goddess Natura appears in a dream vision to the narrator and her complaint is against a particular group that is causing her harm, a group that is acting *contra Naturam*, against Nature, namely, clerics who commit sodomy. In this work, however, Alain extends the concept of sodomy to all kinds of improper couplings other than sexual acts; sodomy becomes here, and subsequently elsewhere, a metaphor for all relationships considered *contra naturam* between 'beyng thinges.' The Parson's statement 'Al that is enemy and destruccioun to nature is agayns nature' (ParsT 865) is a manifestation of this generalization. But there is something that should not be lost to us in this generalization or extension of the meaning of sodomy, because it was not lost to those, such as Chaucer, who followed Alain: from its very beginning in *The Complaint of Nature* the paradigm of sodomy is itself based on the paradigm of language: Proper sex is to be understood in terms of proper grammar; improper sex in terms of improper grammar.

Eugene Vance discusses some of the literary manifestations of the extended sense of sodomy in his chapter 'The Differing Seed: Dante's Brunetto Latini.' He demonstrates that Dante uses 'the problem of sodomy in its most extended [medieval] sense: that is, as a problem involving not just an individual's *natural* physical relationship to his species but his natural relationship to the body politic and, by extension, to letters' (*Signals* 238-9). Elsewhere, Vance offers another convincing piece of evidence which supports the view that the understanding of the extended senses of sodomy was widespread. In the *Jeu de la feuillé*, 'a learned anti-clerical thirteenth-century play' (210), 'improper couplings' (215) are suggested, attempted, and/or succeeded in between father and daughter, and father and son. Notably, such couplings are mirrored in the verbal realm; improper couplings pass 'back and forth between *verba* and *res* with great spontaneity' (215).

It is Jan Ziolkowski who best describes the wide-ranging correlations between sexual, linguistic, and all other intentional human behaviour, such as that shown by Vance to be operating in the *Jeu de la feuillé*. Working from the 'grammar of sex' articulated by Alain de Lille, Ziolkowski demonstrates just how widespread the use of the extended sexual metaphor was during the period. The abuse of words, the abuse of sex, and impropriety generally are all contiguous: 'To Alan, an abuse of action and an abuse of words have the same consequence: both destroy the order of creation' (103). While Alain focuses on sexual behaviour, Ziolkowski points out that 'In the *De planctu Naturae*, Alan emphasized that *willfully* misplaced love upsets grammar, verbal meaning, and truth as a whole' (101, emphasis added). We see in Alain the same general understanding we have seen elsewhere that *the will*, not language itself, is the source of propriety or impropriety in human speech:

> In both his literary and theological works Alan pointed out that grammar is a manifestation, even a direct gauge, of a person's free will because the constructions or words one uses reflect personal decisions: 'voces significantes sunt ad placitum et ex beneplacito inponentis (*Summa 'Quoniam homines'*, p. 142: 'Significant utterances are significant by the will and goodwill of the speaker'). Seeing that both good grammar and good morals are contingent upon the discretion of humanity's free will, the state of humanity's grammar provides an apt metaphoric parallel to the state of humanity's morality (and sexuality) in the *De planctu Naturae*. (106-107)

In this chapter, as in others, I offer evidence that Chaucer understood that the propriety and impropriety of language was a paradigm applicable to all human behaviour. We see now that he shares this understanding with Dante, the author of the *Jeu de la feuillé*, and Alain de Lille. Indeed, given Chaucer's many 'direct borrowings' (Baker 432) from 'Aleyn['s]' 'Pleynt of Kynde' (PF 316), Alain is an obvious source of such ideas for him. Earlier in this book I indicated that another core understanding shared by Alain, Dante, and Chaucer is the knowledge that language is conventional and so subject to the human will. I also pointed to Chaucer's poem 'Lak of Stedfastnesse' in which the narrator laments that in his time 'word and deed . . . Ben nothing lyk' (Sted 4-5). Liam O. Purdon states concisely that in this poem Chaucer 'indicates that abuse of words not only distorts reality but also eventually engenders further linguistic and moral abuse' (146).[3] 'Lak of Stedfastnesse' is a statement of this belief; the *Friar's Tale* is a demonstration of it.

SUMMONERS AND THE GRAMMAR OF SEX

The *Friar's Tale* can be broadly considered from the perspective of improper coupling. We have already seen that the protagonist is a corrupt, materialistic summoner, whose only goal is to couple with material reality, and that the nature of this relationship is revealed verbally as 'briberyes' which the summoner improperly disguises as 'rentes.' The devil whom the summoner encounters is disguised as a yeoman; that is, the devil has coupled himself improperly with the visual 'word' for 'yeman.' In joining company with the devil the summoner improperly becomes one of his 'sworen bretheren' (1405). While there are other such non-verbal couplings and miscouplings, the constant paradigm of the poem is the coupling of word and thought, and word and thing. In fact, through the words of all the characters and the narrator, the poem, as we have seen, becomes an object lesson in this matter.

If we extend the paradigm of coupling and miscoupling we will notice that the summoner's abuse of his office for personal profit is itself an improper coupling, a form of simony. Indeed, in the extended grammar of sex it is a sodomy. In one of his English sermons John Wyclif inveighs against prelates or high church officials, who in the abuse of their offices 'ben gostly sodomytis worse than bodily sodomytis of sodom and gomor' (*English Works* 55); in a Latin treatise, *On Simony*, he specifically describes simony as 'this sodomy':

> For just as in carnal sodomy contrary to nature the seed is lost by which an individual human being would be formed, so in this sodomy [i.e. simony] the seed of God's word is cast aside with which a spiritual regeneration in Christ would be created.[4]

Wyclif would consider, then, that the summoner has 'sodomized' his office. This concept is particularly apt for the summoner because the prime targets of his official improprieties are themselves agents of improper sexual couplings.

There were two courts of law in fourteenth-century England, the civil courts and the church courts. As the Friar accurately describes the office, the church courts under the direction of the archdeacon,

> . . . dide execucioun
> In punysshynge of fornicacioun,
> Of wicchecraft, and eek of bawderye,

---

[3] Purdon, unfortunately, makes the error common to many of those critics discussed in Chapter One in thinking that 'lack of steadfastness' may reside in language itself, rather than in the will of the speaking subject.

[4] Translated by Terrence A. McVeigh, cited in Vance, *Signals* 241.

> Of diffamacioun, and avowtrye,
> Of chirche reves [robberies], and of testamentz,
> Of contractes and of lakke of sacramentz,
> Of usure, and of symonye also.   (1303–1309)

The summoner, a subordinate of the archdeacon, worked in the combined roles of investigating officer, issuer of summonses, and prosecuting attorney. Of all offences, the greatest attention of the ecclesiastical courts was directed towards sexual misbehaviour: 'certes, lecchours dide he [the erchedeken] grettest wo' (1310). The Parson tells us that the sin of lechery is 'ful plesaunt to the devel, for therby wynneth he the mooste partie of this world' (ParsT X 849). So too, lechery was the sin most 'ful plesaunt' to corrupt summoners for thereby did they win most of their bribes. The summoner of the *Friar's Tale* was masterful at sniffing out 'an hurt deer from an hool' (1370), that is, 'lecchours' susceptible to extortion. Once he has recorded someone's offence with one of his informing 'wenche[s]' (1362), the summoner promises his victims that he will 'striken hire [the wench's name] out of oure lettres blacke' (1364) for a consideration, that is, a 'briberye.' As we saw in Chapter One, this is one of many instances in Chaucer's work of the 'white' and 'black' motif of improper coupling of sign and that which it signifies.[5] Here we have the improper use of words, verbal sodomy, both spoken and written, as simultaneously an act and a paradigm of moral and official impropriety.

The tale's introduction indicates that the summoner, before meeting the particular devil of the tale, has been 'coupling,' socially, spiritually and/or physically, with the devil through many agents, various tempters such as pimps and dispensers of sexual favours. The theme of improper couplings is reinforced and the metaphor made real again by the conclusion of the tale. The tale offers an explicit grotesque inversion of the Christian's goal of uniting or coupling spiritually with God, as a 'bride of Christ.' In medieval art 'certain of the punishments of hell are closely connected with the private parts of Satan' (Baird 105). So, as Baird suggests, the devil's promise hints at this end before he sweeps the summoner off to hell,

> Thou shalt with me to helle yet tonyght,
> Where thou shalt knowen of oure privetee
> Moore than a maister of dyvynytee.   (1636–38)

The context here suggests a special sense of 'privitee,' one common to Chaucerian punning. This sense seems confirmed when, a mere sixty lines further, the pilgrim Summoner in his tale 'quits' the Friar by graphically describing the punishment of *friars* in hell in no subtle terms:

> Right so as bees out swarmen from an hyve,
> Out of the develes ers ther gonne dryve

---

[5] Striking out the 'lettres blacke,' that is, making the letters white, will not erase the black sin of any true offence. Only the sacrament of penance may do that, and it is towards the sacrament of penance that the summoner should be leading those whom he is instead extorting. On the black and white motif in Chaucer see above 27–33.

> Twenty thousand freres on a route,
> And thurghout helle swarmed al aboute,
> And comen agayn as faste as they may gon,
> And in his ers they crepten everychon.   (SumT III 1693–98)

Because the pilgrim Summoner is the immediate *raison d'être* for the Friar's treatment of summoners in his tale, it is fruitful to consider him in terms of the grammar of sex. Like the summoner of the *Friar's Tale*, the pilgrim Summoner is, in medieval Christian terms, an improper coupler *par excellence*. Because of his abuse of his office, his excessive coupling with food and drink as revealed through his physiognomy (his 'fyr-reed' [GP I 624], 'saucefleem' [625] face [Curry, *Mediaeval Sciences* 37–47]), and his indiscriminate mating habits (he was 'lecherous as a sparwe' [GP I 626]), he is obviously a sodomite in the extended sense. But, more subtly, an accumulation of detail also strongly implies that he is a sodomite in the usual sense. The strongest evidence is his guilt by association through his relationship with his friend the Pardoner.

Whatever the relationship between the Summoner and the Pardoner, like the relationship between the Friar's summoner and the devil, it most certainly is not one aimed at mutual spiritual improvement. The Pardoner is another master of improper couplings, verbal and otherwise. We are told in the *General Prologue*: 'Ful loude he [the Pardoner] soong "Com hider, love, to me!" / This Somonour bar to hym a stif burdoun' (GP I 672–73), meaning a bass harmony in song, but also carrying a strong phallic connotation, for 'bourdon' and 'burdoun' appear frequently in Middle English meaning 'a pilgrim's staff,' 'a stout staff' (OED).[6] The innuendo of sexual impropriety between these two pilgrims is enhanced by the details preceding the Pardoner's song and which are not usually noted, but which point to irregularity in the Summoner's sexual habits. We are told of the Summoner that 'Ful prively a fynch eek koude he pulle' (GP I 652); such a statement, it has been argued, connotes elsewhere in literature, and so quite possibly here, 'illicit sexual intercourse' (Cawley 173). The act which Cawley is too discreet to name is obviously masturbatory sex between two people. The 'prively' of this statement reinforces this connotation. Moreover, it occurs within a context that suggests that a 'good felawe' could 'have his concubyn / A twelf month ' (GP I 650–51), if only he would engage 'prively' in 'fynch' pulling

---

6 The sexuality of the Pardoner, as well as his other traits, has been the subject of constant debate since W.C. Curry's groundbreaking article in 1919 ('Secret'). Based on physiognomy Curry argues that the Pardoner was a *eunuchus ex nativitate*. Beryl Rowland, Muriel Bowden (274–76) and R.P. Miller have discovered numerous flaws in this argument, and each has come up with variations of his or her own, but they all share the common ground with Curry that something is 'not right' with the Summoner's sexuality. Others (Gilliam; Dinshaw) have produced interpretations which further support this view while exploring other interesting aspects of its implications. Eugene Vance ('Pardoner') has argued that the Pardoner is both a spiritual and sexual sodomite on grounds similar to those I am putting forth here for the Summoner. Perhaps the most balanced article is that of Monica E. McAlpine ('Pardoner's Homosexuality'), in which she argues that the Pardoner is a homosexual in an age when the sexual acts often associated with homosexuality and not homosexuality itself were the issue. McAlpine interprets tolerance in the narrator's portrait and hope for the Pardoner's salvation in his prologue and tale.

with the Summoner. Furthermore, the Summoner, according to the narrator, was willing to 'punish' those whom he could summon in the 'purse': 'He wolde techen him to have noon awe / . . . of the ercedekenes curse / . . . / For in his purs he sholde ypunyshed be' (GP I 654–57). 'Purse' may carry two senses: the usual sense, so that the Summoner's victim could escape punishment through a monetary bribe, and a sense common to the fabliaux, 'purse' as 'testicles' (Vance, *Signals* 215). So, it is implied, a victim could also escape the archdeacon's curse, excommunication, with a bribe from this other kind of purse. Indeed this punishment itself suggests the sin of sodomy. The punishment for minor offences was a flogging; 'corporal punishment was the rule' (Hahn 77). Fornication, resulting as it did from a natural desire of male and female to copulate, was among these lesser offences. So we see the archdeacon of the *Friar's Tale* ordering floggings that cause 'lecchours . . . [to] syngen if that they were hent' (1310–11). However, because sodomy in its usual sense of sexual acts between people of the same gender was an act *contra naturam*, it could result in the ultimate punishment of excommunication. Because the excommunicant was denied access to the sacraments, such a curse meant probable damnation to hell as well as forcing him to endure the immediate condition of being a social pariah (Gauthier 111–112).

The specific details of the improper couplings of the Summoner of the *Canterbury Tales* and the summoner of the *Friar's Tale* remain open to debate, but it cannot be denied that the two characters may be considered from the point of view of the paradigms of language and the 'grammar of sex.'

THE COUPLINGS OF A FOOL

A number of the verses in the first chapter of St Paul's epistle to the Romans seem to be epitomized by the summoner of the *Friar's Tale*:

> For the wrath of God is revealed from heaven against all ungodliness and unrighteousness of men, who hold the truth in unrighteousness . . . *Professing themselves to be wise, they became fools,* And changed the glory of the uncorruptable God into an image . . . [they] changed the truth of God into a lie, and worshipped and served the creature more than the Creator . . . the men, leaving the natural use of the women, burned in their lust one toward another . . . God gave them over to a reprobate mind . . . [they were] filled with all unrighteousness, fornication . . . covetousness . . . full of envy, murder, debate, deceit, malignity; whisperers . . . proud, boasters, inventors of evil things . . .
>
> (Rom. 1:18–30).

This key text for the doctrinal linking of sexual and other improprieties in the Middle Ages may be seen as a model for the Friar in his characterization of the summoner and should be added to those many other biblical texts which have been shown to be referred or alluded to in the tale (Correale; Hatton; Jacobs and Jungman).

In the tale there is a strong emphasis on the summoner's promotion of, and indulgence in fornication, the 'black truth' disguised by the 'worde white' of his office through which he was supposed to be promoting the avoidance of this sin. The equation between fornication and idolatry, based on the text of St Paul, was highly conventional in the Middle Ages (see Vance, *Signals* 231-2). Moreover, the summoner's indulgence in fornication and other fleshly appetites is achieved either directly as fleshly bribes or via the 'gold and silver' 'briberyes' which he constantly pursues. The devil promises the summoner 'gold and silver' (1400), an allusion, possibly, to Exodus 20:23, 'Ye shall not make with me gods of silver, neither shall ye make unto you gods of gold.' The summoner is revealed and reveals himself to be an absolute materialist, an idolater who 'worshipped and served the creature more than the Creator' (Rom. 1:25). As we shall see, the summoner is also 'proud,' 'despiteful,' 'covetous,' 'malicious,' full of 'envy,' 'debate,' 'deceit,' 'malignity,' and a 'whisperer.' But the most important verse in this chapter from St Paul, because it could serve as the epigraph of the entire *Friar's Tale*, is 'professing themselves to be wise they became fools' (Rom. 1:22). It is also a verse which might help us settle a critical debate on the *Friar's Tale*.

The *Friar's Tale* has produced two fundamental interpretations of the character of the summoner of the tale. The oppositions between these interpretations can, I believe, be resolved now by utilizing the methods described in this book. The result may be a third and better interpretation of the summoner of the *Friar's Tale* than either of the previous interpretations allows. This third interpretation is validated by Chaucer's intentionalist realism and deliberate play with three-level semantics. Such an understanding of intentionality and exploitation of verbal play and interpretation facilitate the development of individual psychology; character is revealed through a speaker's own words and the words of various other narrators and characters.

One previous interpretation sees the summoner of the *Friar's Tale* solely as a type of the 'hopelessly "carnal". . . and the resulting picture is not a picture of "psychological" entity [that is, an individual summoner], but a concrete manifestation of a moral concept' (Robertson, *Preface* 268). This view sees the summoner as naive and stupid in the sense of possessing a low level of intelligence and general awareness. The other previous interpretation lauds the 'realistic characterisation' (Richardson, 'Hunter' 156) of the summoner, and would see the summoner as not being stupid in the sense of having low intelligence, but as being cynical, unbelieving, or even Faustian. It is important to note that these two generally opposed approaches are not opposed on a key issue: they both accept the carnality and materialism of the summoner.

The first interpretation, the summoner as a 'concrete manifestation of a moral concept,' might be called 'typological realism.' I think that there is no doubt that such an approach is fruitful, and I do not think that one may deny that on one level the summoner is a type of idolatrous materialist who is coupled to the illusion of material reality. So, too, the widow of the tale, as mentioned in the last chapter, is a type of the ideal widow, one of those proper couplers who only 'desiren the embracynge of Jhesu Crist' (ParsT X 943). There are also allusions to the summoner being a type of other types, such as the 'false theef' (FrT III 1338) of Calvary, who is a type of those who, like the summoner, will not repent; and 'Judas' (1350), a type of those who, like the summoner, worship gold and silver instead of their true master. But there is no reason why the summoner of the *Friar's Tale* cannot be a product of realistic characterization and, just like the false thief and Judas, be seen simultaneously as a type and an individual who 'professing himself to be wise, has *become* a fool.'

The view that the summoner is merely acting stupidly in his encounter with the devil goes back in modern criticism least as far as R.K. Root in 1906: the summoner believes the devil is the devil but has no fear of him because he, the summoner, has become totally, morally decrepit. According to this view the summoner's mental decrepitude is a function of his moral decrepitude, 'given over to a reprobate mind,' as St Paul would say. This view was more fully articulated by Germaine Dempster in 1932. Robertson, however, adds, as we have seen, a theoretical cast to this view, his typological realism, which affects his general understanding of characterization in Chaucer's works.[7]

The main point of Richardson and others is that the summoner is not simply stupid, rather he just does not *believe* that the devil is the devil.[8] Richardson's approach to Chaucerian character, like that of Robertson, has a long history. In fact Richardson's reading of the Friar's summoner is a particular case of the approach to character in Chaucer argued long ago by John M. Manly, namely, that often we should not see this or that Chaucerian character as 'a type, but as a typical individual' (95). The non-believing summoner has the advantage of making the *Friar's Tale* more coherent, more clever, and the characterization more subtle and complex than the simply stupid summoner of the Robertsonian

---

[7] Robertson's narrow and uni-dimensional interpretation of the summoner is affected here by his attempt to fit him into his general approach to Chaucerian representation of character. Just as the 'carnal' Wife of Bath is, according to Robertson, naively unaware that she is misreading scripture, so too the Friar's summoner is basically a type of 'the carnal' and 'the self-deceived' who should not be seen as *a* summoner, an individual, at all. Robertson creates an opposition between two extremes of representation, absolute individual ('a "psychological"' entity) and absolute type ('a moral concept') and champions the latter view: the summoner is simply *not* an individual, he is a type. Robertson errs, I believe, in limiting the possibilities of characterization to the extremities.

Robertson founds his arguments on an historical basis that is difficult to maintain, for they presuppose an extreme realism as being the norm for the Middle Ages, which simply is not the case, as we saw in Chapter Two. The subtle 'intentionalist' characterization of the devil, the summoner, and, perhaps most surprisingly, the widow, which I offered in the last chapter and extend below, allows a new approach to the issue of psychological realism in Chaucer.

[8] The most thoroughly articulated view of this occurs in Hahn and Kaeuper who argue that 'the Summoner does not for a moment believe in the devil' (97), and that 'Most critics have assumed that the Friar's insults are aimed chiefly at the Summoner's intelligence and so have overlooked what is clearly a satire on the fiendish professional cynicism of summoners' (91n82). Leneghan argues that 'the summoner's ignorance is willful' (293), which view supports the contention that the summoner is not merely stupid. Richardson, in another article, argues that the pilgrim Summoner 'is essentially a non-believer, a gross materialist oblivious to all spiritual concerns, and that the Friar endows his protagonist with the same deficiency' ('Friar and Summoner' 233). Some critics fence-sit (the Friar's summoner 'doesn't care or doesn't believe' or 'is too stupid or too carnal' [Szittya 390]). Leicester offers a third neither/nor, both/and approach: 'The summoner's character *is* inconsistent' (22). However, Leicester does a disservice to both sides of the debate by reducing them to the 'cynical Faustian, or merely very stupid summoner' (27) schools, and does not deal directly with the cogent arguments of Richardson, who seems to argue for a cynical *and* stupid summoner. I try in this chapter to focus this combined view under the term 'foolish,' used in a sense that does not include mental deficiency.

approach, which makes of him a uni-dimensional, universal type. The 'non-believing summoner' approach is strengthened through a consideration of intentional attitudes, a particular realization of the fact that Chaucer and many in his period were sensitive to distinctions as to how different people, and even the same person at different times, might perceive the same object. In the summoner's case his interpretation of his perception of external reality is determined by intentional attitudes. In the case of the devil-in-disguise, that attitude is *belief*, an attitude not conditioned by any degree of intelligence, or lack of it. There is an extreme discrepancy between the 'object' *which* the summoner perceives, that is, the devil, and the object *as* he perceives 'it,' that is, *as* a hunting yeoman pretending to be a devil. The irony is successful because the audience is made fully conscious of this discrepancy. When the devil says he is a devil, the summoner chooses to believe the meaning of the signs of the devil's costume rather than the meaning of the signs of his words. Chaucer *and* the summoner know that signs are anything that can be used to lie *or* tell the truth. The summoner's problem is that here, as in so many other aspects of his life, he makes the wrong choice, all the while thinking himself extremely wise in making the 'right' one.

Interpreters who see the summoner of the *Friar's Tale* solely through the lenses of typological realism have not considered Chaucer in terms of phenomenological psychology. This is also true, of course, for those who laud, here and elsewhere, Chaucer's realistic characterization. But the typological realist dismisses the psychological realist primarily on the grounds of anachronism, not realizing that there are roads to psychological realism which bridge both medieval and modern understandings of the workings of the human mind. The advocates of a total typological view of the summoner of the *Friar's Tale* dismiss claims of psychological realism in a medieval text with the assertion that there is no need to answer questions about psychological individuality because such questions are irrelevant. The usual position held is that looking for psychological consistency in a character such as the summoner is to apply the norms of modern psychological realism where they should not be applied: 'Robertson urges us to ask medieval questions about medieval texts' is the usual position. Such a strategy ignores the fact that medieval creators and interpreters of texts, be they poets, philosophers, grammarians, logicians, theologians, spiritual physicians, or some combination of these, were very often interested in the intersection where intention and language meet. The same is true of many modern creators and interpreters of texts, be they poets, novelists, literary critics, linguists, cognitive or biological scientists, philosophers, or some combination of these. Chaucer's play with intentionality through fields of association in the *Friar's Tale* shows that this is clearly an interest for him. What the summoner believes is, for Chaucer, a matter of mental intentionality, a psychological relation to extramental reality which often is revealed, both deliberately and unconsciously, through signs, as 'signs' are understood today, the same way 'signs' were understood in the Middle Ages.

Anyone who wishes to maintain a totally typological view of the 'naive, believing summoner' must ignore the ability of medieval writers and readers to appreciate and assume the phenomenological attitude. An appreciation of this dissolves many of the so-called problems of the *Friar's Tale*:

(1) Why does the summoner not recognize the 'yeoman' as a devil despite all the visual and verbal hints of his identity? [9] He *believes* the 'yeoman' is a yeoman. (2) Why does he not become concerned when the devil reveals his identity? He *believes* the 'yeoman' is a yeoman pretending to be a devil; the devil is a 'lying yeoman'. This is completely consistent with the fool who thinks himself wise. Paul says of such a fool that he 'changed the truth of God into a lie.' Ironically, but consistently with his 'up-so-doun' understanding of reality, the summoner has 'changed the truth of the devil into a lie.' As discussed above, many in Chaucer's audience could have appreciated this play as a perfect inversion of the popular Liar paradox. In the *Friar's Tale* the devil tells the truth; the summoner thinks that he is lying; therefore, everything he says that is true is taken as a lie. (3) Why does the summoner question the devil on his techniques? He is testing, teasing, and playing with the 'yeoman's' ability to support and elaborate his 'lie'.
(4) Why does the summoner not react to the insults or thinly veiled threats of the devil ('a lowsy jogelour kan deceyve thee' (1467); 'thy wit is al to bare / To understonde' (1480–81)); the promised 'chayer' (1518) in hell)? These are part of the 'game' the summoner thinks the 'lying yeoman' is playing. Indeed, the summoner's lie, 'I am a yeman, knowen is ful wyde' (1524), is in one sense equivalent to saying, 'Well if you're a devil, then I'm a yeoman.'
(6) Why does the summoner suggest to the devil that he claim the carter's horse and cart and hay after the carter has cursed them to the devil, unless he is naive about words and intentions? Before he makes this suggestion, the summoner says to himself, with the 'lying yeoman' in mind, 'Heere shal we have a pley' (1548). And 'pley' he does, with the 'lying yeoman', not the carter, with whom neither devil nor summoner exchanges a word.
(7) Why does the summoner condescend to teach the devil a lesson in extortion? Because the summoner believes the 'stupid yeoman' is in need of a lesson, and proudly wishes to flaunt his art.

In summary, the typological view reduces the summoner to a type of sinner who is naive and stupid due to his spiritual corruption. The view of realistic characterization agrees that the summoner is spiritually corrupt, but sees him not as stupid, but cynical and non-believing. As I have already indicated, I think there are grounds for a synthesis of the two views. We have noted that both approaches share one fundamental assumption: the spiritual corruption or carnality of the summoner. The resolution is to see the summoner as 'stupid' but not naive or unintelligent, for someone can be 'stupid' but not necessarily lack intelligence; anyone can be a fool. The paradox of the believing-the-devil-is-the-devil view and its contrary is resolved in the broader concept of foolishness, foolishness based on what is, from a Christian perspective, a foolish belief.

Aside from the play with the Liar paradox, the question 'Why does the devil reveal himself and tell the truth about the nature of devils?' is answered correctly, I think, by D.W. Robertson, Jr. when he states that the devil 'knows that there is no need to deceive a man who has already thoroughly deceived himself' (*Preface* 267). I think, in general, those who reject Robertson's

---

[9] These hints are discussed in the previous chapter.

reduction of the summoner to a type would, nevertheless, accept this interpretation. The devil reacts truthfully, this being the best means to fool, and so *lie* to, the summoner. And, after all, his ruse works: the summoner takes him not for a truthful devil, but for a lying yeoman. The summoner actually ends up scornfully pitying the stupid 'lying yeoman'. We can hear this in his words to the devil, 'taak heer ensample of me' (1580), before he begins his 'game,' that is, his work, with the widow.

In such an approach what have been two opposing views may coincide, not only with each other, but, I believe, with Chaucer's view. Richardson points out that there is an implicit comparison of the summoner's psychological condition to that of the 'wood hare.' The Friar says: 'this Somonour wood were as an hare' (1327). In his sexual frenzy the March hare becomes oblivious to predators, he becomes 'mad,' and, like the 'wood' hare,

> the summoner reveals his heedlessness and stupidity – indeed, his madness
> – by completely disregarding the most obvious warnings of his impending
> fate. *He entraps himself unwittingly*. His complete unscrupulousness, his
> greed, his hypocrisy, and, above all, his stupidity and his pride in his own
> supposed cleverness lead him to seal his own doom. He condemns himself;
> he attempts to deceive the arch-deceiver.
>
> (Richardson, 'Hunter' 159, emphasis added)

The difference between the 'psychological realist' approach to the summoner and the typological approach disappears in the words I have emphasized: 'He entraps himself unwittingly.' The summoner's stupidity is not the stupidity of swearing brotherhood with the devil, which reduces the 'character' of the summoner to that of an idiot; it is the stupidity of the fool: 'the pride in his own supposed cleverness' (Richardson 159): 'Professing themselves to be wise, they *became* fools.' The characterization of a fool demands much more subtlety than the characterization of a person with minimal intelligence, a demand to which Chaucer more than adequately responds.

A strong external argument for considering the summoner as a fool through corruption rather than lack of mental capacity is the fact that in numerous details the summoner shares the biblical profile of such a fool. Recalling the discussions above of various medieval understandings of mode of presentation, one may observe that the summoner consistently sees as ends those very things which should be seen as means. The 'gold and silver' and other objects of the material realm that he seeks are among those 'idols' of which Paul speaks in his letter to the Romans. Such a fool is one of those who because they 'trust in their wealth . . . [their] way is their folly' (Ps. 49:6–13). Such fools were among those who would embark on Sebastian Brandt's *Narrenschiff*, or 'Ship of Fools,' eighty years after Chaucer departed on his final journey. Is the summoner the unbelieving fool of Psalm 53:1, 'The fool hath said in his heart, There is no God. Corrupt they are and have done abominable iniquity: there is none that doeth good'? Focused as he is on means, the summoner certainly does not see his final end, and this indicates, perhaps, a lack of belief in God. This message may be delivered through an ironic twist: he does not *believe* the devil is a devil. Moreover, the summoner behaves like the fools of the Psalm: '[the] workers of iniquity . . . eat up my people as they eat bread: they have not called upon God' (53:4). The summoner abuses an office intended to bring moral trangressors to repentance and redemption by using it 'to eat up people.' In return for some sort of bribe, the summoner releases sinners from the obligation to admit guilt and repent. The fool also deceives himself through pride, 'The pride of thine heart has deceived thee' (Obad. 3), and the summoner in his belief that he is far superior to this fellow who claims to be the devil certainly falls into this trap. Of the proud, Fals-Semblant says in *The Romaunt of the Rose*:

> I dwelle with hem that proude be,
> And full of wiles and subtilte,
> That worship of this world coveiten . . .   (6171–73)

Pride is the 'devil' that dwells in the heart of that wily fellow, the summoner, who acts both 'slyly' ('A slyer boye nas noon in Engelond' [FrT 1322]) and 'subtilly' (FrT 1323), and is obviously among those 'That worship of this world coveiten.' The devil of the *Friar's Tale* knows the summoner, because as 'pride' (and the devil is the Prince of Pride) he has been with him long. The summoner is a fool because he does not recognize the devil: his own foolish pride.

We can interpret authorial intention in this tale. The summoner is presented *as* a materialist fool whose 'truth', like so much else in this poem of inversions, is not truth: 'the [false] truth [held] in unrighteousness' (Rom. 1:18). This mode of presentation reveals the Christian presuppositions upon which the 'authors' (the Friar and Chaucer) are constructing their tale – although whether the Friar as an author believes in and/or fully understands the message of this mode of presentation, or point of view, is debatable.

The *Friar's Tale* presents the master liar, and thus the master semiotician among all creatures, the devil, at play, that is, at work: he tells the lying summoner the truth about devils, knowing that the summoner would not take his words as the 'truth' spoken by a qualified master in the subject. The summoner does not recognize 'truth' in whatever form it takes, or whatever its origin; he outsmarts himself: thinking himself wise, the summoner becomes a fool.

CONCLUSION

But nathelees, whil I have tyme and space,
Er that I ferther in this tale pace,
Me thynketh it acordaunt to resoun
To tell yow al the condicioun
Of ech of hem, so as it semed me;   (GP I 35–39)

However 'modernism' and 'postmodernism' may be defined, a central feature
of modern art has been its exploration, exploitation, and demonstration of
intentionality. Six hundred years ago Chaucer, too, was demonstrating
intentionality, and using this feature of signs to reveal the psychological
'condicioun' of his characters.

While the temporal distance between medieval thinkers and modern
thinkers may seem great, on the important issue of intentionality, the
conceptual distance between many of them is slight. There is nothing
fortuitous or accidental about this. Franz Brentano's insights into intentionality began with his study of the matter in scholastic philosophy. According to
Edmund Husserl (who had been a student of Brentano), without the doctrine
of intentionality as conceived by Brentano 'phenomenology could not have
come into being at all' (Chisholm 366).

The study of intentionality reveals a shared (and derived) medieval-modern
concern. A belief in Judeo-Christian cosmogony made the 'modern'
awareness and exploration of intentionality possible – and here 'modern' must
include Chaucer and his contemporaries. One does not have to subscribe to
this cosmogony, its metaphysics, or its teleology (I, for one, do not), in order
to understand and accept the definition of intentionality that these permitted
and permit.

Considering metaphysical assumptions and beliefs may be, for some, a dry
business. But such assumptions have actual consequences; they permit (or do
not permit), for example, great religiously-inspired art, scientific discovery,
and invention. Such assumptions and beliefs also permit atrocities such as acts
of 'ethnic cleansing,' acts authorized by metaphysical beliefs or presuppositions about the nature of human beings, about the ontological superiority of
certain tribes, groups, races, and/or of a spiritual superiority (an acquired
ontological quality) arrived at by professing a certain faith or religion. For
believers, metaphysical authorization can transform criminal mass murderers
into tribal or religious heroes and saints. So too, much violence and
discrimination against women is authorized by creation myths (accepted by

133

both men and women) which describe an ontological hierarchy in which women are depicted as, or may be interpreted as being, morally, intellectually, and/or spiritually inferior to men.

A more positively productive effect of Judeo-Christian creationist cosmogony is the understanding of intentionality. Here, the broad thesis of intentionality holds that all created beings are intentional objects, intentional objects that are Object-directed by, from, and to the eternal creative Being. Whether or not this is true may be questioned, and so remains a thesis that finally becomes a matter of belief, disbelief, or agnosticism. But in its narrower application to language, to signifying, to consciousness, the thesis of intentionality becomes fact (lending, no doubt, persuasive power to the broader thesis).

It all begins with the remarkable linguistic doctrine of the Judeo-Christian cosmogony that the 'Word' is the initial, creative, intentional 'Being,' the source of all that exists. From a belief in the 'Word' arises the existential metaphysics of speech; from this belief springs the analogy that God is to God's language as human beings are to human language. Such a belief requires a semiotic explanation of 'reality', a wide-ranging semiological metaphysics, and encourages a search for a 'reading' of God. This reading turns inward to self-discovery, to discovering the 'word' (ourselves) which is the image of the 'Word': hence, psychological discovery. The reading also turns outward for an interpretation of extra-mental reality. The study and interpretation of all God's 'words,' all created reality, becomes a legitimate, important, and honourable pursuit: hence, scientific discovery. The representation of intentionality is manifested in art: in impressionist, cubist, or abstract expressionist painting; in passages of well-worked prose by Faulkner, Woolf, Joyce, Proust, and many other writers; in the poetry of Chaucer's *Friar's Tale*. Such art is probably the best proof of the intentionalist fact because it exploits and consciously demonstrates this fact.

Chaucer's exploration, study, and interpretation of his world, inside and out, is manifested in a poetry that reveals an understanding of intentionality; that is, an understanding of the *directed* relationship between word and thing, and the effects of that on the consciousness, and on the 'condicioun', the human *being*, of each individual. This is the intentionalist realism that assumes the originary function of both the 'Divine' and human wills. Because of this assumption all speech acts are understood as willful, conscious acts.

In exploring the speech-act Chaucer explores consciousness, and how language and signs reveal consciousness and reveal the world. In so doing he is able to create realistic description and characters who evince consciousness. What is consciousness? Earlier I cited Maurita J. Harney: 'Consciousness consists in acts of intending some object. Perceiving, imagining, wishing for, thinking of, are different ways of intending some object – they are all *intentional* acts' (Harney 141–42), and 'linguistic expression is one of many possible intentional acts' (142). The theme of the intentionality of linguistic and other signifying expressions, and, consequently, of the intentionality of other acts such as wishing for, and thinking of some 'object,' is an issue in the *Friar's Tale*. It is also an issue in the *The Parliament of Fowls* and the *Clerk's Tale*, and its notes are heard frequently elsewhere – particularly in the *Merchant's Tale*, the *Franklin's Tale*, the *Manciple's Tale*, and *Troilus and Criseyde*.

Through his poetry, Chaucer causes us, his readers, to distinguish between the object which language intends and how that object is intended, and forces us to adopt what is called today the reflective phenomenological attitude. Through a play with the senses of signs, Chaucer focuses his reader's attention on the different perceptions different individuals have of the same object, and so the psychologies, the 'condiciouns,' of individual characters are developed.

Finally, Chaucer's works show us how, through intentional acts, we all intend ourselves, direct ourselves, create what we become. We ourselves are responsible for whatever we create, including, most importantly, our own particular being. Chaucer's ethical world is one that is based on an exhilarating (because of the danger) but demanding Christian existential concept of individual freedom and responsibility.

What are the differences between the way something exists and the way or ways it is thought of and spoken of? What do the conceptions of such differences reveal of the thinker and speaker? What do intentional acts, of all sorts, do to the thinker and speaker? These are modern questions and these were medieval questions. The answers to these questions can be found in Chaucer's art, and the answers were the same then as they are now.

WORKS CITED

Alanus de Insulis (Alain de Lille). *The Plaint of Nature*. Trans. James J. Sheridan. Toronto: Pontifical Institute of Medieval Studies, 1980.

Alexander, Archibald. *Theories of the Will in the History of Philosophy*. New York: Charles Scribner's Sons, 1898.

Alford, John A. 'The Grammatical Metaphor: A Survey of its Use in theMiddle Ages.' *Speculum* 57 (1982): 728–760.

Anderson, James. F. 'Existensial Metaphysics.' *New Catholic Encyclopedia*. New York: McGraw Hill, 1967.

———. *St Augustine and Being: A Metaphysical Essay*. The Hague: Martinus Nijhoff, 1965.

Apter, Michael J. *The Experience of Motivation: The Theory of Psychological Reversals*. New York: Academic P, 1982.

Arendt, Hannah. *The Life of the Mind: Volume Two: Willing*. New York: Harcourt, 1978.

Aristotle. *Aristotle: Selected Works*. Trans. Hippocrates G. Apostle and Lloyd P. Gerson. Grinnell, IA: Peripatetic, 1982.

———. *Metaphysics*. *Selected Works* 331–414.

———. *Physics*. *Selected Works* 169–240.

———. *On Propositions (On Interpretation)*. *Selected Works* 59–78.

———. *Poetics*. *Selected Works* 631–665.

———. *Posterior Analytics*. Trans. Hugh Tredennick. Cambridge, MA: 1960.

Ashworth, E.J. 'Can I Speak More Clearly Than I Understand.' *Historiographia Linguistica* 7 (1980): 29–38.

Augustine of Hippo, Saint. *City of God*. Trans. Henry Bettenson. Harmondsworth: Penguin, 1972.

———. *Concerning the Teacher (De magistro) and On the Immortality of the Soul (De immortalitate animae)*. Trans. George G. Leckie. New York: Appleton-Century-Crofts, 1938.

———. *Confessions*. Trans. R.S. Pine-Coffin. Harmonsworth: Penguin, 1961.

———. *Contra Faustum Manichaeum*. PL 42, 207–518.

———. *De catechizandis rudibus. On the Chatechising of the Uninstructed*. Trans. S.D.F. Salmon. Schaff 282–314.

———. *De doctrina christiana*. Ed. Guilelmus M. Green. Vindobonae [Vienna]: Helder-Pichler-Tempsky, 1963. *On Christian Doctrine*. Trans. D.W. Robertson Jr. Indianapolis: Bobbs-Merrill, 1958. 1–228.

———. *De mendacio. On Lying*. Trans. H. Browne. Schaff 457–77.

———. *De ordine*. PL 32, 977–1020. *Divine Providence and the Problem of Evil*. Ed. and trans. Robert P. Russel. New York: Cosmopolitan Science and Art Services, 1942.

————. *De Trinitate*. PL 42, 819–1098. Trans. Marcus Dods. *The Works of Aurelius Augustinus*. Vol. 7. Edinburgh: Clark, 1871–76.

————. *On Continence*. Trans. C.L. Cornish. Schaff 379–393.

————. *On the Good of Marriage*. Trans. C.L. Cornish. Schaff 397–413.

————. *De natura boni contra Manichaeos*. PL 42, 551–572.

Baird, Joseph L. 'The Devil's "Privitee".' *NM* 70 (1969): 104–6.

Baker, Donald C. 'The Parliament of Fowls.' *Companion to Chaucer Studies*. Ed. Beryl Rowland. Rev. ed. New York: Oxford UP, 1979. 185–201.

Beichner, Paul E. 'Baiting the Summoner.' *MLQ* 22 (1961): 367–376.

Benveniste, Emile. *Problèmes de linguistique générale*. 2 vols. Paris: Gallimard, 1966–74.

Birney, Earle. ' "After His Ymage": The Central Ironies of the "Friar's Tale".' *Medieval Studies* 21 (1959): 17–35.

Bloch, R. Howard. *Etymologies and Genealogies: A Literary Anthropology of the French Middle Ages*. Chicago: U of Chicago P, 1983.

Boehner, Philotheus. *Collected Articles on Ockham*. Ed. Eligius M. Buytaert. St Boneventure, NY: Fransciscan Institute, 1958.

Boethius. *Consolatio Philosphiae*. Ed. Jame J. O'Donnel. Bryn Mawr: Bryn Mawr College, 1984.

————. *De ordine*. Ed. R. Jolivet. Paris: Desclée de Brouwer, 1948.

Boman, Thorlief. *Hebrew Thought Compared with Greek*. Trans. Jules L. Moreau. London: SCM, 1960.

Bourke, Vernon J. *Will in Western Thought: An Historico-Critical Survey*. New York: Sheed and Ward, 1964.

Bowden, Muriel. *A Commentary on the General Prologue to the* Canterbury Tales. New York: Macmillan, 1956.

Bowers, John M. *The Crisis of Will in* Piers Plowman. Washington: Catholic University of America P, 1986.

Bredin, Hugh. 'Roman Jakobson on Metaphor and Metonymy.' *Philosophy and Literature* 8 (1984): 49–103.

Brentano, Franz. *Psychology from an Empirical Standpoint*. Ed. Oskar Kraus. Trans. Antos C. Rancurello et al. London: Routledge, 1973.

Brown, Caroline K. and Marion F. Egge. 'The Friar's Tale and the Wife of Bath's Tale.' *PMLA* 91 (1976): 291–2.

Brown, Stephen F. 'A Modern Prologue to Ockham's Natural Philosophy.' *Sprache und Erkenntnis im Mittelalter*. Vol. 1. Eds. Jan P. Beckmann et al. Berlin: Walter du Gruyter, 1981. 107–129.

Bruyne, Edgar de. *Etudes d'esthétique médiévale*. 3 vols. Brugge: De Tempel, 1946.

Caputo, John. *Heidegger and Aquinas: An Essay on Overcoming Metaphysics*. New York: Fordham UP, 1982.

Carlo, William E. *The Ultimate Reducibility of Essence to Existence in Existential Metaphysics*. The Hague: Martinus Nijhoff, 1966.

Carroll, Lewis. *Through the Looking-Glass*. London: Macmillan, 1968.

Cawley, A.C. 'Chaucer's Summoner, the Friar's Summoner, and the Friar's Tale.' *Proceedings of the Leeds Philosophical and Literary Society*. Literature and History Section. 8 (1957): 173–180.

Chenu, M.-D. *Nature, Man, and Society in the Twelfth Century: Essays on the New Theological Perspectives in the Latin West*. Ed. and trans. Jerome Taylor and Lester K. Little. Chicago: U of Chicago P, 1968.

Chisholm, Roderick M. 'Franz Brentano.' *Encyclopedia of Philosophy*.

Chydenius, Johan. *The Symbolism of Love in Medieval Thought*.Commentationes Humanarum Litterarum 44.1. Helsingfors [Helsinki]: Societas Scientarum Fennica, 1970.

————. *The Theory of Medieval Symbolism*. Commentationes Humanarum Litterarum 27.2. Helsingfors [Helsinki]: Societas Scientarum Fennica, 1960.

————. *The Typological Problem in Dante: A Study in the History of Medieval Ideas*. Commentationes Humanarum Litterarum 15.1. Helsingfors [Helsinki]: Societas Scientarum Fennica, 1958.

Clark, David W. 'William of Ockham on Right Reason.' *Speculum* 48 (1973): 13–36

Cloud author. *The Cloud of Unknowing and Related Treatises*. Ed. Phyllis Hodgson. Exeter Eng.: Catholic Records, 1982.

Coleman, Janet. *Piers Plowman and the* Moderni. Rome: Edizioni di storia e letteratura, 1981.

Colish, Marcia L. *The Mirror of Language: A Study in the Medieval Theory of Knowledge*. Rev. ed. Lincoln, NE: U of Nebraska P, 1983.

Correale, Robert M. 'St Jerome and the Conclusion of the Friar's Tale.' *English Language Notes* 2 (1965): 171–74.

Courtenay, William J. *Schools and Scholars in Fourteenth-Century England*. Princeton: Princeton UP, 1987.

Curry, Walter Clyde. *Chaucer and the Medieval Sciences*. 2nd ed. London: Allen, 1960.

————. 'The Secret of Chaucer's Pardoner.' *JEGP* 18 (1919): 593–606.

Curtius, Ernst Robert. *European Literature and the Latin Middle Ages*. Trans. Willard R. Trask. Princeton: Princeton UP, 1973.

Cursor Mundi: A Northumbrian Poem of the XIVth Century in Four Versions. Ed. Richard Morris. EETS. London: K. Paul, 1874–1893.

Dante Alighieri. *Il Convivio*. Ed. Maria Simonelli. Bologna: R. Patron, 1966.

————. *Paradiso, Vol. I: Italian Text and Translation*. Ed. and trans. Charles S. Singleton. Princeton: Princeton UP, 1975.

Delasanta, Rodney. 'Chaucer and the Problem of the Universal.' *Mediaevalia* 9 (1986 for 1983): 145–163.

————. 'Nominalism and Typology in Chaucer.' *Typology and English Medieval Literature*. Ed. Hugh Keenan. New York: AMS, 1992, 121–139.

Dempster Germaine. *Dramatic Irony in Chaucer*. 1932; rpt. New York: Humanities Press, 1959.

Derrida, Jacques. 'Differance.' *Speech and Phenomena: And Other Essays on Husserl's Theory of Signs*. Trans. David. B. Allison and Newton Garver. Evanston, Ill.: Northwestern UP, 1973, pp. 129–160.

Devitt, Michael. *Realism and Truth*. 2nd ed. Oxford: Blakwell, 1991.

Dictionary of Philosophy. 1962 ed. Ed. Dagobert D. Runes. Totowa NJ: Littlefield, 1967.

A Dictionary of Philosophy. 2nd rev. ed. Ed. Anthony Flew. London: Pan; London: Macmillan, 1983.

Dilman, Ilham. *Quine on Ontology, Necessity and Experience*. London: Macmillan Press, 1984.

Dinshaw, Carolyn. *Eunuch Hermeneutics*. *ELH* 55 (1988): 27–51.

Dolan, Michael James. 'Chaucer and the Continental Tradition: A Study of Neoplatonic Influences.' Diss. Cornell U, 1974.

Dreyfus, Hubert L. 'Introduction.' Dreyfus, ed. 1–27.

Dreyfus, Hubert L., ed. *Husserl Intentionality and Cognitive Science*. Cambridge, MA: MIT P, 1982.

Dronke, Peter. 'Francesca and Heloise.' *Comparative Literature* 27 (1975): 113–35.

Drummond, John J. *Husserlian Intentionality and Non-Foundational Realism*. Dordrecht: Kluwer Academic, 1990.

Duns Scotus, John. *Duns Scotus on the Will and Morality*. Trans. Alan B. Wolter. Washington: Catholic UP, 1986.

Eco, Umberto. *Semiotics and the Philosophy of Language*. Bloomington: Indiana UP, 1984.
──────. 'Signification and Denotation from Boethius to Ockham.' *Franciscan Studies* 44 (1984): 1–29.
──────. *Theory of Semiotics*. Bloomington: Indiana UP, 1976.
Edelman, Gerald M. *Bright Air, Brilliant Fire: On the Matter of the Mind*. New York: Basic Books, 1992.
Eriugena, Johannes Scotus. *Periphyseon (The Division of Nature)*. Trans. I.P. Sheldon Williams and John O'Meara. Montreal: Bellarmin; Washington: Dumbarton Oaks, 1987.
Faur, José. *Golden Doves with Silver Dots: Semiotics and Textuality in the Rabbinic Tradition*. Bloomington: Indiana UP, 1986.
Ferster, Judith. *Chaucer on Interpretation*. Cambridge: Cambridge UP, 1985.
Føllesdal, Dagfinn. 'Brentano and Husserl on Intentional Objects and Perception.' Dreyfus, ed. 31–41.
──────. 'Husserl's Notion of *Noema*.' Dreyfus, ed. 73–80.
──────. 'Husserl's Theory of Perception.' Dreyfus, ed. 93–96.
Franciscan Studies 44 (1984) and 45 (1985).
Freccero, John. 'The Fig Tree and the Laurel: Petrarch's Poetics.' *Diacritics* 5 (1975): 34–40.
Frege, Gottlob. 'On Sense and Reference.' *Translations from the Philosophical Writings of Gottlob Frege*. Trans. and eds. P.T. Geach and Max Black. Oxford: Oxford UP, 1952. 56–78.
Gadamer, Hans-Georg. *Truth and Method*. New York: Crossroads, 1985.
Gallacher, Patrick J. *Love, the Word, and Mercury: A Reading of John Gower's* Confessio Amantis. Albuquerque: U of New Mexico P: 1975.
Gardner, John. *The Poetry of Chaucer*. Carbondale: Southern Illinois UP, 1977.
Gauthier, Albert. 'La Sodomie dans le droit canonique médiéval.' *L'Erotisme au moyen-âge*. Ed. Bruno Roi. Montreal: Belarmin, 1977.
Gersh, Stephen. *From Iamblichus to Eriugena: An Investigation of the Prehistory and Evolution of the Pseudo-Dionysian Tradition*. Leiden: E. J. Brill, 1978.
Gilson, Etienne. *Being and Some Philosophers*. 2d ed. Toronto: Pontifical Institute of Medieval Studies.
──────. *God and Philosophy*. New Haven: Yale UP, 1941.
Goldmann, Lucien. *Le Dieu caché: étude sur la vision tragique dans les pensées de Pascal et dans le théâtre de Racine*. Paris: Gallimard, 1955.
Gosselin, Mia. *Nominalism and Contemporary Nominalism: Ontological and Epistemological Implications of the work of W.V.O. Quine and of N. Goodman*. Dordrecht: Kluwer Academic, 1990.
Gurwitsch, Aron. 'Husserl's Theory of the Intentionality of Consciousness.' Dreyfus, ed. 59–71.
Haak, Susan. ' "Realism." ' *Synthese* 73 (1987): 275–299.
Hahn, Thomas. 'The Devil and His Panne.' *Neuphilologische Mitteilungen* 86 (1985): 348–52.
Hahn, Thomas, and Richard W. Kaeuper. 'Text and Context: Chaucer's *Friar's Tale*.' *Studies in the Age of Chaucer* 5 (1983): 67–101.
Hallie, Philip P. 'Stoicism.' *Encyclopedia of Philosophy*.
Handelman, Susan. 'Jacques Derrida and the Heretic Hermeneutic.' *Displacement: Derrida and After*. Ed. Mark Krupnick. Bloomington: Indiana UP: 1983. 98–129.
Harney, Maurita J. *Intentionality, Sense, and the Mind*. The Hague: Martinus Nijhoff, 1984.
Harris, Roy, and Talbot J. Taylor. *Landmarks in Linguistic Thought: The Western Tradition from Socratates to Saussure*. London: Routledge, 1989.

140   *Works Cited*

Harvey, Ruth E. *The Inward Wits: Psychological Theory in the Middle Ages and the Renaissance*. London: Warburg Institute, 1975.

Hatton, Tom. 'Chaucer's Friar's "Old Rebekke." ' *Journal of English and Germanic Philology*. 67 (1968): 266–271.

Heath, P. L. 'Carroll, Lewis.' *Encyclopedia of Philosophy*.

Heidegger, Martin. *The Basic Problems of Phenomenology*. Trans. Alfred Hofstadter. Bloomington: Indiana UP, 1982.

Henninger, Mark G. *Relations: Medieval Theories 1250–1325*. Oxford: Clarendon Press, 1989.

Henry, Desmond Paul. *That Most Subtle Question (Quaestio Subtilissima): The Metaphysical Bearing of Medieval and Contemporary Linguistic Diciplines*. Manchester: Manchester UP, 1984.

Hollander, Robert B. *Allegory in Dante's* Commedia. Princeton: Princeton UP, 1969.

Husserl, Edmund. *Logical Investigations*. Trans. J. Findlay. New York: Humanities, 1970.

Jackson, Darrel B. 'The Theory of Signs in St. Augustine's *De Doctrina Christiana*.' *Augustine: A Collection of Critical Essays*. Ed. R.A. Markus. New York: Anchor-Doubleday, 1972. 92–147.

Jacob's Well, an englist tretise on the cleansing of man's conscience. EETS. London: K. Paul, 1900.

Jacobs, Edward C., and Robert E. Jungman. 'His Mother's Curse: Kinship in *The Friar's Tale*.' *Philological Quarterly* 64 (1985): 256–58.

Jakobson, Roman. 'Glosses on the Medieval Insight into the Science of Language.' *Mélange Linguistiques offerts à Emile Benveniste*. Louvain: Peeters, 1975.

——. *Main Trends in the Science of Language*. London: George Allen, 1974.

——. 'Two Aspects of Language and Two Types of Aphasic Disturbances.' *Fundamentals of Language*. Roman Jakobson and Morris Halle. 2nd rev. ed. The Hague: Mouton, 1971. 69–96.

Javelet, Robert. *Image et resemblance au douzième siècle*. 2 vols. Paris: Editions Letouzey, 1967.

Johansson, Ingvar. *Ontological Investigations: An Inquiry into the Categories of Nature, Man, and Society*. London: Routledge, 1989.

Johnson, Anthony L. 'Jakobsonian Theory and Literary Semiotics: Toward a Generative Typology of the Text.' *New Literary History* 14 (1982): 33–61.

Joós, Ernest. *Intentionality – Source of Intelligibility: The Genesis of Intentionality*. New York: Peter Lang, 1989.

Jordan, Robert M. *Chaucer's Poetics and the Modern Reader*. Berkeley: U of California P, 1987.

Keen, Samuel McMurray. 'Gabriel Marcel.' *Encyclopedia of Philosophy*.

Klene, Jean. 'Chaucer's Contribution to the a Popular Topos: the World Upside-Down.' *Viator* 11 (1980): 321–334.

Klibansky, Raymond. *The Continuity of the Platonic Tradition during the Middle Ages*. Munich: Kraus International, 1981.

Kneale, William, and Martha Kneale. *The Development of Logic*. Oxford: Clarendon, 1962.

Kolve, V.A. ' "Man in the Middle": Art and Religion in Chaucer's *Friar's Tale*.' *Studies in the Age of Chaucer* 12 (1990): 5–46.

——. ' "Christ as Gardener in Medieval Art and Drama," and "Christ as Pilgrim in Medieval Drama." ' Maxwell Cummings Lectures. McGill University, Montreal, Feb. 7 and 8, 1991.

Küng, Guido. 'The World as Noema and as Referent.' *Journal of the British Society for Phenomenology*. 3:1 (1972): 15–26.

Lavely, John H. 'Personalism.' *Encyclopedia of Philosophy*.

Leff, Gordon. *William of Ockham: The Metamorphosis of Scholastic Discourse*. Manchester: Manchester UP, 1975.

Leicester, H. Marshall, Jr. ' "No Vileyns Word": Social Context and Performance in Chaucer's *Friar's Tale*.' *The Chaucer Review* 17 (1982): 21–39.

Lemos, Ramon N. *Metaphysical Investigations*. Rutherford: Fairleigh Dickenson UP; London: Associated UP, 1988.

Lenaghan, R.T. 'The Irony of the *Friar's Tale*.' *The Chaucer Review* 7 (1972): 281–94.

Levinas, Emmanuel. *Ethics and Infinity*. Trans. Richard A. Cohen. Pittsburg: Duquesne UP, 1982.

————. *The Theory of Intuition in Husserl's Phenomenology*. Evanston: Northwestern UP, 1973.

Long, A.A., and D.N. Sedley. *The Hellenistic Philosophers*. Vol. 1. Cambridge: Cambridge UP, 1987.

Lot-Borodine, M. *La déification de l'homme selon la doctrine des Pères Grecs*. Paris: CERF, 1970.

Lynch, Katheryn L. 'The *Parliament of Fowls* and Late Medieval Voluntarism.' 2 parts. *The Chaucer Review* 25 (1990): 1–16; 85–95.

McAlpine, Monica E. 'The Pardoner's Homosexuality and How It Matters.' *PMLA* 95 (1980): 8–22.

McInerny, Ralph. *The Logic of Analogy: An Interpretation of St Thomas*. The Hague: Martinus Nijhoff, 1961.

MacIntyre, Alisdair. 'Pantheism.' *Encyclopedia of Philosophy*.

McKeon, Richard. 'Poetry and Philosophy in the Twelfth Century: The Renaissance of Rhetoric.' *Critics and Criticism: Ancient and Modern*. Ed. R.S. Crane. Chicago: U of Chicago P, 1952.

Maimonides, Moses. *Guide for the Perplexed*. 2nd. rev. ed. Trans. M. Frielander. 1904; New York: Dover Press, 1956.

Manly, John M. *Some New Light on Chaucer*. New York: Henry Holt, 1926.

Mann, Jill. *Chaucer and Medieval Estates Satire: The Literature of Social Classes and the General Prologue of the Canterbury Tales*. Cambridge: Cambridge UP, 1973.

Marenbon, John. *Later Medieval Philosophy (1150–1350): An Introduction*. London: Routledge, 1987.

Márkus, Geörgy. 'The Paradigm of Language: Wittgenstein, Lévi-Strauss, Gadamer.' *The Structural Allegory: Reconstructive Encounters with the New French Thought*. Ed. John Fekete. Minneapolis: U of Minnesota P, 1989.

Markus, R.A. 'St Augustine on Signs.' *Augustine: A Collection of Critical Essays*. Ed. R.A. Markus. New York: Anchor-Doubleday, 1972. 61–91.

Maurer, Armand. 'William of Ockham on Language and Reality.' *Sprache und Erkenntnis im Mittelalter*. Vol. 1. Ed. Jan P. Beckmann et al. Berlin: Walter du Gruyter, 1981. 795–802.

Mazzotta, Giuseppe. '*The Decameron*: The Marginality of Literature.' *UTQ* 42 (1972): 64–81.

The Middle English Dictionary. Eds. Hans Kurath et al. Ann Arbor: 1952– .

Miller, R.P. 'Chaucer's Pardoner, the Spiritual Eunuch, and the *Pardoner's Tale*.' *Speculum* 30 (1955): 180–199.

Moody, Ernest A. 'Buridan and the Dilemma of Nominalism.' *Harry Austryn Wolfson Jubilee Volume*. English Section. Vol. 2. Jerusalem: American Academy for Jewish Research, 1965. 577–596.

————. 'Medieval Logic.' s.v. 'Logic, History of.' *Encyclopedia of Philosophy*.

Montgomery, Marion. *The Trouble with You Innerleckchuls*. Front Royal, VA: Christendom, 1988.

Moran, Dermot. ' "Officina omnium" or "Notio quaedam intellectualis in mente divina aeternaliter facta': The Problem of the Definition of Man in the Philosophy of John Scotus Eriugena.' Wenin 1:195–204.

Mroczkowski, Przemyslaw. ' "The Friar's Tale" and its Pulpit Background.' *English Studies Today, Second Series*. Ed. G.A. Bonnard. Bern: A. Francke, 1961. 107–120.

Murphy, James J. *Rhetoric in the Middle Ages: A History of Rhetorical Theory from Saint Augustine to the Renaissance*. Berkeley: U of California P, 1974.

Murtaugh, Daniel M. 'Riming Justice in *The Friar's Tale.' NP* 74 (1973): 107–112.

Myles, Robert. ' "This litel worde IS": The Existential Metaphysics of the *Cloud* Author.' *Florilegium* 8 (1986): 140–168.

Nash, Ronald H. *The Light of the Mind: St Augustine's Theory of Knowledge*. Lexington: UP of Kentucky, 1969.

Nims, Margaret F. '*Translatio:* "Difficult Statement" in Medieval Poetic Theory.' *UTQ* 3 (1974): 215–230.

Oates, Whitney J., ed. *The Stoic and Epicurean Philosophers: The Complete Extant Writings of Epicurus, Epictetus, Lucretius, Marcus Aurelius*. New York: Random House, 1940.

Owens, Joseph. 'The Accidental and Essential Character of Being.' *Mediaeval Studies* 20 (1958): 1–40.

The Oxford English Dictionary. 2nd ed.

Passon, Richard H. ' "Entente" in Chaucer's *Friar's Tale.' The Chaucer Review* 2 (1968): 166–173.

Patterson, Lee. *Negotiating the Past: The Historical Understanding of Medieval Literature*. Madison: U of Wisconsin P, 1987.

———. 'The "Parson's Tale" and the Quitting of the "Canterbury Tales".' *Traditio* 34 (1978): 331–380.

Patrologia Latina. Ed. Jacques-Paul Migne. 221 vols. Paris: 1841–1905.

Peck, Russell E. 'Chaucer and the Nominalist Questions.' *Speculum* 53 (1978): 745–60.

Pinborg, Jan. 'Roger Bacon on Signs: A Newly Recovered Part of the Opus Maius.' *Miscellanea Mediaevalia* 13 (1981): 403–412.

Plato. *The Collected Dialogues of Plato*. Eds. Edith Hamilton and Huntington Cairns. Princeton: Princeton UP, 1961.

———. *Cratylus*. Trans. Benjamin Jowett. *Collected Dialogues*. 421–474.

———. *Laws*. Trans. A.E. Taylor. *Collected Dialogues*. 1225–1513.

———. *Plato's Parmenides: Translation and Analysis*. Trans. and analysis R.E. Allen. Minneapolis: U of Minnessota Press, 1983.

———. *Republic*. Trans. Paul Shorey. *Collected Dialogues*. 575–844.

———. *Timaeus*. Trans. Benjamin Jowett. *Collected Dialogues*. 1115–1211.

Plotinus. *The Enneads*. Tr. Stephen MacKenna. 2d ed. rev. by B.S. Page. London: Faber, 1956.

Pratt, Robert A., ed. *The Tales of Canterbury Complete*. Boston: Houghton, 1974.

Pseudo-Dionysius. *Pseudo-Dionysius: The Complete Works*. New York: Paulist Press, 1987.

Pulsiano, Philip. 'Redeemed Language and the Ending of Troilus and Cryseyde.' *Sign, Sentence, Discourse: Language in Medieval Thought and Literature*. Eds. Julian N. Wasserman and Lois Roney. Syracuse, NY: Syracuse UP, 1989. 153–174.

Purdon, Liam O. 'Chaucer's *Lak of Stedfastnesse*: A Revalorization of the Word.' *Sign, Sentence Discourse: Language in Medieval Thought and Literature*. Eds. Julian N. Wasserman and Lois Roney. Syracuse: Syracuse UP, 1989. 144–152.

Ricoeur, Paul. 'Naming God.' *Union Seminary Quarterly Review* 34:4 (1979): 215–227.

———. 'The Model of the Text: Meaningful Action Considered as a Text.' *New Literary History* 5 (1973–74): 91–117.

———. *The Rule of Metaphor*. Trans. Robert Czerny et al. Toronto: U of Toronto P, 1975.

Richardson, Janette. 'Friar and Summoner, The Art of Balance.' *The Chaucer Review* 9 (1975): 227–236.

———. 'Hunter and Prey: Functional Imagery in "The Friar's Tale." ' *Chaucer's Mind and Art*. Ed. A.C. Cawley. Edinburgh: Oliver and Boyd, 1969. 155–165.

Rist, J.M. 'Augustine on Free Will and Predestination.' *Journal of Theological Studies* 20:2 (1969): 420–447.

———. *Plotinus: The Road to Reality*. Cambridge: Cambridge UP, 1967.

Robertson, D.W., Jr. *A Preface to Chaucer: Studies in Medieval Perspectives*. Princeton: Princeton UP, 1963.

———. 'Why the Devil Wears Green.' *Modern Language Notes* 49 (1954): 470–72.

Robinson, F.N., ed. *The Works of Geoffrey Chaucer*. 2nd ed. Boston: Houghton, 1957.

Robinson, John Mansley. *An Introduction to Early Greek Philosophy: The Chief Fragments and Ancient Testimony, with Connecting Commentary*. Boston: Houghton, 1968.

Root, Robert Kilburn. *The Poetry of Chaucer: A Guide to its Study and Appreciation*. Boston: Houghton, 1906.

Rosen, Charles. 'The Miraculous Mandarin.' *The New York Review of Books*. 40:17 (Oct. 21, 1993): 72–77.

Ross, James F. 'Analogy as a Rule of Meaning for Religious Language.' *Aquinas: A Collection of Critical Essays*. Ed. Anthony Kenny. London: Macmillan, 1969. 93–138.

Rowland, Beryl. 'Chaucer's Idea of the Pardoner.' *The Chaucer Review* 14 (1979): 140–154.

Sajama, Seppo, and Matti Kamppinen. *An Historical Introduction to Phenomenology*. London: Croom Helm, 1987.

Sapir, Edward. *Selected Writings of Edward Sapir in Language, Culture and Personality*. Ed. David G. Mandelbaum. Berkeley: U of California P, 1963.

Saussure, Ferdinand de. *Course in General Linguistics*. Eds. Charles Bally and Albert Sechehaye. Trans. Roy Harris. LaSalle IL: Open Court, 1986.

Schaff, Philip, ed. *Nicene and Post-Nicene Fathers*. Vol. 3. Edinburgh: T and T Clark, 1890–; rpt. Grand Rapids, MI: Wm. B. Eerdmans, 1988.

Searle, John R. *Intentionality: An Essay in the Philosophy of Mind*. Cambridge: Cambridge UP, 1983.

———. 'The Logical Status of Fictional Discourse.' *New Literary History* 6 (1974–75): 319–332.

———. *Speech Acts: An Essay in the Philosophy of Language*. Cambridge: Cambridge UP, 1969.

———. 'What Is an Intentional State?' Dreyfus, ed. 259–276.

Shepard, Odell. *Pedlar's Progress: The Life of Bronson Alcott*. Boston: Little, Brown, 1937.

Shoaf, R. Allen. 'Dante's *Commedia* and Chaucer's Theory of Mediation.' *New Perspectives in Chaucer Criticism*. Ed. Donald M. Rose. Norman, OK: Pilgrim Books, 1981. 83–103.

Skeat, Walter W., ed. *The Complete Works of Geoffrey Chaucer*. Vol 7. Oxford: Clarendon, 1897.

Steinmetz, David C. 'Late Medieval Nominalism and the *Clerk's Tale*.' *The Chaucer Review* 12 (1977): 38–54.

Strohm, Paul. *Social Chaucer*. Cambridge: Harvard UP, 1989.

Swiezawski, Stefan. 'Les intentions premières et les intentions secondes chez Jean Duns Scotus.' *Archives d'histoire doctrinale et littéraire du moyen âge* 9 (1934): 205–60.

———. 'La pensée philosophique du moyen âge tardif face au problème de la liberation de l'homme.' Wenin 1: 3–15.

Szittya, Penn R. 'The Green Yeoman as Loathly Lady: The Friar's Parody of the Wife of Bath's Tale.' *PMLA* 90 (1975): 386–94.

Tachau, Katherine H. *Vision and Certitude in the Age of Ockham: Optics, Epistemology and the Foundations of Semantics 1250–1345.* Leiden: E.J. Brill, 1988.

Tatlock, John S.P., and A.R. Kennedy. *A Concordance to the Complete Works of Geoffrey Chaucer.* Gloucester MA: Peter Smith, 1963.

Taylor, P.B. 'Chaucer's *Cosyn to the Dede.*' *Speculum* 57 (1982): 315–327.

Thomas Aquinas. SCG. *De Veritate Catholicae Fidei Contra Gentiles.* In *Opera Omnia.* Parmae Edition. 1865; rpt. New York: Musurgia, 1949. *Summa Contra Gentiles.* 2v. Various Translators. Notre Dame: U of Notre Dame P, 1975. First published as *On the Truth of the Catholic Faith.* New York: Doubleday, 1955.

———. *In Librum de Causis-Expositio.* Ed. Ceslai Pera. Turin: 1955.

———. *On Interpretation: Commentary by St Thomas and Cajetan.* Trans. J. Oesterle. Milwaukee: Marquette UP, 1962.

———. *Summa Theologica.* 61 vols. Latin text with English Translation. Blackfriars. New York: McGraw, 1963.

Tomasic, Thomas. 'Negative Theology and Subjectivity: An Approach to the Tradition of the Pseudo-Dionysius.' *International Philosophical Quarterly* 9 (1969): 406–430.

Trentman, John A. 'Mental Language and Lying.' Wenin. 2:544–553.

———. 'Ockham on Mental.' *Mind* 79 (1970): 586–90.

———. 'Speculative Grammar and Transformational Grammar: A Comparison of Philosophical Presuppositions.' *History of Linguistic Thought and Contemporary Linguistics.* Ed. Herman Parret. Berlin: Walter de Gruyter, 1976. 279–301.

Trevelyan, G.M. *English Social History.* Harmondsworth: Penguin Books, 1967.

Tuchman, Barbara W. *A Distant Mirror: The Calamitous 14th Century.* New York: Ballentine, 1978.

Ullmann, Stephen. *Meaning and Style: Collected Papers.* Oxford: Blackwell, 1973.

———. *The Principles of Semantics.* 2nd ed. with add. material. Glasgow: Jackson, 1963.

Usk, Thomas. *The Testament of Love. The Complete Works of Geoffrey Chaucer. Supplement.* Vol. 7. Ed. Walter W. Skeat. Oxford: Clarendon, 1897. 1–145.

Vance, Eugene. 'Augustine (Aurelius Augustinus), Bishop of Hippo (354–430).' *Encyclopedic Dictionary of Semiotics.*

———. 'Chaucer's Pardoner: Relics, Discourse and Frames of Propriety.' *NLH* 20 (1989): 723–45.

———. *Mervelous Signals: Poetics and Sign Theory in the Middle Ages.* Lincoln: U of Nebraska P, 1986.

Verbeke, Gerard. *The Presence of Stoicism in Medieval Thought.* Washington: Catholic University of America P, 1983.

Vinsauf, Geoffrey de. *Poetria nova.* Trans. Margaret F. Nims. Toronto: Pontifical Institute of Mediaeval Studies, 1967.

Vlastos, Gregory. *Platonic Studies.* Princeton: Princeton UP, 1981.

Walsh, W.H. 'Metaphysics, Nature of.' *Encyclopedia of Philosophy.*

Wenin, Christian, ed. *L'homme et son univers au moyen âge.* 2 vols. Louvain-la-neuve: Editions de l'institut supérieur de philosophie, 1986.

William of Ockham. *Ockham: Philosophical Writings.* Ed. and trans. Philotheus Boehner. Edinburgh: Nelson, 1957.

Williams, David. *The Canterbury Tales: A Literary Pilgrimage.* Boston: Twayne Publishers: 1987.

———. 'From Grammar's Pan to Logic's Fire: Intentionality and Chaucer's Friar's

Tale.' *Literature and Ethics: Essays Presented to A.E. Malloch*. Eds. Gary Wihl and David Williams. Kingston: McGill-Queen's UP, 1988. 77–95.

Wasserman, Julian N. and Louis Roney, eds. *Sign, Sentence, Discourse: Language in Medieval Thought and Literature*. Syracuse: Syracuse UP, 1989.

Wolter, Alan B., ed. and trans. *Duns Scotus on the Will and Morality*. Washington: Catholic UP, 1986.

Wyclif, John. *The English Works of Wyclif*. Ed. F.D. Matthew. EETS. London: Trubner, 1880.

Ziolkowski, Jan. *Alan of Lille's Grammar of Sex: The Meaning of Grammar to a Twelfth Century Intellectual*. Boston: The Medieval Academy of America, 1985.

INDEX

affectio commodi (affection for the advantageous), 50
affectio iustitiae (affection of justice), 50; see also: will
Alanus de Insulis (Alain de Lille), 57, 84; *De planctu Naturae*, 121–122
Alexander, Archibald, 21, 43
Alford, John A., 6, 7, 8, 9, 10, 10n8, 13, 18, 72
Analogy, 8, 84, 86
Anaximander, 57
Anderson, James. F., 48, 60, 60n5, 61, 63, 64
Angels, 47, 50, 106n16; see also: devils
Anthropomorphic model of Being, 69, 73; see also: *imago Dei*; personalism
Anti-essentialism, 19, 63, 63n11, 86; see also: metaphysics, essentialist; metaphysics, existentialist
Anti-realism, 2, 3, 8, 11, 13, 15–16, 18
Appetite, 49, 50, 51, 62n6, 127; see also: intentionality, natural; tendency
Apter, Michael J., 52
Aquinas, see Thomas Aquinas
Arendt, Hannah, 17, 42, 43, 48, 50
Aristotle, 3, 7–9, 11, 12, 12n8, 13, 30, 34n1, 36, 37, 47, 48, 50, 51, 55, 62, 62n9, 63n11, 73, 74, 79, 81, 90; *Metaphysics*, 61; *On Interpretation*, 39, 44n10; *On Propositions*, 8; *Physics*, 62; *Posterior Analytics*, 65n13
Ashworth, E.J., 44n10, 84, 90
Augustine of Hippo, St, 2, 3, 5, 7, 10, 10n8, 11–14, 12n9, 17, 18, 19, 22, 26, 27, 28, 36, 39, 40, 41, 42, 43, 44, 45, 46, 46n11, 48, 49, 52–53, 57, 60, 61, 63, 64, 65, 67n15, 69n17, 70, 77–80, 83n2, 88–89, 111, 111n13; *Contra Faustum*, 26; *De doctrina christiana*, 12, 39, 49, 67n15, 77, 78, 88, 89, 111; *De*

magistro, 12, 36; *De mendacio*, 28; *De Trinitate*, 41, 70, 77, 89; *On Continence*, 78–79; *On the Good of Marriage*, 78; *On the Nature of the Good*, 60; see also: psychology, Augustinian; realism, Augustinian; will, primacy of
Austin, John L., 110
Authorial intentionality, 53–54, 79, 132; see also: intentional fallacy
Authorial responsibility, 25, 79–81; see also: reader responsibility
Avicenna, 36, 83, 83n2

Bailey, Harry, Host of the Tabard Inn, (C.T.), 54, 96n9
Baird, Joseph L., 124
Baker, Donald C., 122
Barthes, Roland, 13
Beckett, Samuel, 13, 59n2
Beichner, Paul E., 116
Benveniste, Emile, 34, 38, 39, 39n7, 87
Bernard Silvestris (Silvestre), 57
Birney, Earle, 96n6
Black and white motif in Chaucer, 27–33, 124, 124n5, 127; see also: *wordes white*
Bloch, R. Howard, 10–13, 18, 26
Boehner, Philotheus, 3, 5, 21, 27n20, 37, 38
Boethius, 7, 8, 11, 17, 18, 23, 24, 27, 36, 41, 43, 48, 49, 50, 51, 82, 90, 120; see also: Chaucer, *Boece*
Boman, Thorlief, 64, 65, 69, 71, 72, 72n22
Bourke, Vernon J., 42
Bowden, Muriel, 125n6
Bowers, John M., 28
Bredin, Hugh, 92n3
Brentano, Franz, 33, 35, 35n2, 45, 133
Brito, Radulphos, 84
Brown, Caroline K., 113n20